Blockchain and Artificial Intelligence

Blockchain and Artificial Intelligence

Intelligence

—

The World Rewired

Edited by
Tom James

DE GRUYTER

ISBN 978-3-11-125830-0
e-ISBN (PDF) 978-3-11-066445-4
e-ISBN (EPUB) 978-3-11-066134-7

Library of Congress Control Number: 2021941384

Bibliographic information published by the Deutsche Nationalbibliothek
The Deutsche Nationalbibliothek lists this publication in the Deutsche Nationalbibliografie;
detailed bibliographic data are available on the internet at http://dnb.dnb.de.

© 2023 Walter de Gruyter GmbH, Berlin/Boston
This volume is text- and page-identical with the hardback published in 2021.
Cover image: Ryzhi/iStock/Getty Images Plus
Typesetting: Integra Software Services Pvt. Ltd.
Printing and binding: CPI books GmbH, Leck

www.degruyter.com

Preface

Over the centuries there have been key defining moments where jump shifts in technology suddenly opened up new opportunities for the human race or changed how we interacted with our world.

This book takes a look at how the emergence of two such technologies – artificial intelligence (AI) and blockchain – is already starting to redefine how the world around us works and how that world interacts with us.

The first time that the two words "Artificial" and "Intelligence" were put together was on the 31st of August 1955, when Prof. John McCarty from the University of Dartmouth, together with M. L Minsky, N. Rochester and C. E. Shannon, asked the Rockefeller foundation to fund a summer of research on Artificial Intelligence (AI).

Artificial intelligence is any task performed by a program or machine, which would otherwise require human intelligence to accomplish it. It is the science and engineering of making computer systems demonstrate human-like intelligence, especially visual perception, speech recognition, decision-making, and translation between languages.

There are two types of AI, General AI and Narrow AI. We are still currently experiencing Narrow AI – AI programs capable of solving one specific problem. General AI is still work in progress; it can be defined as an artificial intelligence program capable of tackling every kind of problem it is presented with. This is similar to an extremely powerful human, and you can think of it as the robot from *Terminator* (but hopefully a peaceful version of it).

AI has already affected our lifestyle either directly or indirectly and is shaping the future of tomorrow. It has become an intrinsic part of our daily life and has greatly impacted our lifestyle with the increased use of digital assistants on mobile phones, driver-assistance systems, chat bots, texts and speech translators, and systems that assist in recommending products, services, films we watch, music we listen to and customized learning.

The second technology addressed in this book, that of blockchain, is perhaps best known for "Bitcoin" and other crypto currencies like "Ethereum" but separate to its application as a currency of exchange, the underlying technology called Blockchain, the programming language if you like, that makes it all possible, is in itself a very powerful tool with many applications in the financial services industry and elsewhere.

Although the mechanics of blockchain are extremely complex, the basic idea is simple: to decentralize the storage of data so that such data cannot be owned, controlled or manipulated by a central system. It gives the potential to create blocks of data, that are irrefutable, immutable, and so can be trusted as they are spread across a network of computers making it far harder to hack or attack multiple systems and change the data on all of them. Because of this decentralized nature, it provides a very high level of security for data.

https://doi.org/10.1515/9783110664454-202

This technology could change the way that ownership, privacy, uncertainty and collaboration are conceived of in the digital world, disrupting sectors and practices as diverse as financial markets, content distribution, supply chain management, the dispersal of humanitarian aid and even voting in a general election. This is why the field of blockchain in the IT sector is growing very fast.

Blockchain technology provides one of the most secure and safe online transactions and has shaken every industry. Due to its numerous benefits, many companies and professionals have started to adopt blockchain technology. It is estimated that blockchain technology has already been adopted by more than one-third of the companies in the world.

Blockchain technology is very transparent as everything is visible to all the participants from the beginning. This reduces the chance for any kind of discrepancy in the system because nothing is hidden. It is also considered the most reasonable in the world from a cost perspective to use for developing solutions, with a lot of the languages freely available as open source for developers to use. If one compares it with traditional software development models, it is a lot less expensive and many companies are now looking to take advantage of this fact and save costs in their economic model; it is starting to prove especially beneficial for the banking and financial industry, something we look at in this book.

The most obvious area where AI and blockchain have already had a huge impact is information technology operations, but there are many areas where they are already changing how businesses interact with us as human beings. Having researched the key business areas where the two technologies are having a combined impact for this book, I selected the most interesting areas which are touching the vast majority of our working and private life in some way. For example, the accounting industry where AI is already revolutionizing the analysis of what is usually a big data problem; maritime and shipping where blockchain and AI are helping the documentation that moves commodities and vessels around the world and analysing weather patterns and routing of vessels; human resources in selecting and finding the best candidates from thousands of resumes; marketing with targeted advertising and information. This list goes on; many of the areas where AI and blockchain are touching our lives already are subtle and so I hope you will enjoy reading this book and find it a useful eye opener to the applications and developments in AI and blockchain that are impacting the world we live in.

Tom James

Acknowledgments

A huge thanks must go to my editorial and research team which includes my son Kiren Chong-James in the UK, Aditya Kumar in India, and Justine Butler in the UK. Your dedication to the project and support was invaluable. Thank you!

I must also give a massive thank you to all of my family who encouraged me to keep pushing on with this book project despite the many difficulties and delays caused by the Covid lockdowns around the world.

Last but certainly not least I would like to dedicate this book to my old school friend, Andrew Fox, who sadly passed away well before his time during the Covid Pandemic in 2020. His passion for computers when we attended school together inspired me to start learning computer languages and work with them since the early 1980s.

https://doi.org/10.1515/9783110664454-203

Contents

Tom James
Chapter 1
Marketing

Artificial Intelligence

Artificial intelligence (AI) frameworks continually take a shot at the foundations of famous items and services like Netflix, Amazon, and Google. As great as these disruptions have been, recent years have seen in a brief time AI clearing an even more profound path into promoting and helping brands improve each progression of the client's venture. As business and technological innovations in AI have gained wider adoption, instruments accessible only once to big business organizations have now opened the door to small- and medium-sized organizations.

Imaginative ideas of an engineered cognizance created by people – a wild development along the lines of science fiction motion pictures – are probably not going to be realized soon. Current AI, though simpler than a sci-fi sapience, are no less disruptive to the world. Today's AI are frameworks capable of performing assignments that would otherwise regularly require human intelligence and oversight. Capable of incorporating aspects of critical thinking, perceiving feelings, playing complex strategy games, and even diagnosing diseases, AI are increasingly matching or surpassing their human counterparts. One only needs to participate in an AI showcasing arrangement to illustrate how much the gap between information science and execution is vanishing.

What is AI in Marketing?

Artificial intelligence marketing (AIM) is a technique for utilizing client information and AI innovations like machine learning to predict your best course of action.

Computer-based intelligence in promoting is the utilization of client information, AI, and other computational ideas to anticipate an individual's activity or inaction. It can take on colossal quantities of information and help advertisers effectively portion them into processable categories. After all relevant information is considered, advertisers can further organize information groupings to make modified content for their crowds. With AI, organizations can make incredibly well-informed promotion strategies to focus on the correct potential clients. This will enable computerized advertisers to take care of clients with the correct content on the correct channel at the correct time.

https://doi.org/10.1515/9783110664454-001

Why is AIM Important?

AI is leaving an enormous impression in advanced marketing. An investigation by Smart Insights shows that out of 100 senior advertisers from various enterprises, 55% of organizations are executing or previously considering utilizing AI in their marketing.

AIM is a practice that allows advertisers to crunch tremendous quantities of marketing information during investigations of internet-based life, messages, and the wider web. Additionally, shorter time periods spent on data collection and processing assists advertisers with boosting effort execution and return on investment (ROI). This gives advertisers and organizations more opportunity to concentrate on other significant assignments.

This is practiced by utilizing big data analytics, machine learning, and different procedures to pick up knowledge and insight into intended interest groups. With these parcels of knowledge, you can make increasingly powerful client contact focuses. Regardless of whether you are participating in email marketing or providing client service, AI takes out a significant part of the mystery associated with client interactions.

AIM will help content advertisers comprehend who precisely their intended interest group is, and accordingly make an individual encounter personalized for clients. On a grander scale, it very well may be utilized to automate forms that were once subject to people. Content generation, PPC promotions, and even website design are all potential applications for AI marketing. It is easy to see why AI will continue to grow in significance beyond 2021.

How to Use AI for Marketing

AI has increasingly been integrated into every industry with benefits not just limited to decreasing human intercession in complex and simple tasks. Usage of AI has concurrently led to an increase in the quality of productive output, by helping people carry out their responsibilities better, with less effort. As such, fields like social media, consumer electronics, robotics, travel and transportation, finance, healthcare, security, surveillance, e-trade, etc., today are already profiting by means of AI.

A good example of where we might see the dynamic benefits of AI is in the creation of a website. Ordinarily, building up a site without at least some expertise in HTML, CSS, and JavaScript is inconceivable for a business. Be that as it may, AI has made it conceivable. Well-known web designers like Wix utilize AI to construct sites. The only human interaction required is in providing the substance, pictures, and page format. Then your expertly crafted site is good to go. Such benefits in skill and efficiency form the new normal in digital marketing.

Digital Marketing

Digital marketing and AI are intrinsically linked. In computerized marketing, there is an imperative to process huge quantities of information. AI encourages computerized advertisers to process information faster, which provides them with the free time and attention to make advanced methodologies more effectively.

Online advertising is one of the most significant components of computerized marketing. It encourages organizations to contact their intended interest group as quickly as possible. A larger part of online promotions we see today are controlled by a muddled conveyance framework fueled by AI, which is classified as "programmatic advertising." The program encourages the purchasing and selling of advertisement spaces. It conducts barters where these advertisement spaces are sold and purchased in timespans measured in fractions of milliseconds.

"Personalization is the new cool." According to Evergage, 96% of advertisers concur that personalization is the way to convey an awesome client experience. AI has made it conceivable to make sense of the preferences, standards of conduct, interests, and exercises of a huge number of individuals consistently. It does so by gathering and breaking down client information while considering factors including (but not limited to) physiography, socioeconomics, gadgets, and geography. The greater the personalization, the greater the odds of change.

AI helps achieve this personalization by doing the math and examining information, two tasks in which AI frameworks are exceptionally proficient. Computer-based intelligence utilizes measurable models and programming to foresee a client's future activities by considering their past conduct and attributes. Along these lines, AI encourages advertisers to find out about their clients, for example, finding out what cost do they expect for a specific item. In view of the information, likewise, AI can anticipate what sort of highlights clients expect in the item update. Advertisers can use this information to make slogans and run battles with the end goal of pulling in more clients and expanding the odds of transformation.

Right now, in the era of auto-created messages, individuals are anticipating customized/personalized messages that are pertinent and personally appealing to them. Computer-based intelligence can assist you with sending a modified email for your email marketing efforts by examining client conduct and inclinations. Simulated intelligence dissects many gigabytes of information to identify the correct title and headline that will catch a client's eye. Likewise, it can locate the correct time, day, and recurrence to send the email, which further raises the odds of transformation.

Sales Forecasting

Sales forecasting is enormous business. If you can reliably foresee the demand of a specific item or administration service you will sell in a given day, you can more readily stock inventory, staff your offices better, and learn more from your business' records, which in doing so you will gain a competitive advantage in the market.

To further assist in forecasting, you can utilize AIM for processing social affairs information about past arrangements. AIM will contemplate the information from messages, gatherings, and certain event calls. AIM can relate the information to the result of the potential deals of your present and future campaigns.

Customer Experience

Through the information assembled by AIM arrangements, it tends to be simpler for advertisers to comprehend what their client's needs are, and when they need it. Advertisers can also make client profiles to make it simpler for them to categorize individuals who are keen on their item from the individuals who are yet considering or unlikely to ever buy (see Figure 1.1).

> By 2025, as many as 95 percent of all customer interactions will be through channels supported by artificial intelligence (AI) technology – Microsoft

AI can be effectively utilized to provide savvy, advantageous and educated client involvement at all points along the client venture. This will bring about reconsidered client encounters and start-to-finish client experiences that are incorporated into an experience, which feels progressively natural to clients.

AI's greatest effect without a doubt will be to change client assistance by making it mechanized, quick, and hassle free. Salesmen, call center specialists, and workers in other client assistance jobs can't be relied upon to ingest and comprehend a client's whole history before every discussion, as this would be an unreasonably time-consuming task for any person. AI, however, is presently making this task a conceivable reality.

AI is helping organizations make encounters that regularly incorporate information of consumer patterns with shoppers' day-to-day routines. Customers will no longer change their example of correspondence while collaborating with brands to fulfill their requirements. Wise expectation and customization will cause clients to feel as though every item or brand experience was custom-made only for them.

Organizations will have the option to evaluate individual customer inventories and purchaser practices to anticipate and order merchandise to homes before they're even aware they are coming up short. Self-driving vehicles will utilize their frameworks to identify the most efficient favored courses and in-vehicle amusement selected from a personal profile based upon past conduct will enhance everyday drives and excursions. Requesting assistance will become a simpler process as AI with the ability to understand and emulate feelings will make client-experience collaborations smoother and streamlined across all channels.

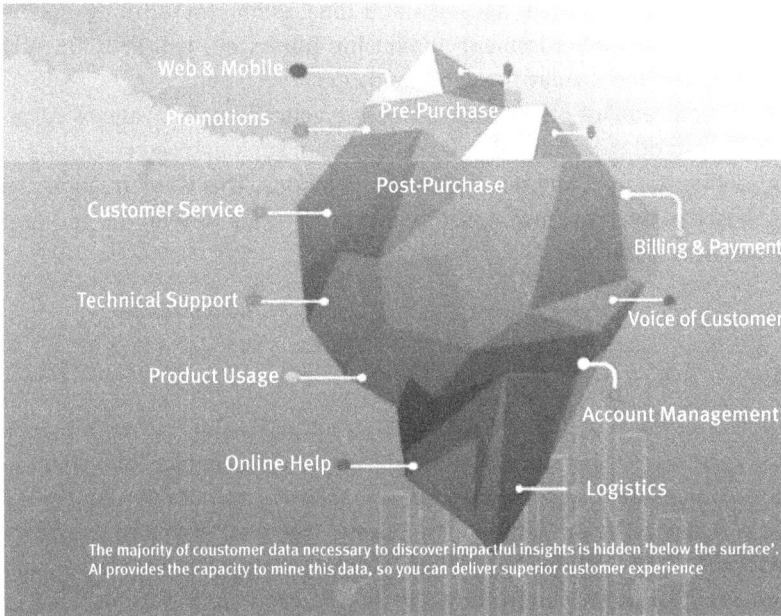

The majority of coustomer data necessary to discover impactful insights is hidden 'below the surface'. AI provides the capacity to mine this data, so you can deliver superior customer experience

Figure 1.1: The Big Data Map of customer data necessary to discover impactful insights for business.
Source: www.pointillist.com; https://www.pointillist.com/blog/role-of-ai-in-customer-experience/

The intensity of AI-empowered client analytics is that it can filter through a greater and progressively complex information space, and in this manner reveal a lot more business opportunities – even opportunities you may not have been aware you ought to be searching for. Therefore, you can invest your energy organizing these bits of knowledge into useful categories as opposed to manually and endlessly poring over a deluge of hidden information.

Programmatic Ad Targeting

Fundamentally, programmatic ad targeting is computerizing all or parts of the promotion purchasing process utilizing programming-driven innovation. The customary method for purchasing/selling advertisements is a long, monotonous procedure that begins with contacting a sales rep, setting up the conditions of an agreement and afterward having it executed. The eventual fate of AI in digital marketing changes that into a simpler robotized process.

With the information from cookies of mobile applications and sites utilized/visited, the AI can target individual clients that match the sponsor's or business' measures. The models the AI constructs to evaluate probability of success and failure can be based upon anything from area, age, sex, and time, among other things. If the model predicts value, the advertisement purchasing framework will consequently offer on the impression and display the winning content.

Facebook's advertisements offer a case of this in practice. Facebook allows advertisers and publicists to utilize information investigation in computerized marketing to make custom profiles to target and retarget their promotions. This is information you share via web-based networking media platforms when you consent on the end-user license agreement (EULA).

Chatbots

Be it for enquiries purchasing, or just making a good complaint, messaging apps like Facebook Messenger, Viber, and WhatsApp have made it simpler for a client to connect with organizations and mention what's at the forefront of their minds. It's free and simple to use for many individuals. Despite the great potential to engage with customers, the tragic reality about utilizing messaging applications for organizations, particularly for large organizations, is that it very well may be difficult or impossible to answer each time a client communicates something specific. Envision answering to a great many messages inside your work hours, and a large portion of them are posing a similar inquiry!

So, what do you do to stay aware of your clients and answer their inquiries? Enter the chatbot – an AI program that can reenact a discussion with a client in normal language.

Chatbots allow organizations to set preordained responses to clients and customers' inquiries as often as possible, for example, by assisting them with finding and purchasing an item they like. This essentially decreases the time that is required for human intercession and reaction, therefore, setting aside time and cash to be spent elsewhere.

From style to well-being or insurance, wise chatbots are already being employed to give engaging client care. At times, they're even greater at making customized content than people.

Chatbots approach a huge number of client information focuses. They can aggregate location-specific requests to identify designs, spot tedious issues, and anticipate what's causing issues for a specific client. Frequently, this makes them more proficient than any human client care rep.

However, chatbots aren't constrained to coordinating client care operations. For example, look at the conversation in Figure 1.2 and guess which one looks more humanlike?

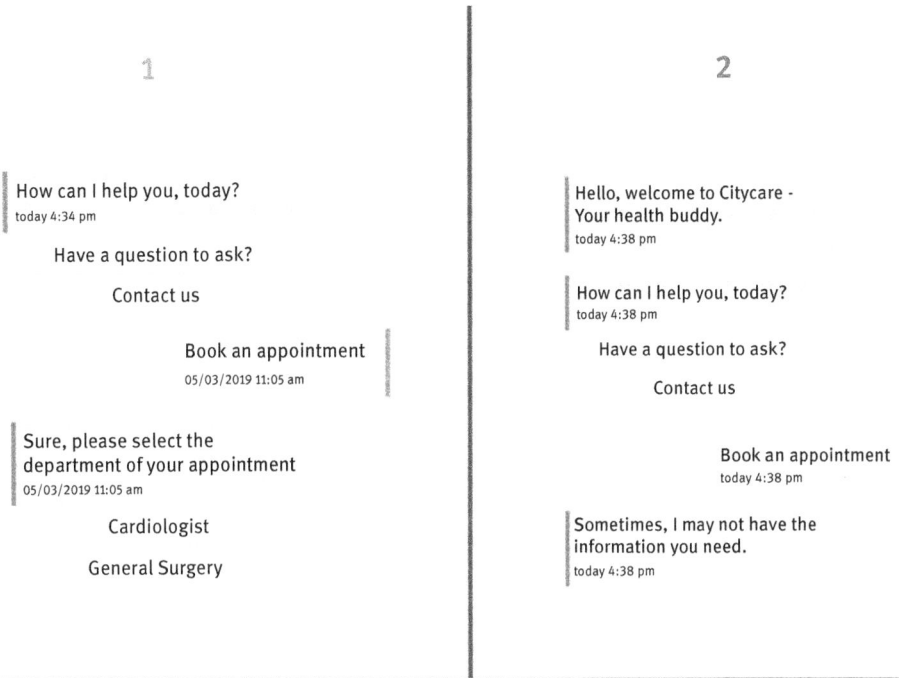

Figure 1.2: Conversation with a chatbot.
Source: *Chatbots Magazine.*

Number 1. Isn't that so?

AI gives a human touch to each discussion a chatbot strikes up. The bot comprehends the client's question and triggers an exact reaction, by using a framework that simulates the way people can see each other's anxiety and give a reaction in a like manner.

Table 1.1: Chatbot with AI vs. Chatbot without AI.

Chatbot with AI Vs. Chatbot without AI	
Answer FAQ	
Yes	Yes
Understand unique query	
Yes	No
Personalize response	
Yes	No

Table 1.1 (continued)

Chatbot with AI Vs. Chatbot without AI	
Learn from past conversations	
Yes	No
Improve future conversations	
Yes	No

Source: Author.

From Table 1.1 we can conclude:

1. A Chatbot with AI powers makes your bot fit and keen to answer complex questions. The collaboration is conversational, natural, and energetic.
2. Chatbot gains from each discussion it has with the clients. It experiences the past cooperation to improve the present reaction. This action assists with improving the proficiency of bot reaction. In addition, assists with understanding your client's decisions and inclinations.
3. Keen connections spare the client's time by helping them to locate the correct data and address their inquiries.

Speech Recognition

Need to feel what it's like to have an AI assistant like Jarvis from the Marvel film "Iron Man"? All things considered, Jarvis is conceivably still far ahead of present-day technological capabilities, however, that doesn't mean the creation of a true AI assistant won't occur at some point in the future. At present, we have comparatively promised AIs with speech recognition capabilities – Siri, Google Assistant, or Alexa among others – each constituting an AI chatbot with voice recognition capabilities capable of assisting users with various queries.

These AIs can perceive certain expressed words and convert them into the content to be executed in the correct order. Speech recognition is even utilized in applications, for example, Google Maps, Shazam, and different handheld devices.

So, by what method would marketers be able to exploit speech recognition for their campaigns? According to projections on virtual assistant ownership, >55% of families will have a savvy speaker by 2022 up from only 13% in 2018. Furthermore, deals from vocal shopping orders are predicted to soar to US$40 billion in 2022, up from just US$2 billion out of 2018. Assuming the predictions are accurate, this speaks volumes (pun intended), as far as the need to utilize speech recognition in any marketing effort goes.

The general speech and voice recognition market is estimated to reach US$21.5 billion by 2024 from US$7.5 billion out of 2018, at a compound annual growth rate (CAGR) of 19.18%. The development of the speech and voice recognition market can be ascribed to the high development potential in medicinal services application, developing interest for voice confirmation in versatile financial application, fast expansion of multifunctional gadgets or smart speakers, and the developing effect of AI on the precision of speech and voice recognition (see Figure 1.3).

Attractive Opportunities in Speech and Voice Recognition Market

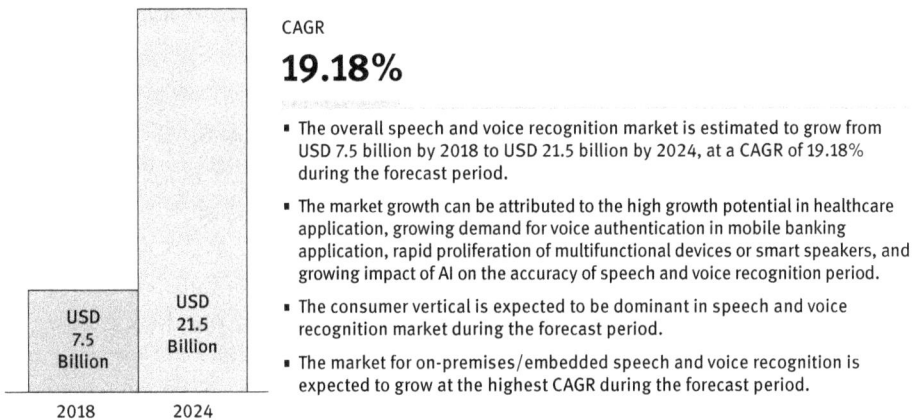

CAGR

19.18%

- The overall speech and voice recognition market is estimated to grow from USD 7.5 billion by 2018 to USD 21.5 billion by 2024, at a CAGR of 19.18% during the forecast period.

- The market growth can be attributed to the high growth potential in healthcare application, growing demand for voice authentication in mobile banking application, rapid proliferation of multifunctional devices or smart speakers, and growing impact of AI on the accuracy of speech and voice recognition period.

- The consumer vertical is expected to be dominant in speech and voice recognition market during the forecast period.

- The market for on-premises/embedded speech and voice recognition is expected to grow at the highest CAGR during the forecast period.

USD 7.5 Billion — 2018

USD 21.5 Billion — 2024

Figure 1.3: Attractive opportunities in speech and voice recognition market.
Source: Markets and Markets Analysis.

When contrasted with speech recognition, the voice recognition advertising industry is estimated to develop at a higher rate from 2021 to 2024 inferable from the developing utilization of voice recognition in multifaceted validation frameworks in Banking, Financial Services, and Insurance (BFSI), government, and defense verticals (Figure 1.4). In North America and Western Europe, an enormous number of banking clients use telephone banking services. A significant number of these money-related foundations are embracing voice-based validation answers for acknowledging or dismissing versatile exchanges from a client. Moreover, the market for voice recognition innovation is observed to grow higher in the administration, finance, and enterprise verticals during the following two–three years. This warrants emphasizing the information security worries due to cyberattacks and data breaches by intruders increasing concurrent to the high development of the voice recognition showcase.

SPEECH AND VOICE RECOGNITION MARKET, BY REGION (USD BILLION)

21.5

7.5

2016   2017   2018-e   2019   2020   2021   2022   2023-p   2024

■ Americas   ■ Europe   ■ APAC   ▫ RoW

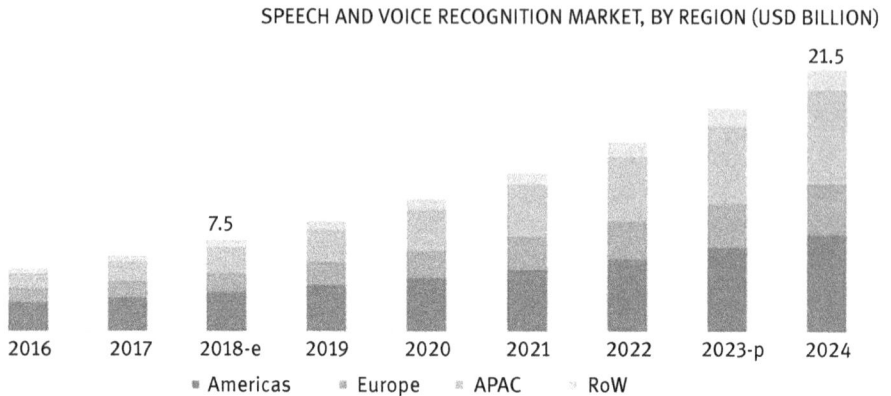

Figure 1.4: Speech and voice recognition market, by region (USD billion).
Source: Industry Experts, Secondary Research, and Markets and Markets Analysis.

Content *Generation*

The manual age of substance and content generation is full of dull procedures. Instead, envision having a site that can create its own substance. You don't need to recruit essayists or editors, and you'll have a self-supporting site that can procure results for you. Life would be simpler for you as an advertiser. Imagine a scenario where you realized that AI calculations would already be able to go this far.

This is called content generation. You've presumably perused generated content without knowing or seeing it. Tragically, AI is not yet able to make long and smoothly composed articles by CEOs, industry pioneers, bloggers, and other skilled scholars offering expert information and analysis. Where it excels (as of this composition), is in generating straightforward stories and narratives. For example, stock updates, monetary reports, sports news, etc.

If you need assistance in creating customized content for your site, there's another method to do, it's called content intelligence. In contrast to content generation, this furnishes makers with information-driven input and bits of knowledge for progressively powerful substance that will yield better outcomes (see Figure 1.5).

At present, content marketing has expanded into a worldwide industry. It's pervasive to the point that some allude to it as the main kind of marketing.

Computer-based intelligence is approaching the point where it can possibly both minister and produce content, at that point placing it before the comparative skill of ideal individuals on the right platforms. This innovation is now robotizing the content age on an essential level, yet in the end, AI could create practical subjects for authors, or even create beginning drafts of substance dependent on specific parameters.

Content Marketing Vision

Version 1: Intuition-based Content Marketing
- o Content is created & promoted based on intuition.
- o Marketers don't know how their content is performing.

I have no idea what I'm doing.

Version 2: Insight-based Content Marketing
- o Content is created & promoted based on insights on past-performance data.
- o Marketers measure content performance tied to revenue.

How am I performing today?

Version 3: Predictive Content Marketing
- o Content is created & promoted through forecasted predictions on performance.
- o Marketers receive predictions on how their content will perform in the future.

If I do X, how will it perform?

Version 4: Autonomous Content Marketing
- o Content is partially-created & promoted autonomous based on predictive analytics with massive personalization.
- o Marketers simply input their content ideas, budget requirements, and desired results.

Here is what I want. Do it for me.

Figure 1.5: Content marketing vision.
Source: www.curata.com

On the strategy side, AI can possibly assist advertisers with mapping out a start-to- finish content procedure. As of today, some marketing techniques are providing this component. I anticipate it will also have the option to create far reaching reports providing details regarding content activities, with next to zero human work included.

Dynamic Pricing

This AI is frequently referred to as customized evaluating. It's an appraisal system wherein an item's cost is dictated by demand as well as supply. A genuine model is the costs of ride-sharing applications that increases as the number of requests rises or when you can't discover a rebate when you have to buy an item on the web.

An application's bot or site's bot can screen your predictive analytics use cases, for example, cookies, history, web searches, and different exercises, to furnish you with constant reestimations. This implies you get lesser discounts as well as more significant expenses for the item/service you need right now. It sounds unreasonable, but there are always different sides to a story.

Clients can profit by dynamic pricing when the demand for an item is low. A genuine case of this is when lodgings/hotels go unsold. To help increase the odds of a secured business opportunity, dynamic pricing can offer serious value for clients to create business opportunities.

80% of study members considered value the absolute most significant factor in a buy.

Even though they are mind boggling models, these dynamic pricing AI models are grounded in an exceptionally basic idea:

Convey the correct cost for each client while expanding income for the business.

Have you at any point wondered how Uber, Amazon, and Airbnb entered established markets and pulverized all their rivals in business? One of the significant common factors of success for these three tech goliaths is that they've integrated dynamic pricing as a central spoke for their marketing operations, matching the immediate supply to the immediate demand in the market for the optimum price.

Here's a model of this in action: the charge of an Uber ride is considerably lower than an ordinary taxi. When there's a cultural event likely to drive up demand, for example, when there's a match or a ball game coming up and the demand spikes, the costs also will see a rise to match demand. To watch the game, you must pay progressively because of the demand. The upside is, provided you tolerate the increased fare you will also benefit from the consistent availability of Ubers to hire despite the recent increase in demand. Since the fares are better there will be more drivers around the ballpark, thus allocating the availability of services where the demand has also increased. As these cultural events end, the demand returns to the market normal and the accessibility increases as the cost decreases to match the lowered demand.

What are the Core Benefits of AI in Marketing?

AIM has been gaining more attention among advertisers considering the benefits it provides. As indicated by an ongoing PwC study, 72% view AI as a "business advantage."

Increasingly Intelligent Searches

As cutting-edge innovation arrangements develop more brilliant and intelligent frameworks, it's important to remember that customers are getting more intelligent as well. Because of online networking and rapid-fire search engines (says thanks to Google!), individuals find what they are searching for quicker than any time in recent memory. AI and large information arrangements can really break down these search arrangements and assist advertisers in identifying and prioritizing areas where they should center their endeavors.

More Astute Ads

Advertisers are plunging their toes into more astute promotions, with account-based marketing arrangements and AI assistants providing valuable assistance with rapid analysis of huge sums of internet data. With another medium of information accessible, online advertisements can become even more effective and wide-reaching. AI arrangements can delve profoundly into keyword searches, social profiles, and other online information for human-level results.

Refined Content Delivery

With AI, advertisers can take information and targeting to an entire new level. Audience analytics can go past the regular socioeconomics level, to comprehend customers on an individual basis. Presently, marketing personnel can utilize AI to both recognize potential customers or purchasers and convey the perfect content that is generally applicable to them. With big data, machine learning, and AI joined, there is very little a wise marketer can't accomplish.

Depending on Bots

Client assistance and retention is another territory where AI in the future will play an emerging critical role. Before long, chat functions and other direct-to-consumer engagement will be controlled by AI bots. Numerous organizations can spare representative time and expenses with these strategies. AI bots additionally approach a whole web of information, data, and search narratives, making them substantially more effective than their human partners.

Continued Learning

Perhaps the most promising feature of AI is that it can really be "educated," learning how to fuse recently revealed experiences into new campaigns, enhancing efforts to target the most significant and promising of clients. Over time, these AI arrangements will turn out to be progressively more intelligent, more conversational, and more capable of adept real-time decision-making.

What is the Future Ahead for AI in Marketing?

The future of AI in marketing is likely to see impact marketing methodologies, including plans of action, deal procedures, and client assistance alternatives, such as client practices. These looming changes may be best comprehended utilizing three illustrative cases from assorted businesses.

In the transportation business, driverless, AI-empowered vehicles might be coming around the bend, promising to adjust both business models and client conduct. Taxi and ride-sharing organizations must advance to avoid from being outcompeted by AI-empowered transportation models; demand for accident coverage (from individual clients) and breathalyzers (less individuals will drive, particularly in the wake of drinking) will probably decrease, though demand for security frameworks that shield vehicles from being hacked will increase in demand. Driverless vehicles could also affect the engaging quality of land, since (1) driverless vehicles can move at quicker speeds, thus drive times will lessen, and (2) drive times will be increasingly beneficial for travelers, who can securely work while being headed toward their daily goals. In that capacity, living in remote areas may turn out to be progressively appealing, versus the case today (see Table 1.2).

Table 1.2: Industry usage of AI.

Industry or Usage Context (specific firm or AI application)	Description
AI in driverless cars (e.g., Tesla)	In the future, AI- enable cars may allow for car journeys without any driver input, with the potential to significantly impact various industries (e.g., insurance, taxi service) and customer behaviors (e.g., whether they still buy cars).
Online retailing AI (e.g., Birchbox)	AI will enable better predictions for what customers want, which may cause firms to move away from a shopping-then-shipping business model and toward a shipping-then-shopping business model.
Fashion-related AI (e.g., Stitch Fix)	AI applications support stylists, who curate a set of clothing items for customers. Stitch Fix's AI analyzes both numeric and image/other non-numeric data.
Sales AI (e.g., Conversica)	AI bots can automate parts of the sale process, augmenting the capabilities of existing sales teams. There may be backlash if customers know (upfront) that they are chatting with an AI bot (even if the AI bot is otherwise capable)
Customer service robots (e.g., Rock'em and Sock'em; Pepper)	Robots with task-automating AI respond to relatively simple customer service requests (e.g., making cocktails).
Emotional support AI (e.g., Replika)	AI aims to provide emotional support to customer by asking meaningful questions, offering social support and adjusting to users' linguistic syntax.
In-car AI (e.g., Affectiva)	In-car AI that analyse driver data (e.g., facial expression) to evaluate drivers' emotional and cognitive states.

Table 1.2 (continued)

Industry or Usage Context (specific firm or AI application)	Description
Customer screening AI (e.g., Kanetix)	AI used to identify customers who should be provided incentives to buy insurance (and avoid those who (1) are already likely to buy and (2) those unlikely to buy).
Business process AI (e.g., IBM Interact)	AI used for multiple (simple) applications, such as customized offers (e.g., Bank of Montreal).
Retail store AI (e.g., Café X, Lowebot, 84.51, Bossa Nova)	Robots that can serve as coffee baristas, respond to simple customer service requests in Lowe's stores, and identifying misshelved items in grocery stores.
Security AI (e.g., knightscope' K5)	Security robots patrol in office or malls, equipped with superior sensing capabilities (e.g., thermal cameras).
Spiritual support AI (e.g., BlessU-2; Xian'er)	Customizable robot priest/monk offering blessings in different languages to the user.
Companion robot AI (e.g., Harmony from Realbotix)	Customizable robot companion, which promises reduce loneliness to the user.

Source: SpringerLink Research.

Secondly, AI will influence deals formed between different businesses. Most sales reps depend upon making a phone call (or comparable medium) as a basic staple of the business procedure. The future will see salesmen helped by an AI specialist that screens tele-discussions continuously. For instance, utilizing propelled voice investigation capacities, an AI operator may have the option to gather from a client's tone that an unmentioned issue stays an issue and give real-time feedback to control the (human) sales rep's next methodology. In this sense, AI could increase a salespersons' abilities, yet it also may trigger unintended contrary outcomes, particularly if clients feel awkward about an AI observing discussions. Additionally, later, firms may basically rely upon AI bots, which – now and again – work just as human sales reps, to reach deal possibilities. Yet, the peril of human bias remains; if clients find that they are communicating with a bot, they may get awkward, feel uncanny, or intimidated, activating negative outcomes.

Thirdly, the plan of action right now utilized by online retailers for the most part expects clients to put orders, after which the online retailer dispatches the items (the shopping-then-transportation model). With AI, online retailers might have the option to anticipate what clients will need; expecting that these items match their client's demands, retailers may progress to a delivery then-shopping plan of action. That is, retailers will utilize AI to recognize clients' inclinations and deliver things to clients without a proper request, with clients having the alternative to return what they do not need. This move would change retailers' marketing techniques, plans of action, and client practices (e.g., data search). Organizations like Birchbox, Stitch Fix, and Trendy Butler as of now use AI to attempt to foresee what their clients need, with shifting degrees of accomplishment.

Blockchain

The underlying foundations of blockchain innovation can be traced back to 1991 when Stuart Haber and W. Scott Stornetta proposed an idea called a blockchain. It was a framework that comprised of a chain of blocks protected by cryptography and verified by digital timestamps that couldn't be changed.

In 2008, an anonymous person (it is uncertain whether they were an individual or group of people operating under a pseudonym) named Satoshi Nakamoto utilized this idea to present Bitcoin – a cryptocurrency that empowered individuals to complete exchanges without the need for a middle person, for example, a bank.

Through the span of 10 years, a few digital forms of money entered the market, for example, Ethereum, Litecoin, Ripple, EOS, etc. In any case, it is important not to mistake Bitcoin or other cryptocurrencies as the sole application for blockchain technology. Cryptocurrencies are just a single use of the enormous potential behind blockchain, which is the most secure way yet to encode sensitive data.

Blockchain might be a moderately recent innovation, yet it's already changing the world. An ongoing overview by Deloitte found that 83% of respondents see convincing uses for blockchain in 2019, up from 74% in 2018.

Advertisers are also standing by enthusiastically to perceive how blockchain will affect or streamline their work. Many companies have gone to blockchain and marketing specialists to figure out how the innovation is presently being utilized in the marketing field, and how marketers can best leverage blockchain technology later.

What is Blockchain in Marketing?

A portion of the key principles of blockchain technology – transparency, security, and availability – are conceivably set to disrupt almost every industry, including marketing and advertising. In any case, what precisely is blockchain marketing?

Blockchain marketing imagines an altogether new advertising and marketing condition where purchasers can possess and sell their information legitimately to advertisers and promoters. This implies bypassing social media platforms like Facebook and Instagram completely, so there's more trust and convenient use of shopper information.

Blockchain technology is being used to create an information trade among shoppers and brands. "Developed from the beginning to emphasize the connection among brands and shoppers, blockchain marketing outperforms the middleman." This is essential since social media platforms like Facebook ordinarily gather information by following client action, yet the subsequent data is low quality, and comes with an associated customer mistrust with this sort of social media observation (see Figure 1.6).

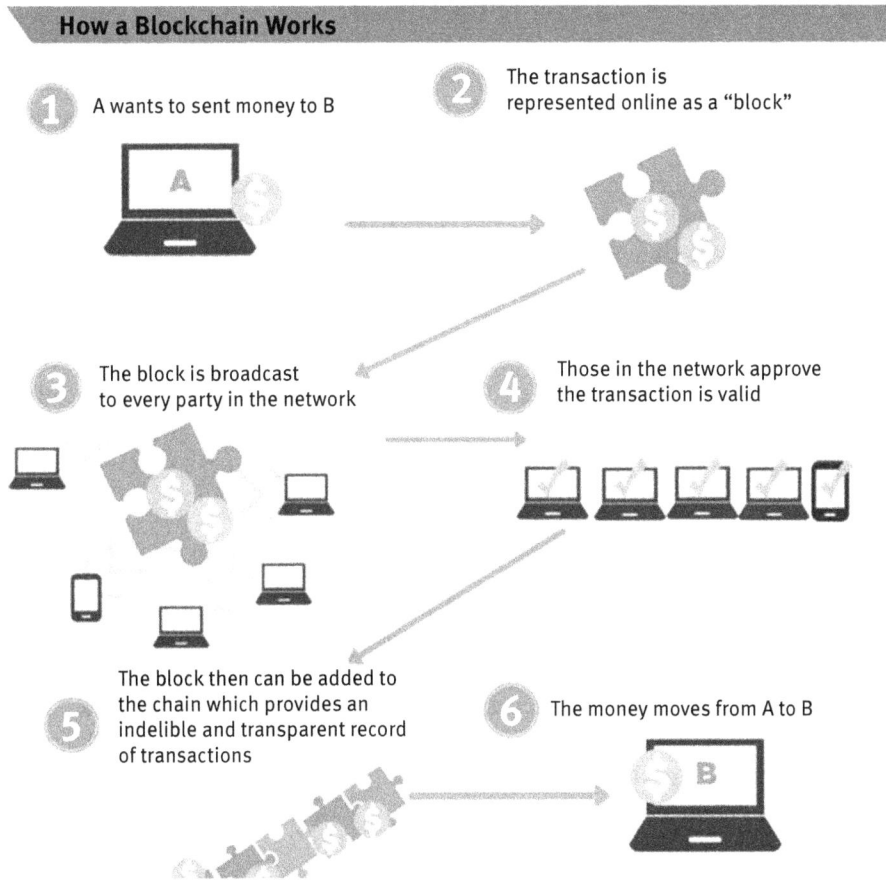

How a Blockchain Works

1. A wants to sent money to B

2. The transaction is represented online as a "block"

3. The block is broadcast to every party in the network

4. Those in the network approve the transaction is valid

5. The block then can be added to the chain which provides an indelible and transparent record of transactions

6. The money moves from A to B

Figure 1.6: How a blockchain works.
Source: webforum.org

When the World Wide Web first brought the individuals of earth close together, it had an equalizing impact (generally): Anyone with access to a PC, an ISP, and power could profit by the web, regardless of once great geographical barriers or market access. Something remarkably similar will occur with information. Each person on the planet will have rights concerning who utilizes their information, and the instrument that will make this privacy achievable is blockchain encryption.

This coming democratization of information won't just give clients much more say about how their information is utilized, it will also push advertisers to think of better approaches to cooperate with clients and improve their shopping experience in some way. Furthermore, you will have the option to accumulate more precise information about every client, even more so than you ever could with cookies.

Why is Blockchain Marketing Important?

To see how blockchain will change the marketing scene, we should take a gander at the three principal reasons why blockchain technology is rapidly being adopted:

1. *Decentralization*

In a concentrated or customer server model, there's (at least one) entity known as the server that has all the data, and you (the customer) must communicate with the server to access the data. For instance, if you must send cash to somebody by means of the web, you have to do so by engaging with a mediator, for example, a bank. Alongside the addition of a broker, the unified model is vulnerable to numerous dangers like information leaks.

By contrast, a person-to-person (P2P) server is decentralized. There's no single host of the data. Actually, as observed before, each hub in the system stores the data locally. Thus, if you need to send cash to somebody, you can do so straightforwardly without directing it through a broker.

2. *Unchanging Nature*

The second benefit is security through the immutable nature of blockchain records. When a block is verified, the information stored can't be adjusted or deleted. Any attempt to deceive a block in the blockchain will altogether change the information alongside the hash of its past blocks. Since the entire blockchain has now transformed, it can't be confirmed by any other hub. Anybody attempting to hack into the blockchain needs to modify records at every hub, which is practically impossible.

3. *Transparency*

Since blockchain is a distributed digital ledger, all members in the blockchain have access to the exchanges that have occurred. This may sound alarming at a first glance, however there's no compelling reason to be alarmed. Though all the exchanges are accessible to the blockchain members, the identity of each transaction's members remains anonymous.

On a larger scale, blockchain innovation can possibly handle a few hidden separation points in marketing and advertising: transparency of supply chains and ad fraud.

In 2018, promoters lost an expected $19 billion to extortion, as indicated by Juniper Research. Subsequently, the absolute greatest names in tech are turning to blockchain for solutions to battle scams and criminal schemes, endeavoring to construct transparency by making a basic budgetary compromise for digital media buying. Others are taking a deep look at how blockchain can be utilized in the buying procedure itself, maybe permitting gatherings to exchange directly utilizing their own cryptocurrency.

How to Use Blockchain for Marketing

Blockchain innovation is set to disrupt all sectors – BFSI, real estate, media, retail, medicinal services, and legal, just to name a few. Big corporate names, like IBM, Microsoft, Oracle, Intel, and Apple have seen the potential and have begun to make advances into utilizing blockchain technology.

With so much promotion encompassing the innovation, we should look at the blockchain techniques and best practices that are changing the marketing scene.

Influencer Marketing

Brands are intensely focusing their resources into big name and smaller scale influencers to spread their message to a more engaged, younger crowd, inaccessible to many forms of traditional advertising. Despite the apparent strengths of influencer marketing bypassing adblocks and attaching a personality to a product or brand, influencer marketing gets a terrible reputation in marketing strategy because of sleuth of issues. Trouble in following the ROI, an absence of transparency with cases of sponsorships or marketing deals not being disclosed to audience subscribers and scams such as phony supporters being used to lure in marketers with a false image of popularity and market reach.

Blockchain can adequately resolve these issues by presenting smart contracts in the ecosystem. Smart contracts will encourage the payout upon the completion of a certain activity or upon delivery of the ideal outcomes.

This innovation can also be utilized to confirm the performance and authenticity of the influencer. For example, Socialmedia.market is an Ethereum-based influencer marketing stage that empowers promoters to work with influencers and offers a dispute solution framework.

Improved Cost and Operations Efficiency

Any CFO or COO will value a portion of the ground-floor enhancements blockchain brings to the table. For example, the speed with which exchanges can be completed carefully will significantly expand the quantity of exchanges per second, from a thousand to millions per second, and every one of those exchanges provides a brand with value.

As indicated by an Accenture report, receiving blockchain could cut framework costs by 30%. Maybe more interesting is that blockchain expels the requirement for outsiders to be engaged with transactions, emails, or other kinds of promoting. Blockchain gives brands an immediate link to every client, and capital that once used to be given to middlemen would now be able to be applied to more productive expansion of the company.

Boosts for the Brand

Further stringent development of data protection rights will in future constrain brands to treat client privacy with closer regard. The current arrangement where clients concerned about their privacy may have to opt out of hundreds of cookies every time, they try to use an online service simply results in a disregard for customer privacy, or customers abandoning services altogether. Blockchain technology will streamline this process of information sharing or protection. Brands should be unequivocal about getting authorization to gather data and straightforward in explaining what will be done with such data. This sort of straightforwardness will inculcate trust, and with data breaches being such a common issue, brands need all the assistance they can get to avoid falling short of legal requirements. Blockchain can improve consumer trust in different ways as well. For example, blockchain would make it viable for a marketing brand to pen down case studies showcasing how it ensures data transparency in a manner freely verifiable (see Figure 1.7).

Smart Contracts

IBM succinctly defines smart contracts (otherwise called cryptocontracts) as lines of code that are put away on a blockchain and naturally execute when preordained terms and conditions are met.

Smart contracts are frequently self-executing, identifiable, irreversible and contain the details of the understanding between the purchaser and the merchant. Their self-executing characteristic wipes out the requirement for middlemen.

Previously all used through the business-to-business (B2B) condition, smart contracts use blockchain to vet and confirm each contract, which is then connected to each exchange identified with that contract. Brands can trade money, offers, or other incentives in a completely straightforward way. Also, this opens the path for cross-promotional marketing among brands and would apply to channels like social media where influencers assume such a major role.

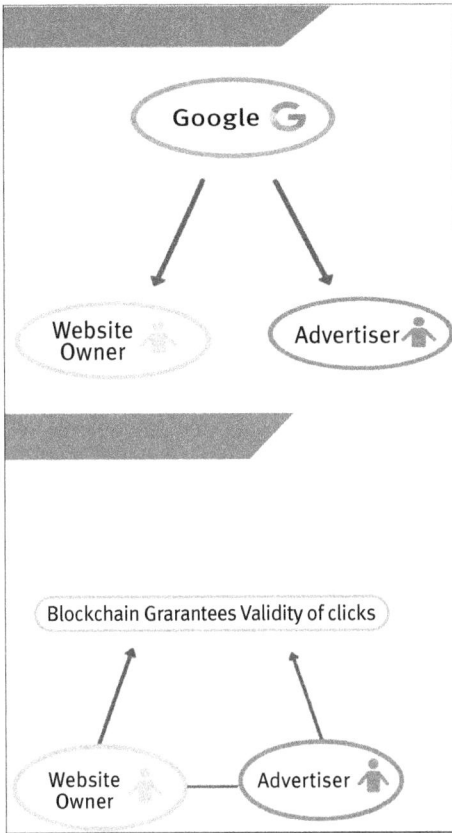

Figure 1.7: Data transparency.
Source: Search Engine Land.

For instance, while working with an expert/consultant, organizations can utilize a smart contract that will consequently discharge the installment upon the effective consummation of the expectations. Along these lines, there's no requirement for extra advances, for example, invoicing.

Loyalty Programs

Clients join loyalty programs since they are either effectively faithful to your brand or are hoping to get redeemable discounts. The average American family is a part of 29 diverse loyalty programs yet utilizes just 12 of them.

The issue with loyalty programs for clients is in the redemption of points. Clients need to monitor distinctive loyalty programs and reclaim them before the offer lapses. In this way, instead of being a win-win situation for brands and clients, it turns out to be detrimental for both, since brands and customers alike are missing out by creating a liability and lost gain, respectively.

Loyalty programs filled by blockchain can take care of this issue by presenting a frictionless framework. As blockchain is decentralized, different brands can work together by permitting clients to reclaim loyalty points with any brands within the system. Since the loyalty points are stored continuously, clients can reclaim them on the go. In such a way, everybody in the system wins.

Example: Loyalcoin, Sandblock, and KeyoCoin are a part of the loyalty program arrangements created on blockchain innovation.

Incentives and Discounts

Based on loyalty program participation, numerous brands have had difficulties with making sense of how to get clients to react to discounts, just as they have pondered how to determine what the optimal discount rate ought to be. If the brand offers too little, clients won't go through the hassle of attempting to reclaim a coupon through their application. Offer a discount that is too generous, and the brand's margin goes down. What's more, if nobody's reacting to your incentive program, your brand isn't gathering any client data.

Blockchain addresses this problem by simplifying the relationship between customer loyalty, reward, and data collection. For example, an organization called GAT-COIN plans to consolidate blockchain and mobile targeting to assist retailers with pulling in and retaining new clients. Through an omnichannel stage, brands can issue "trader tokens" to a huge crowd of clients in an assortment of flavors, from prepaid money tokens to discount, gift, and travel tokens.

Paying Users to View ads

We live in the consideration economy where if you're not catching the clients' consideration, you're losing it. Brands pour truckloads of cash in internet promoting to such an extent that the market for worldwide digital advertisement consumption is anticipated to grow up to 333.25 billion USD before the current year is over.

Since blockchain is so difficult to degenerate and records precise narratives of online conduct, this innovation of information technology is ideal for making it possible to uncover one of the greatest conundrums in internet promoting: how can you ever be truly certain that anybody is looking at your online content? Metrics like clicks can be spoofed by bots, whilst someone can watch an advertisement and never leave a click.

Utilizing blockchain, a brand could now really pay clients to watch promotions and accordingly confirm that the advertisement was conveyed and seen by a genuine individual. This would incorporate enhancing the recurrence of advertisements to guarantee that you're not over-delivering them. In all likelihood clients would be paid in a blockchain currency that could be traded out through a loyalty program.

Blockchain can assist you with benefiting as much as possible from your venture by demonstrating your advertisements to the intended interest group that is generally interested in your offerings. For instance, a blockchain-based web browser called Brave empowers its clients to choose the sorts of advertisements they get to see. Brave has presented Basic Attention Token (BAT), an Ethereum-based utility token that gets circulated among publishers and customers depending upon the promotions seen. In this way, basically, the advertiser is giving clients value in exchange for their attention, guaranteeing that the advertisement spending plan is effectively spent.

Other examples: Kind Ads and Impetus One offer highlights in a similar vein.

Content Licensing

There are other client engagement applications, like safely paying clients for utilization of any of their brand products or content, such as photographs or recordings that incorporate your brand. This is particularly pertinent to social media influencers yet could be expanded in scope to any copyrightable material utilized, in a crusade to guarantee that makers of videos, pictures, or music have conceded legitimate rights of use to other content producers and are well compensated for their work.

Verification Services

The open-source nature of blockchain affords it a vast range of potential future applications. Blockchain can enable frameworks that are decentralized, scalable, and secure. For example, valid authentication controlled by private-public encryption framework is a built-in feature of blockchain. This feature, combined with the simple availability of peer-to-peer functions, empower blockchain to give the best in-class arrangements in data accreditation and document verification. Numerous new businesses have just begun to take a shot at blockchain based data verification solutions. Stampery is one such company that furnishes coordinated data verification with auditable forensics.

Educational institutions can also use blockchain to execute worldwide frameworks intended to authenticate educational documents, consequently empowering students, selection representatives and other legitimate entities to freely check records in a flash.

Blockchain-based Social Platforms

Social media applications have amassed billions of clients since the most recent decade. Although social media has given clients a lot of chances to associate with their family, peers, most loved brands, and celebs, it comes at the expense of their data. Since promotion deals are the essential income stream for social media apps, they track activity to improve their focused research capacities. This information combined with the latest data leaks has made clients wary in regard to utilizing social media.

Example: Blockchain-based social media stages give power back to clients. Apps, for example, Peepeth and mastodon.social are taking care of precisely the same issue.

What are the Core Benefits of Blockchain in Marketing?

With verified profiles dependent on trusted data, brands can essentially improve their marketing programs. The present client profiles are siloed in certain brand databases like Facebook and Google; however, marketing can be substantially closer and important if it's planned over numerous sources.

Even though the marketing proverb "right message, perfect individual, opportune time" isn't new information to anyone, blockchain provides a new more predictable route for this to be validated. What's more, it includes a truly necessary layer of consent. Blockchain-empowered marketing allows the customer to choose when, where, and how brands can associate with them.

The advantages don't end at consent. Purchasers can also expect a few different advantages that span investment funds and security. Since advertising will be especially effective and less expensive to brands, individuals will really get a good deal on items. Since data protections and transparency across profiles, advertising, and exchanges will be fundamentally upgraded, digital fraud will eventually vanish.

Here are four different ways your marketing efforts can profit by blockchain innovation:

1. *Diminished Costs*

Since blockchain is a decentralized, peer-to-peer technology, you can reduce costs right off the bat by expelling third parties/middlemen from the condition. Promotion networks are infamous for redundancy and waste, begging to be spent for the sake of charges or benefit cuts. The incorporation of smart contracts guarantees that you're paying just for the details of the understanding met. This empowers brands to manage publishers, specialists, external merchants, or clients and pay them without depending on the middlemen. And while blockchain may acquire some foundational costs, this is offset by the fact that the exchange costs are nearly zero.

2. *Crowd Targeting*

By decentralizing the advertising ecosystem, brands can straightforwardly interface with the correct publishers and take their message to the target audience. Since clients get paid for survey advertisements, brands can also be guaranteed that they'll get the most value for their money.

For instance, a near-field communications (NFC) label sewn into a luxury handbag and associated with an application can empower a brand to push messages to the handbag's owner, who is associated on the blockchain to that individual item. An opted-in bag owner can be welcomed to an exclusive occasion/event with her bag going about as the ticket/entry pass to that occasion/event, or get discount codes for another handbag when the manufacturer of that handbag realizes the present one is approaching the end of its life expectancy.

Blockchain-empowered focusing can also be utilized with specific areas, maybe driving footfall into another store to redeem a voucher. This mix of offline and online drivers gives advertisers a ground-breaking weapon to add to their arsenal.

3. *Increased Efficiency*

In general, work that includes desk work will be tedious and repetitive. Take receipt/invoice preparing for instance. When you raise a receipt, you must hang tight for the payment. You must wait until a middleman releases the payment. Blockchain handles these issues by empowering exchanges to occur progressively. Since the data is open to both gatherings, it isn't important to keep up discrete records, and the execution of smart contracts encourages immediate payment when the terms in the understanding are met.

4. *Decentralized Applications*

With regard to conventional mobile applications, the standards are directed by the Play Store or App Store. The equivalent goes for any platform that has a solitary position controlling the entire platform.

Since no single authority administers decentralized applications, no one party can dictate terms of operation to another – application makers are not left to the mercy of application hosts. Steem empowers brands to make applications and gives them a chance to earn and build such a decentralized network. Ethereum, EOS, NEO, Tron, Cardano, etc., are also a few stages that empower you to fabricate applications on their platform.

What is the Future Ahead for Blockchain in Marketing?

Interest from buyers to control their own data will only increase in the following years, and blockchain with its consent-based access and difficult to split security is a great choice in data management technology moving forward. Nevertheless, blockchain alone won't be sufficient. It's one piece of an innovative arrangement. Compatible frameworks and applications should be worked to make it generally conceivable to utilize blockchain encryption, however, purchasers (especially in the United States) will also have to be educated about its nature and demand its implementation.

In the following years blockchain encryption is going to ascend as a worldwide security arrangement and as a route for individual clients to have power over their digital profiles and digital footprints. Blockchain can change society, creating brand transparency, greater privacy controls, and access to more useful client related data.

We're still quite a few years off from across-the-board blockchain marketing adoption. Certain factors could increase or decrease the rate of adoption. Company or department enthusiasm, knowledge of blockchain marketing technology, changing government standards and consumer expectations all set the pace for innovation adoption. Most importantly, as marketing companies adopt blockchain marketing, it has the effect of pressuring competing companies to adopt or become uncompetitive. Subsequently the common position for marketing associations is to prepare their organization for a blockchain adoption wave. This implies putting resources into appropriated capacities – finding approaches to empower a higher level of decentralization, transparency, protection, and value-based throughput – with the goal that organizations can completely bolster blockchain use cases in preparation for the future.

Further Reading

Artificial Intelligence

https://www.mageplaza.com/blog/ai-marketing-what-why-how.html
https://emarsys.com/learn/blog/artificial-intelligence-marketing-solutions/
https://www.forbes.com/sites/forbesagencycouncil/2019/08/21/how-artificial-intelligence-is-transforming-digital-marketing/#f67d11421e1b
https://contentmarketinginstitute.com/2017/08/marketers-use-artificial-intelligence/
https://medium.com/datadriveninvestor/10-applications-of-artificial-intelligence-in-digital-marketing-a562a37db2bd
https://www.pointillist.com/blog/role-of-ai-in-customer-experience/
https://chatbotsmagazine.com/why-artificial-intelligence-plays-an-important-role-in-chatbot-development-7a6da9fd1817
https://www.marketsandmarkets.com/Market-Reports/speech-voice-recognition-market-202401714.html
http://www.curata.com/blog/content-intelligence/
https://hackernoon.com/ai-and-dynamic-pricing-secret-weapon-of-tech-giants-today-yln32ut
https://link.springer.com/article/10.1007/s11747-019-00696-0

Blockchain

https://www.martechadvisor.com/articles/blockchain/what-is-blockchain-how-to-use-it-in-
    marketing/
https://emarsys.com/learn/blog/blockchain-changing-marketing/
https://www.singlegrain.com/blockchain/blockchain-explained/
https://cmo.adobe.com/articles/2018/12/how-blockchain-will-change-marketing-in-2019.html#gs.
    4cudtc
https://www.leanplum.com/blog/blockchain-marketing/
https://www.cmswire.com/digital-marketing/how-blockchain-is-disrupting-digital-marketing-and-
    where-its-headed/
https://www.forbes.com/sites/danielnewman/2019/09/18/how-blockchain-is-changing-digital-
    marketing/#592306b216eb
https://medium.com/digital-realm/blockchain-document-verification-f9e40b708100

Tom James

Chapter 2
Sales

Artificial Intelligence

Artificial Intelligence (AI) has changed everything – and sales are no exemption. AI is helping salespeople support lead volume, quality, and close rate.

It influences how clients purchase – and how salespeople need to sell.

AI fills purchasing decisions we make each day, from the shows we watch and the routes our driver takes to the things we order on the web.

Suggestion, area, and association algorithms are our behind-the-scenes purchasing influencers, and they make AI fascinatingly creepy and cool for the same reason: our gadgets know and learn a great deal about us, creating analysis of behavioral patterns we may not even be aware we're following.

With the increasing adoption of AI, we can expect to see an automation of a significant part of the sales procedure. Accordingly, sales groups will be freed to concentrate on closing deals. Thus, sales pioneers anticipated that their groups' AI appropriation would become 155% by 2020, as per Salesforce. Salesforce additionally found that high-performing sales reps are 4.9 times more likely to utilize AI than others. Whether we find AI to be creepy or cool, no salesperson can afford to ignore the changes AI will bring to sales.

What is AI in Sales?

Sales are hard. Transformation rates are low and the sales cycle is longer. Your clients don't simply take out their credit cards to purchase things. They need handholding and a great deal of approval. You must make calls, meet them face to face, answer their interests, and keep on managing them after sales to guarantee that you construct a solid relationship with them. AI can make this somewhat simpler.

AI today doesn't aim to supplant sales reps, instead serving in an ancillary role as a partner to human-led sales efforts by:
1. Assisting with mechanizing dreary assignments like data entry and scheduling a meeting or complicated job that doesn't require personal connections like sales determining/forecasting.
2. Identifying patterns in client reactions to empower salespeople to organize all the better and improve as a sales individual.
3. Give group pioneers detailed research on all correspondence between sales reps and potential customers including emails, calls, and talks.

https://doi.org/10.1515/9783110664454-002

AI reforms sales by assuming control over the monotonous undertakings of finding and arranging leads, checking the necessary requests, and speaking with clients and potential clients (among others) so your sales group can concentrate on expanding their conversion rates.

"The power of selling is moving away from the individual and toward the machine – machines that can now prospect, follow up, present, and propose without human intervention," says Victor Antonio, author of *Sales Ex Machina: How Artificial Intelligence is Changing the World of Selling*. Sometimes, the machine will devastate sales capacities, while other times it will drastically move the locus of the concentrate further into the sales cycle.

Why is AI Sales Important?

Frameworks that utilize AI can be trained to accomplish certain outcomes, at that point turned loose on totally new information to accomplish those outcomes again and again, finding out increasingly more about what works and what doesn't each time.

This implies modern AI can dissect client and prospect information, anticipate which possibilities are destined to close, prescribe the most significant sales moves to make, gauge results, improve valuing, and a whole lot more.

Because of this capacity to expand and improve sales execution, McKinsey examiners writing in *Harvard Business Review* gauge that AI can make $1.4 to $2.6 trillion of significant worth in promoting and sales.

That is premised on the basis that there are a lot of approaches to utilize AI to hit your numbers quicker or surpass them altogether, if you have perfect, organized, and useful information at your disposal.

AI projects can look over a great many occasions to discover examples and connections that we just would not see on an everyday basis. It may identify that sending a particular pitch deck to forthcoming customers before calling them brings about better transformations. Or it may see that sending a week by week follow-up email can yield results about two months after beginning contacted. These are little practices that a sales expert may miss yet can quickly adapt to in time.

The impact is to ally sales experts with a second brain, one that does the math and recognizes designs without requiring any help. This can possibly make each salesperson in the workplace reach peak productivity and rates of success, not only those with the best impulses.

How to Use AI for Sales

AI is helping salespeople support lead volume, quality, and close rate. AI can computerize and enlarge a significant part of the sales procedure, subsequently allowing sales groups to concentrate on closing deals. The way AI is changing sales exercises and techniques, influencing client relations, and creating organizations between sales agents and AI, has attracted acute business attention. Here is an outline of some of the ways AI can improve sales forms and give excellent outcomes.

Price Optimization

Realizing what discount, if any, to give a customer is constantly a challenge. You need to win the arrangement without leaving cash on the table. Today, an AI calculation could analyze and recommend the perfect discount rate to guarantee that you're well on the way to win the arrangement by analyzing patterns of each past arrangement that was won or lost. Patterns could draw from any number of recorded factors including size of the arrangement in dollars, item particular consistence, number of contenders, organization size, an area/locale, customer's industry, customer's yearly incomes, public or privately-owned business, level of leaders (influencers) included, timing (e.g., Q2 vs. Q4), new or existing customer, etc.

Forecast Sales

Sales supervisors face the overwhelming test of attempting to anticipate where their group's complete sales numbers will fall each quarter. Utilizing an AI calculation, supervisors are currently ready to foresee with a high level of exactness the next quarter's income, which would thus support an organization's efforts to oversee stock and assets more readily.

Upselling and Cross-selling

The quickest and most affordable approach to develop your top-line income is to offer more to your current customer base. As encingly simple as that sounds, the million-dollar question is, who is bound to purchase more? You can spend a great deal of cash on advertising to the individuals who won't purchase, or you can utilize an AI calculation to help distinguish which of your current customers are bound to purchase a superior rendition of what they presently own (up-sell) or advertise a product or service to an existing customer using other products or services (cross-sell). The net impact is an expansion in income and a drop in advertising costs.

Qualified Lead Scoring

A salesperson with a rich pipeline of qualified potential customers needs to settle which choices to make on a daily, or even hourly basis, concerning where to focus their opportunity with regard to closing arrangements to hit their month to month or quarterly share. Ordinarily, this dynamic procedure depends on gut sense and analysis of inadequate data. With AI, the calculation can incorporate verifiable data about a customer alongside web-based life postings and the salesperson's client co-operation history (e.g., emails sent, voicemails left, instant messages sent, etc.) and rank the chances or leads in the pipeline as per their odds of closing effectively.

Performance Management

Sales supervisors need to consistently evaluate the income pipelines of each of their salespeople with an eye towards supporting deals that may slow down, or more un-fortunately, fail to work out. Utilizing AI, sales supervisors would now be able to utilize dashboards to outwardly observe which salespeople are probably going to hit their targets alongside which exceptional arrangements have the highest poten-tial for successful closure. This will permit supervisors to concentrate on key sales-people and related deals that will enable the organization to hit their quarterly or monthly market share target.

Prioritizing Calls

Salespeople can regularly distinguish which leads to seek after, but realizing which leads to seek first isn't consistently self-evident. AI can provide an empirical reliability to these choices with calculations that incorporate verifiable exchange data, communi-cation details and online networking on rank leads and the odds of closing deals.

Improve Relationship and Value

Earning client lifetime esteem has consistently been a test for sales pioneers and salespeople. Who will renew? Who will leave? Above all, why?

AI can help distinguish the strength of relationships and point salespeople to-ward those who need consideration and those whose esteem is ironclad. A few asso-ciations use AI to do this month to month so it's never past the point where it is possible to expand the lifetime esteem of clients.

Sales Automation

AI cleverly automates some monotonous sales undertakings. For example, devices exist that mechanize information capture to give you back time in your day. A few arrangements give mechanized playbooks to eliminate reaction time.

AI devices can also enlarge your work. One model is AI arrangements that break down sales call information to assist you with scaling tasks.

Pipeline Creation

AI tools can help salespeople fill pipelines quickly. There are AI devices today that find new leads for you within your databases. Others will discover new leads that resemble your present leads. Also, a few devices even give contact data to individuals in your addressable market.

Research

The battle to discover customers, research and stay up with the latest market trends and changes is an assignment that sucks time and vitality from a sales group's day. AI innovation planned explicitly for research can transform that activity into a largely automated process.

There's just one issue. AI can't work without information and it needs a great deal of it to make top notch forecasts. Any manager who's tried knows that getting sales groups to enter information reliably can be harder than getting the 800-pound telephone to make a cold pitch. Salespeople tend to be busy focusing on client engagement. When they must choose between work that results in winning or losing a commission check, they're going to push forward and work legitimately with their records, not invest energy entering information into a CRM framework.

Fortunately, AI and automation tools are incredible assistants for data entry. Innovation can't assuage desk work and data entry entirely (yet), but it can certainly help.

Outreach and SalesLoft stages follow and oversee email correspondence. Items like Yesware and Mixmax guarantee inbox information discovers its way into the corporate client relationship management framework. Once documented, the information would then be able to be curated by people and bots. Salesforce takes note that half of sales estimates are driven by information alone, and that number should increase in the next few years.

Finding the Perfect Client Fit

One of the best things AI can do for you is help you find new possibilities. Making sense of the best possibilities requires accumulating and analyzing information across various sources, searching for associations among each source and afterward quantifying the possibilities. This is achievable with a human team, yet it takes up a ton of time and effort.

Most sales bunches depend on guesswork, floated by simple information grouping to outline their most plausible possibilities. A lot of savvy salespeople (and chiefs) work under the conviction that they should continue rehashing their best sales endeavors – with similar kinds of clients – until they no longer get hits. The senses and guesswork alone however are not enough to identify every possible new selling stream.

AI can help distinguish great fits and improbable possibilities that increasingly customary techniques would miss. For instance, the information may recommend that the executive or vice president of sales is your most logical choice in dealing with organizations within a certain scope of income, yet organizations in that range may have drastically unique go-to-market models.

Communication

Consider all the low-level discussions that go on in sales that AI could deal with. Numerous sales groups have just begun embracing chatbots to do only this – opening reps for more profound relationship building and vital discussions. The opportunities for AI to improve correspondence will only develop as AI improves.

AI as of now generally peruses data on a similar or superior level of skill as people:
- It can sift through muddled reports more precisely – and at far more prominent rates – than even the best partners.
- It can make fundamental emails in manners that are strikingly humanlike.
- It can react to basic messages faster and more precisely than any human could manage.

What's more, the technology is only showing signs of improvement.

Organizations like Drift have discovered that individuals wouldn't fret cooperating with a machine provided they got the assistance they needed. Indeed, 55% of respondents to an ongoing study by Drift said they would appreciate getting a speedy reaction to a simple to-address question from a chatbot.

Platforms like Conversica – a conversational AI administration for arriving at shoppers – are as of now removing the early correspondence ventures from the hands of business advancement delegates. The innovation can respond to essential item questions and timetable gatherings without human mediation. Float's bot is another assistance AI that encourages customers to find solutions to fundamental inquiries without human intervention.

Training

Training salespeople may be one of the boldest and most transformational uses of AI for sales. Reps need assistance understanding what blend of practices really drive arrangements, and AI's prescient capabilities can make this procedure fast and exact. Already, the highest performing sales groups were found to be 2.3 times as likely to use AI guided selling than their lesser performing peers.

AI can help direct training endeavors and help anticipate where a deficiency might be before it shows up. Cell phones fill in as extraordinary training gadgets because your sales reps will usually have a mix of telephones, PCs, and tablets around them constantly.

For example, the microlearning application Qstream can send training questions straight to the telephones of sales reps. They answer the inquiries and the manager surveys them.

This enables the reps to develop their insight rapidly and effectively. Additionally, it tells managers where sales inadequacies lie and if more training is required. Obviously, the best training pairs virtual training with face-to-face training by supervisors and companions. Sales is about connections. Nevertheless, setting up great connections requires some serious energy, innovation, and training. Sales associations that investigate new advances and training strategies will see their reps improve quicker and stand out in the sales world.

What are the Core Benefits of AI in Sales?

Inventive sales pioneers are transforming the selling experience for their groups by applying AI to their sales processes. By outfitting the intensity of AI and applying it to front and middle-office revenue processes, sales pioneers can smooth out their revenue practices, increase sales viability, and improve margins and revenue. They're additionally gaining enhancements in new leads, strategic cross-sells/up-sells, and increasing sales process durations by a factor of at least five.

Here are 5 key advantages/benefits sales pioneers can enjoy by embracing AI innovation:

1. *Make a Sales Dream Team*

For most endeavors, business achievement is to a great extent dependent upon the accomplishment of their sales groups. It's important that sales leaders employ viable sellers and gives them the direction and devices important to succeed. Be that as it may, building a sales "dream team" comprising entirely of A-grade players is uncommon. Getting everyone from the sales group to work like A-grade players is an ambitious objective for any sales head, however, one that AI innovation can assist in accomplishing. For instance, AI can become familiar with the practices reliably displayed by the best salespeople during effective sales. Thus, these practices are displayed and proactively conveyed to all sellers as prescriptive activities that can prompt positive business results. Winning practices that drive faster deal conversion, such as leading client needs evaluations, booking follow-up calls, and following strategic cross-sell/up-sell suggestions are instances of best practices that AI can help advise with to the whole sales group (see Figure 2.1).

TOP BENEFITS OF INTELLIGENT SALES CAPABILITIES
SURVEY OF SALES LEADERS USING INTELLIGENT SALES TECHNOLOGIES

Customer retention	83%
Customer/prospect nurturing	80%
Productivity of sales reps	80%
Sales velocity	74%
Forecast accuracy	73%
Pipeline generation	64%

Salesforce 2017

Figure 2.1: Top benefits of intelligent sales capabilities.
Source: Salesforce 2017 Market Report.

2. Win Bigger Deals, Win More Consistently
In the present business condition, clients are in the driver's seat. Your seller's price quotes must give customer friendly offers and competitive pricing without affecting the profits. AI can gain from your verifiable sales information and guide sellers to the advanced offers and valuing that boosts win probability. AI can also learn client purchasing behaviors and suggest different items or services that provide an incentive for clients and your association, while expanding profit margins. Giving clever direction dependent on current patterns and verifiable sales information places your sellers in the most ideal situation to win greater deals that drive more income, gain more market share, and fuel business development.

3. Reveal More Sales Opportunities
For most sales associations, revealing new doors to open is an endless interest as it is the main driver of income/revenue growth. AI can proactively find new sales

opportunities and openings utilizing AI investigation that recognizes client purchasing propensities, practices and informs dealers as to potential strategic pitch and upsell openings. The best part is that the AI have no need to sleep or take breaks and are always looking for new opportunities! So, AI can gain proficiency with the key attributes of clients that have the best capacity to purchase and guide sellers to concentrate on their best leads. For instance, considering past selling achievement, AI can prescribe explicit approaches to possibilities depending on qualities like industry, number of workers, yearly income, existing resources, and that's only the tip of the iceberg. The outcome is a general increase in revenue stream and more opportunities for sellers.

4. Boost in Sales Productivity
Sales profitability is a main consideration in the general accomplishment of a business. The less time sellers spend on manual procedures, scanning for data, and managerial undertakings, the more time they can spend selling and nurturing relationships with clients and possibilities. As per an investigation recently published in Forbes, sellers spend under 36% of their time actually selling. AI that incorporates chatbot innovation can support sales efficiency by giving conversational client encounters, through content and voice mediums. This type of AI spares merchants time and work to be allocated to more productive tasks by associating with CRM and Middle Office applications, like Configure Price Quote (CPQ) and Contract Lifecycle Management (CLM) through built up channels like Skype, Slack, SMS, and email. For instance, sellers can refresh their chances, plan gatherings, and query client data by instant message. They can alter cites, send recommendations, and favor decreases by voice order on their cell phone or inside the applications themselves. Enhancing sales tools with AI not just assists with client selection, studies have shown utilizing AI can result in up to 90% quicker task completion focus, empowering sellers to concentrate additional time on earning commission and producing income.

5. Ramp Up New Sellers Faster
For recently employed sellers, there is frequently a period before they become completely proficient and adept at income creating. Finding a workable pace on possibilities and existing clients, on items and services to sell, and on sales devices and procedures to utilize requires sales training and time to get accustomed – the "ramp up" period. Organizations are finding that utilizing AI can definitely decrease the measure of time and exertion it takes for sellers to get that pace in their workstyle. For instance, AI innovation that gives conversational user interfaces allows clients to associate with sales applications by means of content or voice, lessening the requirement for sales training to finish basic sales assignments, for example, looking into account data, drafting NDAs, and booking client gatherings. In fact, an ongoing client overview directed by Apttus found that AI can decrease new seller ramp up time by up to 60%.

What is the Future Ahead for AI in Sales?

AI will affect future sales in three critical ways.

The maximum capacity of AI might be ages away, yet there are now immediate pathways to profitably incorporate AI into modern sales tasks today.

It's as of now being utilized at numerous organizations, and it's gradually being embraced by sales.

Almost 90% of agents who use AI state they presently are or are intending to utilize AI for sales anticipating and email showcasing (Figure 2.2).

Initially, it will change the job of client care, the same number of the interactions done today by individuals will be dealt with by means of AI with voice capabilities. Analysis suggests that 90% of future interactions will be done at a more satisfactory level of customer service than people are presently receiving.

Secondly, AI will enable the client to be much more engaged than they are today.

At the point when AI turns out to be completely coordinated with sites, we will see clients having the option to go a lot further through the purchasing procedure before they need to communicate with a human. For some exchanges, there won't be any human communication at all.

Thirdly, AI will permit the salesperson to have the option to deal with progressively complex sales and have the option to do it in an increasingly practical way.

Just as the PC and cell phone have expanded the profitability of salespeople, AI will further develop this trend pattern. The salesperson will presently have the option to lead sales by arranging meetings utilizing AI instead of connecting with their sales supervisor.

Rather than seeing AI as a threat to people's livelihoods, a superior methodology for AI implementation is to inquire as to whether AI can assist with carrying out their responsibilities. Just as every new iteration of the phone changed business, and the PC and the web thereafter, we don't have to think commercial AI integration is the end all human employability.

Keep in mind, AI presently provides incredible advantages we acknowledge, like spell check, web search channels, and email spam channels, just to give some examples. AI will permit the top performing salesperson to maximize their productivity even more; AI will not replace the top performing salesperson. On the other hand, the salesperson who isn't providing value to their employer by means of knowledge, skills, or sales closures to their clients will be long be out of an occupation, yet the implementation of AI is not the cause, only the catalyst.

Specific AI use case adoption worldwide 2017

Adoption of specific artificial intelligence (AI) use cases in 2017, by category

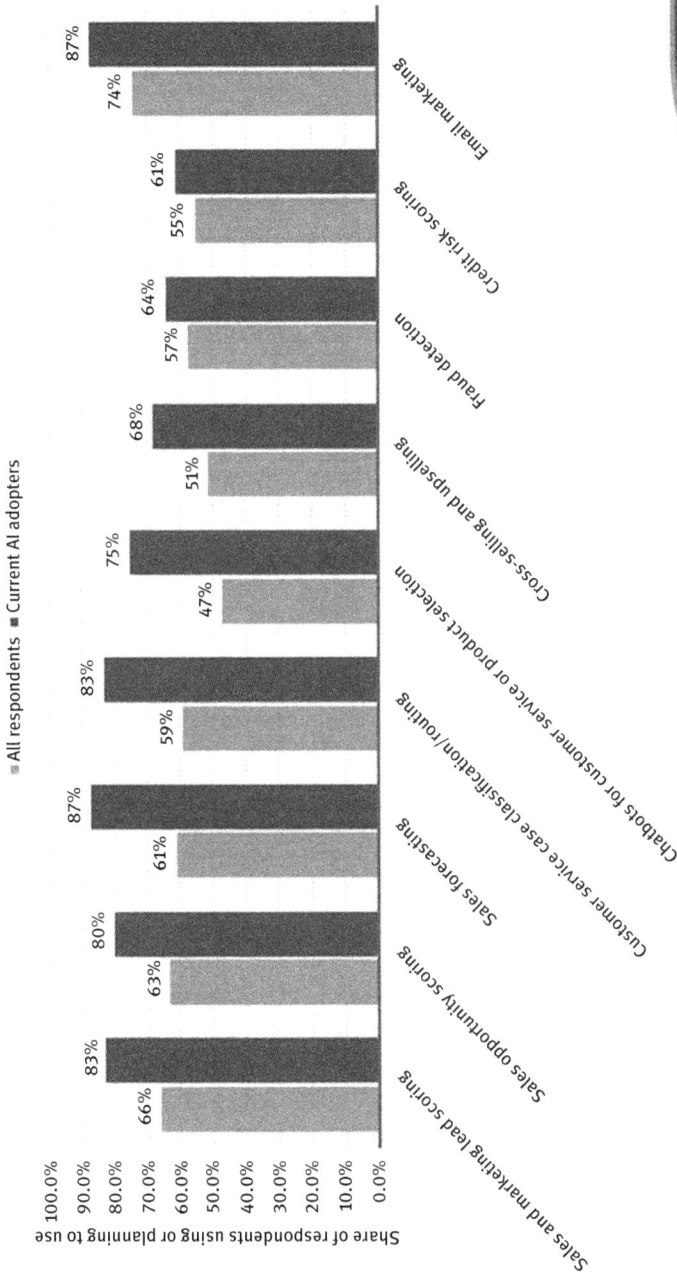

All respondents ■ Current AI adopters

Category	All respondents	Current AI adopters
Email marketing	87%	74%
Credit risk scoring	61%	55%
Fraud detection	64%	57%
Cross-selling and upselling	68%	51%
Chatbots for customer service or product selection	75%	47%
Customer service case classification/routing	83%	59%
Sales forecasting	87%	61%
Sales opportunity scoring	80%	63%
Sales and marketing lead scoring	83%	66%

Share of respondents using or planning to use

statista

Figure 2.2: Adoption of specific artificial intelligence (AI) use cases in 2017, by Statista.

Blockchain

Keeping sales and business trade secrets has now become a major risk in the open world. Presently, salespeople are expected to figure out how to do the math and work with customer relationship management (CRM) in a blockchain. Today, numerous sales managers and sales groups are continually associated with their screens, gadgets, applications, and online devices, with these advances intended to improve sales proficiency.

Yet these advances are assisting with snatching the business opportunities of contenders through the separation of blockchain data. This blockchain process has been set up since the approach of the banking framework was first introduced to screen transactions. Does this forecasted insurgency have broader ramifications on sales? Finding the appropriate response is complicated, so it is recommended that sales chiefs give close attention to unfurling advancements and developments in blockchain security. In the meantime, Coca-Cola has been running different research projects over a year on developing how it can utilize blockchain innovation to improve the transparency of labor conditions among its work force. They intend to handle representative labor understandings and check the utilization of smart contracts using blockchain technology.

What is Blockchain in Sales?

Blockchain in sales: Blockchain offers solutions for issues with the collection of sales records that currently are being overseen through other mechanical arrangements or manual record keeping. In any case, these gradual changes altogether could result in an essentially streamlined end-to-end sales procedure and sales group drive procedure.

Blockchain has notably been used recently for digital currency. It uses advanced calculations and drives a dispersed information structure to oversee electronic money developments, replacing the role of a national bank or government-backed bank with a decentralized network.

The blockchain is the archive and wholesaler of virtual coins. Crypto coins are not conveyed or taken care of, yet they do exchange, increase and multiply because of the blockchain at the middle. On the off chance that you picture a business ledger that refreshes itself progressively, duplicating that image by billions of information spaces will give you some representation of the way blockchain works.

For sales organizations, it very well may be a virtual bank – moving cash, finishing transactions, and more. This differs from online banking where your business is dependent upon guidelines, business hours, and other limitations.

Why is Blockchain Sales Important

Generally, sales profits by blockchain the most. Blockchain implementation is difficult to execute for typical clients. It should be overseen by a group of specialists, which makes it perfect for organizations who have the financial limit and need to deal with the blockchain venture.

The worldwide blockchain market improvement to $20+ billion of every year until 2023 is another indication of how quickly organizations are accepting the future role of blockchain technology. The benefits are obvious; it lessens operational expenses by cutting out middlemen, helping businesses decrease cost as well as diminishing the purpose of contact – improving efficiency and development.

Transaction speeds are additionally improved to another level. For business, it is about efficiency and precision, and blockchain transactions promise to greatly reduce transaction speeds. The benefits are not just limited to corporate administration. The Dubai Blockchain Strategy is one administrative model where the administration of Dubai expects blockchain technology to save $1.5B in reduced costs from document processing alone.

How to Use Blockchain for Sales

While the quickly changing blockchain space can be confusing, there are some important experiences to be picked up, explicitly according to sales. What makes the blockchain so alluring are similar characteristics present in advanced, powerful sales organizations.

Here are some key featured areas of blockchain in sales that could be full of impacts.

CRM

Clients are increasingly wary of giving individual information online because of the widespread publication of information hacks and information misappropriation. Consequently, CRM apparatuses need to develop and consider these worries. A blockchain-based CRM could tackle this issue and address problems that plague current CRM virtual products.

Workers regularly depend on the analysis of enormous sums of information and use different devices to mine data and make the required cuts of data, however, the procedure is tedious and frequently imperfect. Blockchain-based CRM could convey more useful information consistently without relinquishing application adaptability. Therefore, data silos will break down. Instead of numerous duplicates of a client's data being produced in different frameworks, the entire association approaches one lot of qualities for each profile.

For a sales rep this could mean more prominent accomplishment in scoring and qualifying leads. Poor leads could be set apart all through the association and this framework could dispense with redundant work. An open ledger would also guarantee that leads can be followed up with and their situation in the sales pipeline is clear.

Recordkeeping

Another application for blockchain that is being investigated is information stockpiling and recordkeeping. Agreements, correspondences, proposition, notices, receipts, and some other records can be put away carefully on a blockchain, giving organizations a reasonable and precise picture of what occurred and when. This type of straightforward record keeping will also at the same time dispense with bogus self-announcing by sales reps who are simply hoping to meet their standards.

Still, there are numerous issues with this blockchain-driven methodology. We currently have different applications like Dropbox or Box.com that can safely store information and sync it across the framework. Blockchain also depends on a solitary factor validation as opposed to a far more prevalent two-factor approval framework which incorporates highlights like interruption location, volume limits, firewalls, remote IP following, and the capacity to disengage the framework in a crisis.

Speedy Transactions

Transactions and ledger refreshes through blockchain are all quick throughout the ecosystem. Thus, valuable time isn't lost hanging tight for bank transfers to go through. Sales reps could get installments rapidly and get their payments on schedule.

This speed does have some limitations. While Visa can deal with sixty thousand transactions for every second, Bitcoin has overseen just seven. For bigger partnerships that do numerous transactions consistently, this impediment may be unacceptable.

Channel Management

Following up sales after an item has been offered to a merchant is frequently a gigantic test for organizations with aberrant channel accomplices. Organizations have no influence over the end-client experience and little visibility into the sales procedure after the underlying sales have been made. This issue is exceptionally applicable to the innovative business; as per an estimate by Accenture, 80% of all sales are indirect sales. Such organizations are compelled to put resources into gathering sales information through costly third party aggregators.

On a basic level blockchain can totally change the way such sales occur. Since the ledger is openly transparent and available, cutting edge organizations could undoubtedly follow sales down to the end client and get full visibility into their sales procedure.

So, any selection of the blockchain innovation in the indirect sales channel would require critical venture by channel accomplices. Then again, expanded transparency would imply that organizations are less dependent on channel accomplices and third party information agents for information. These two factors may cause some to be hesitant to embrace this innovation.

Blockchain in B2B and B2C

The sales processed through business-to-business (B2B) depend on connections and obligation. B2B sales connections also require more outfield, expertise product knowledge, field work, knocking doors, and they additionally have a more drawn-out sales cycle than business-to-consumer (B2C) sales. The duty is on the reps to guarantee the right information is given to the customer pre- and post-sales.

Only blockchain offers a solitary, shared ledger continuously showing all transactions, endorsements, and confirmations to all gatherings, and in this way empowers increasingly productive and quicker assistance conveyance – providing access to a shared audit trail that will make billing and account receivable processes progressively precise and transparent, which means there ought to be less inquisitive solicitations.

Sales Force Management

Dealing with a sales group is not a simple task. You can possibly either make or break your sales reps and there's huge amounts of conflicting data out there. It's not simple in every case to discover a harmonious balance between encouraging quality execution and pushing sales reps to achieve new objectives.

Successful sales chiefs select top sales pioneers, give them the tools they require to get sales and watch the numbers develop. However, it isn't always as straightforward as that. Sales supervisors can both motivate their groups and assist them with arriving at their objectives or crush their morale, which leads to a drop in your organization's gainfulness.

It very well may be ascertaining what your sales group really needs from you to hit their objectives, make benefits, and drive sales. That is the reason we've assembled these procedures to assist you with running an exceptional sales group through blockchain. As a sales administrator, your prosperity relies upon your group's capacity to meet execution objectives.

What are the Core Benefits of Blockchain in Sales?

Trust

It's been written that the blockchain gives "the exchange of trust in a trustless world." It safely records each transaction that occurs on the system, from a couple of bucks to two or three million. That implies that two individuals who don't have any acquaintance with one another (and don't have to know one another) can trade cash without utilizing a go-between. Utilizing the blockchain to buy merchandise or exchange value is quick, safe, and removes the mediator (and his expenses).

Salespeople realize the role trust plays in the purchasing procedure. Potential clients will occasionally make some grief ensuring all necessary documentation is signed if they believe there's a chance they'll get burned. Building trust, posing suitable inquiries, and being compassionate to worries can secure deals. If all else fails, be transparent and offer some incentive.

In research, investigating whether people prefer to do online research or converse with a salesperson, Forrester discovered about 60% of purchasers favor online research to conversing with a salesperson – sales cycles are getting shorter.

Transparency

Blockchain advocates love to discuss how the innovation keeps prying eyes (state, private, or malicious hackers) away from their transaction history. Yet at its heart, the blockchain is an open, auditable ledger – permanent and immutable. Everybody who utilizes the blockchain is truly on the same wavelength. Need to ensure your gift gets to the proposed beneficiary? The blockchain can help with that. It's the visibility, the unhindered access to data that individuals find appealing. In the past, sales reps were data watchmen. A possible client knew as much about an item as its site and representative presented. That permitted salespeople to introduce their items in the most ideal light, pointing out all the great and hand-waving the awful.

That's doesn't work anymore. Forthcoming customers are on review sites, reading case studies and cross-referencing your answers at meetups with their own information channels. On the off chance that you jump on a call with a possible client, you should be prepared to have a brutally honest discussion about the strengths and weaknesses of your product.

Sales groups that are winning left and right are recognizing their item's defects, speaking openly about product disadvantages, and examining why clients dislike or what clients dislike about their products. Reps pose testing inquiries, talk about advantages and position highlights but also address weaknesses as a vital part of the discussion.

Speed

Expelling third parties in transactions removes transaction fees and waiting times, individuals are worn out on bank transfers taking two to three business days. With the blockchain, those exchanges can be turbocharged. What used to take days presently takes only minutes. The decrease in time makes electronic exchanges of significant worth less overwhelming and increasingly reasonable in a time where everything is accessible on-request. Utilizing blockchain innovation will be a distinct advantage for organizations, considering fast and secure buys without the need of installment processors.

The same can be said for sales, utilizing innovation to abbreviate the sales cycle and diminish grinding. Sales engagement platforms (Outreach.io), video conferencing software (Zoom, GoToMeeting), and digital transaction solutions (CPQ, DocuSign, PandaDoc) make it simple for imminent purchasers to draw in with reps, assess tools, and make buys.

What's more, numerous B2B SaaS suppliers that take into account new businesses or small- and medium-sized businesses (SMBs) have grasped a self-administration model, accelerating the purchasing procedure even more.

What is the Future Ahead for Blockchain in Sales?

Blockchain changes numerous fundamental principles of sales and marketing. It digitizes touch points, makes digital payments, provides significant value and utility, forms trust and decentralizes sales ideas. Advertisers who perceive this will have a rewarding open door before them and a competitive edge over others. Thus, for salespeople and advertisers, it merits investing some time and energy to understand the developments occurring in this field. As of now organizations dependent on blockchain are developing exponentially.

One of the difficulties each business faces is income, and showcasing offices are not insusceptible to it. Bitcoin is a solution. It has some finance related advantages and points of interest. The organization who acknowledges the payment can either utilize an outsider to change over the Bitcoins into cash or withdraw it in the species of Bitcoins. Startup is simple. There are a lot of organizations who help other organizations get Bitcoin set up as a payment option.

Blockchain is stirring up businesses including production networks, corporate obligations, style structuring and computerized publicizing. To acknowledge Bitcoins, all the organization needs is a Bitcoin button at the checkout and an advanced wallet. It works like a cycle whereby the distributers and clients get tokens when they see promotions.

We are encountering a noteworthy shift in the real estate business, as an ever-increasing number of individuals are participating in property transactions utilizing Bitcoin. Numerous industry specialists are amped up for the potential for advanced cash and the blockchain innovation in regard to real estate. However, although digital money transaction is the future, business insiders state that we are not yet at the point where cryptocurrency can replace the role served by traditional currencies and lines of credit. Digital cash experts are less optimistic that the property market will be amenable to adopting digital money any time soon.

As dealers and speculators have participated more and more in Bitcoin trading, Bitcoin's value has increased, and the Securities and Exchange Commission has suspended the operations of certain Bitcoin exchanges. These all prove to be obstacles to wider adoption of cryptocurrencies in businesses like real estate. Nevertheless, were these obstacles to be overcome, cryptocurrencies would allow the real estate business to store online reports, draw up computerized and shrewd agreements, all while keeping the principal parties of the agreements anonymous.

The blockchain is the framework behind cryptographic forms of money. A fundamental handle of how it functions will be adequate for the time being; in the future, this information will barely be sufficient. Cryptographic money is a digital payment kept up by a system of PCs that utilizes cryptography to verify transactions. Contingent upon how speculators hope to bring in cash and how they are organized, some digital forms of money may be considered a form of securities. On the off chance that brokers of these monetary standards prop up the cost and go online to spread rumors of rising value, that may be considered a scam, as seen in Bitconnect. There also exists no consensus among critics whether a cryptocurrency bubble exists, thus many companies maintain strategic distance from mass adoption of cryptocurrencies.

There is also a war over the fate of Bitcoin, the largest and first cryptocurrency to gain traction in society. Two of the greatest among its contenders are Darkcoin and Ethereum. Many of the cryptocurrencies more youthful than Bitcoin can be utilized for substantially more purposes. Consequently, Bitcoin faces a danger from progressively deft contenders. Computerized monetary standards will drive a new organization model for development at uncommon levels. This upset could be either the beginnings of a bubble or the beginning of a budgetary realignment.

Blockchain innovation represents a seismic shift like that provided by email and the web during the 1990s, or the shift provided by Facebook and Twitter 10 years later. The cryptographic forms of money like BitCoin and Ethereum are only a hint of something bigger to come. These block chain technologies have a lot to offer to the mainstream financial world and we have seen this already start to emerge with many financial institutions utilizing the Ethereum block chain language technology in the development of banking applications. This means that Ethereum miners are getting paid not only to process transfers of Ethereum but also to power the processing of other financial application transactions powered by Ethereum.

Charlie Shrem was among the pioneers of digital money. He helped to establish a new business in 2011 called BitInstant that was one of the foremost digital money organizations preparing 33% of all Bitcoin transactions. In 2015, Shrem went to jail for supporting an unlicensed cash transmitter secured using Bitcoins, which was utilized in an online marketplace to purchase narcotics and other controlled substances. It was a crime and prosecution that marked the first of its sort in the crypto world.

Upon his discharge he approached the issue of reinforcing the environment of blockchain. A genuine advancement came when he made a prepaid Dash platinum card; he then joined Intellisys Capital and chose to raise capital via an initial coin offering, however, in the end Intellisys was dissolved. Despite that, a significant number of the blockchain resources are tokens that are used in the same manner that Intellisys used them, dispersing the tokens as starting coins to early contributors. As the value of the coins increase, so too are the early investors rewarded for having invested. Thus, competitors who understand initial coin offerings realize how to compose shrewd agreements, and those who have a decent comprehension of Ethereum will have a serious competitive advantage in the age of blockchain (see Figure 2.3).

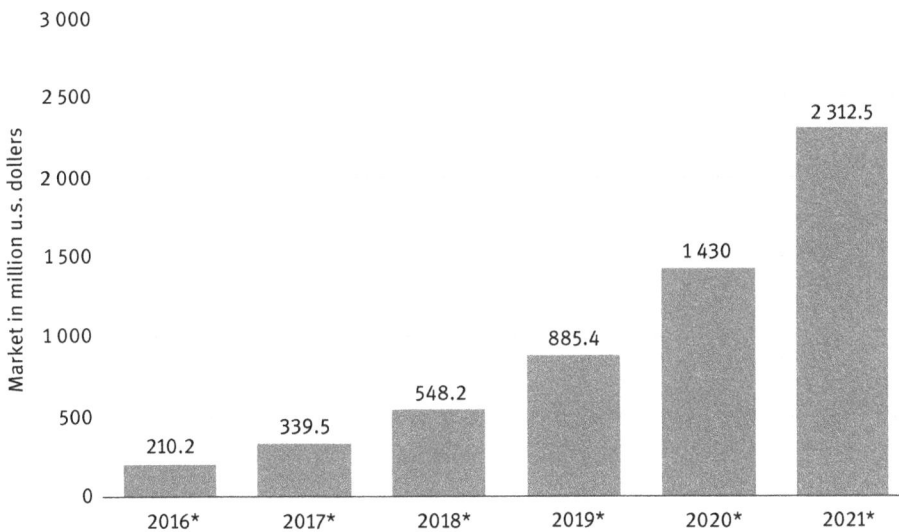

Figure 2.3: Estimated values for Ethereum in distribution.
Source: statista.com

Things are clear. Blockchain isn't the present business zeitgeist. Yet the innovation will continue developing. When the fundamental issues that confine it are settled, it will have some influence on sales, and sales pioneers will keep on observing it intently.

Henceforth, it is certain that blockchain innovation organizations are prepared to reform business practices in pretty much every industry. In any case, the total reception of blockchain by these business procedures will without a doubt require an incredible adoption effort just as it will require time. Considering all that has been mentioned; we are certain that cryptocurrencies will only hasten their development. Additionally, we can expect that administrations will eventually not just acknowledge blockchain applications but implement them once its advantages are fully acknowledged. Once we start to see widespread utilization of blockchain technology for improving financial and public services, it will rapidly alter the way we conduct business in every other branch of industry and commerce.

Further Reading

Artificial Intelligence

https://www.marketingaiinstitute.com/blog/how-to-use-artificial-inteligence-for-sales
https://www.leadfuze.com/sales-marketing-ai/
https://www.salesforce.com/quotable/articles/why-AI-will-be-your-new-best-friend-in-sales/
https://hbr.org/2018/07/how-ai-is-changing-sales
https://www.resourcefulselling.com/ai-is-changing-sales/
https://www.saleshacker.com/ai-for-sales/
https://blog.aimultiple.com/sales-ai/
https://apttus.com/blog/5-ways-sales-leaders-can-benefit-from-artificial-intelligence/
https://www.smartdatacollective.com/5-important-ways-artificial-intelligence-improves-sales/
https://www.raconteur.net/hr/the-role-of-artificial-intelligence-in-sales
https://smartercx.com/heres-how-artificial-intelligence-is-changing-sales-teams/
https://reply.io/ai-in-sales
https://www.marketingaiinstitute.com/blog/ai-for-sales

Blockchain

https://www.leewayhertz.com/how-blockchain-improve-point-of-sale-process/
https://www.outreach.io/blog/what-do-the-blockchain-and-b2b-sales-have-in-common-and-why-it-matters
https://www.forbes.com/sites/larrymyler/2018/01/22/how-blockchain-technology-can-help-b2b-companies-become-more-profitable/#61089dd47ec2
https://www.cbinsights.com/research/industries-disrupted-blockchain/
https://blog.smei.org/blockchain-technology-in-sales-and-marketing/
https://www.daily-sun.com/post/452499/Blockchain-in-Sales
https://www.newgenapps.com/blog/boost-sales-with-blockchain-technology/
https://www.ledgerinsights.com/blockchain-innovation-gartners-sales-hype-cycle/

Tom James and Kiren Chong-James
Chapter 3
IT Operations

Artificial Intelligence

Since the beginning, companies have thought about the difficulties of understanding how well their foundation is acting on the business side of things. They have utilized plenty of tools to distinguish, oversee, and resolve issues that are causing interruptions in administrations. Some of these tools included monitors, network monitors, application monitors, and end-user response time measurement facilities, to name only a few. In any case, with every one of these devices comes a crucial issue confronting associations – how to unite data from the different stages in the association and relate that data so business administrations can be precisely observed and managed.

For almost two decades, software vendors and IT departments were centered on the idea of business service management (BSM). BSM should outline parts of the business administrations they bolstered and use dashboards to show how well those business administrations were running. However, the guarantee of BSM was never satisfied because it was excessively complex in its makeup. In most vendor provided BSM arrangements it was too difficult to even consider creating and updating service definitions, excessively strict in how administration information was gathered and managed, and they depended on too few information hotspots for significant business understanding.

This unfulfilled guarantee of BSM implies that domain-explicit checking approaches still being used today don't present a holistic, cross-domain comprehension of what is going on.

Fortunately, in recent years, investigation stages like Splunk, Elastic, and others have developed to address necessities around IT Operations Analytics (ITOA). Their objective is to give a multistage, cross-discipline, coordinated perspective on what's going on over the IT framework and help associations to wipe out their reliance on these domain explicit instruments with practically zero combination capacities.

According to the Gartner Group, ITOA is a business opportunity for arrangements that carries progressed scientific methods to IT operations management (ITOM) uses for processing cases and information. ITOA arrangements gather, store, dissect and picture IT activities using information from different applications and ITOM tools. This enables IT activities groups to perform quicker main driver investigations, triage, and find quicker issue resolutions.

Digital change includes DevOps and the reception of cloud and new advances like containers. It represents a shift from centralized IT to applications and developers, an expanded pace of advancement and deployment, and the obtaining of new

https://doi.org/10.1515/9783110664454-003

digital clients – machine specialists, internet of things (IoT) gadgets, application programming interfaces (APIs), etc. – that associations beforehand didn't have to support. These innovations and clients are straining conventional execution and service management strategies and tools to the limit. Artificial intelligence operations (AIOps) are the IT operations (ITOps) outlook change required to deal with these changing digital issues.

What is Artificial Intelligence in ITOps?

Traditional IT organization and the management procedures are improving. By utilizing artificial intelligence (AI), IT activities are taking a fascinating turn with regard to the field of AIOps. The expression "AIOps" represents AI for the ITOps. AIOps utilizes AI methods and calculations to screen the information as well as reduce the blackout times. The strength of digital organizations is presenting innovative changes in their tasks to streamline them and wipe out the overhead of traditional operational administration.

Digital organizations are producing abundant and data rich information whose analysis and observation is made without delay. From data collection to storage, or information handling and analysis, all tasks should be as frictionless as possible to manage them in a proficient way. In recent years, the AIOps advertised on market have exploded in growth, which is rapidly reducing delays in problem-solving and identification.

The IT business is changing rapidly as the innovations that are generally utilized in IT activities change from AI to machine learning (ML), big data to IoT and APIs for different use-cases to edge computing. Every one of these developments are streamlining IT tasks, making them progressively simple and smooth tasks to execute.

AIOps stages improve and computerize IT activities, utilizing the accompanying methodologies:

- Utilizing AI calculations and neural systems for better investigation of accumulated information. The information is accumulated utilizing IoT gadgets and tools associated with the source, sending information to the cloud for its storage capacity and cross-platform accessibility.
- The framework naturally deciphers if something isn't right in the activities. The blunders are identified quickly without presenting delays in the tasks that are dependent on other tasks to finish.
- Lessening human force via robotizing the procedures that incorporate the work efforts of people (RPA Robot Process Automation).

As the innovation and order has gotten progressively modern, Gartner has reimagined ITOA as "AIOps," at first calling it Algorithmic IT Ops, and now defining it as

"Artificial intelligence ops." This name mirrors the expanding utilization of AI, prescient analytics, and AI in these arrangements (see Figure 3.1).

ML has come to be known as an order inside software engineering that utilizes measurable strategies to enable PC frameworks to "learn" with information, without being necessarily customized.

AIOps Platform Enabling Continuous Insights Across IT Operations Monitoring (ITOM)

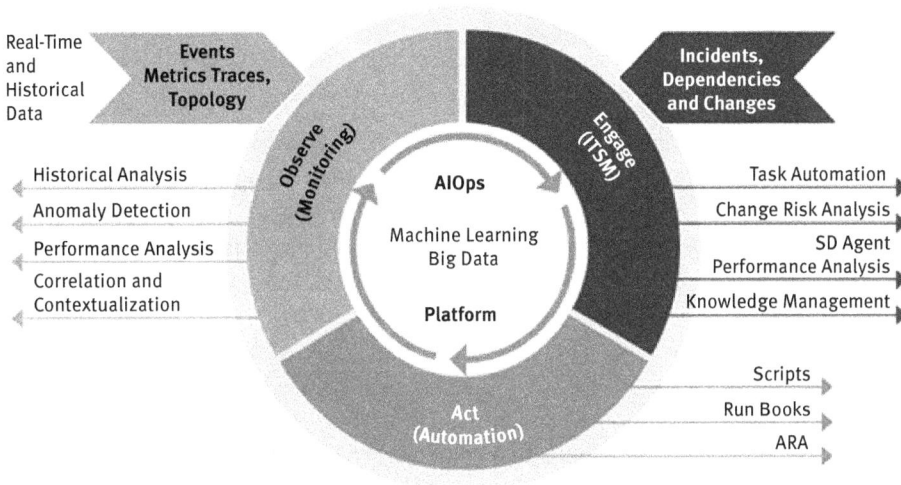

Figure 3.1: AIOps platform enabling continuous insights across IT operations monitoring (ITOM). Source: Gartner Group; https://www.gartner.com/smarterwithgartner/12-steps-to-excellence-in-artificial-intelligence-for-it-operations-infographic/

Basically, it is an activity used in finding out from the information how to settle on various information driven choices. ML can be utilized to rapidly make, send, and constantly screen a high volume of investigative models to utilize information and drive better results. It is the "AI" that when joined with ITOA provides an AIOps stage.

AIOps utilizes ML and advanced analytics to streamline tasks, organize issue goals, and adjust IT to the business. Utilizing metrics and execution pointers that are lined up with key objectives and goals, it goes past receptive and impromptu investigating to proactively sort out and associate applicable metrics and occasions as indicated by the business administrations they support. In addition, platforms that join big data and ML usefulness to upgrade and possibly even supplant an expansive scope of ITOps procedures and undertakings – including observing, occasion relationship and investigation, service management and automation – showcase the great value AI provides for ITOps.

This reallocation of work efforts permits developing IT associations to focus their efforts and newfound free time on solving other issues, such as acquiring a profound understanding of the effect that administration degradation has, not just on the segments in their service stack, but also on service levels and business abilities. It gives a business a streamlined, innovation-oriented point of view. For instance, IT can see "How is the web store performing?" rather than checking the status of the web server and application.

Why is AI ITOps Important?

AIOps is the advancement of IT operational analytics (ITOA). It comes out of a few patterns and influences ITOps in many ways. Conventional ways of dealing with or managing IT's multifaceted nature – especially in regard to offline, manual endeavors that require human mediation – don't work in many varied situations. Following and dealing with this multifaceted nature through manual, human oversight is not, at this point achievable. ITOps has been surpassing human problem-solving scope and scale for quite a long time, and it continues developing.

The size and scope of data that ITOps needs to retain is exponentially increasing. Performance monitoring, service ticket volumes experiencing step-work increases, the addition of IoT gadgets, APIs, mobile applications and digital or machine users, all add up. The scale of data generated is increasing beyond the reasonable scope of manual research and analysis.

Infrastructure issues must be resolved at an ever-faster rate. As associations digitize their business, IT turns into the business. The "consumerization" of innovation has changed client desires for all enterprises. Responses to IT problems – regardless of whether the problems are genuine or not – need to happen quickly, especially when an issue impacts client experience.

Increasingly computing power is moving to the edges of the system. The transparency with which cloud foundation and outsider services can be embraced has engaged line of business (LOB) capacities to assemble their own IT solutions and applications. Control and spending plans have moved from the center of IT to the edge. Furthermore, all the computing power (that can be utilized) is being utilized by out of center IT services.

Developers have more power and impact. However, responsibility ultimately lies with center IT. DevOps and Agile are driving software engineers to take on more checking duty at the application level, however, responsibility for the general well-being of the IT ecosystem and the connection between applications, services, infrastructure remains the domain of center IT. ITOps is assuming greater liability just as their systems are getting increasingly complex.

It ought to be noticed that an affirmation that ITOps is surpassing human scale of analysis doesn't imply that the machines are replacing people. It implies we need big data, AI/ML, and automation to manage the new reality. People aren't replaced, however, ITOps staff should learn new skills and abilities as new jobs will develop to support the changing nature of IT as a whole.

How to Use AI for ITOps

AI will profoundly affect the IT business. The ML and models that carry AI to the forefront show signs of improvement with access to more data. If these calculations can learn from existing clinical reports, and help specialists with diagnoses, the equivalent AI for IT can be utilized to improve IT tasks and diagnostics. All things considered, enterprise IT manages humongous sums of data procured from servers, working frameworks, applications, and clients. These datasets can be utilized for making ML models that help framework overseers, DevOps groups, and IT departments bolster divisions.

Here are a few of the ways AI in IT will fundamentally affect businesses in the future.

Log Analysis

Breaking down logs is the clearest case for AI-driven activities in IT. Each layer of the stack – equipment, working frameworks, servers, applications – creates the data stream that can be gathered, put away, prepared, and investigated by ML calculations. Today this data is utilized by the IT group to perform review trails and root cause analysis (RCA) of an incident caused because of a security breach or a framework failure. Traditional log management platforms, for example, Splunk, Elasticsearch, Data Dog, and New Relic are expanding their foundation with ML. By carrying AI to log investigation, IT can proactively discover oddities in the frameworks before a failure is accounted for.

Having detected the open door in carrying ML to log the board, a couple of new businesses are building AI-driven log analysis platforms. These intelligent tools can associate data from networking gear, servers, and applications to pinpoint the issue periodically.

Moving ahead, the software will develop to be sufficiently keen to self-analyze, self-repair, and recover from failures. ML calculations will be installed directly into the wellsprings of data including working frameworks, databases, and application programming.

Capacity Planning

IT architects invest significant amounts of energy arranging the resource needs of applications. It could be exceptionally testing to characterize the server details for a complex, multilevel application organization. Each physical layer of the application should be coordinated with the quantity of CPU centers, the measure of RAM, stockpiling limit, and system transmission capacities.

In the open cloud environments, this results in recognizing the privilege of virtual machine (VM) type for every level. Cloud suppliers like Amazon EC2, Azure VMs, and Google Compute Engine routinely add new VM families to help deal with the ever-increasing demands of tasks at hand, like processing big data, game rendering, parallel processing, and data warehousing.

AI can act as the patron saint of infrastructure architects by helping them characterize the correct choices in hardware or pick the proper case type in the open cloud. The calculations gain from existing arrangements and suggest the ideal setup for every remaining task at hand.

It's a short time before the open cloud suppliers include an intelligent VM suggestion engine for each outstanding task at hand. This move will diminish the workload on IT engineers by helping them immediately recognize the right configurations and specifications.

Infrastructure Scaling

Because of the versatility of the cloud, executives can define auto scaling for applications. Auto scaling can be designed to be proactive or receptive. In proactive mode, administrators will plan the scale-out activity before a specific occasion occurs. For instance, if an immediate mailer campaign set off at each end of the week brings about extra burden, they can design the infrastructure to scale-out on a Friday night and scale-in on Sunday.

In receptive mode, the fundamental observing infrastructure will follow key measurements, for example, CPU use and memory utilization to start a scale-out activity. At the point when the heap comes back to the normal, the scale-in activity brings back the infrastructure to its unique structure.

With ML, IT administrators can design prescient scaling that gains from the past burden conditions and use designs. The framework will develop to be sufficiently astute at choosing when to scale with no express guidelines. This structure supplements scope organization by modifying the runtime infrastructure needs more precisely.

In the coming months, open cloud suppliers will begin adding prescient scaling to their infrastructure as a service (IaaS) offering.

Cost Management

Evaluating the expense of infrastructure assumes an urgent job in IT architecture. Particularly in the open cloud, cost examinations and estimations are hard to ascertain. Cloud suppliers charge for an assortment of parts including the use of VMs, stockpiling limits, IOPS, internal and external bandwidth use, and API calls made by applications.

AI can precisely calculate and extrapolate the expense of infrastructure. By examining the remaining tasks at hand and their use designs, it becomes conceivable to give a breakdown of the expenses across different parts, applications, offices, and membership accounts. This would help specialty units to be certain about IT spending plans. In the future, intelligent cost management will turn into a true component of open cloud platforms.

Energy Efficiency

Huge digital infrastructure suppliers are proceeding to pool their resources into monstrous data communities. One of the most difficult aspects of overseeing data focuses is power management. The expansion in energy costs coupled with environmental responsibility has spurred the data community industry to improve its operational efficiency.

By applying ML toward power management, data focus chairmen can significantly lessen their energy use. Google is spearheading AI-driven computational power and efficiency through their DeepMind project, a UK-based organization that the company acquired in 2014 for $600 million. Google claims that it figured out how to decrease the measure of energy utilized for cooling by up to 40%. Figure 3.2 shows how the power usage effectiveness (PUE) was balanced dependent upon the ML suggestions.

AI-driven power management will open doors to greater, more efficient endeavors, bolstering the capabilities of data management centers.

Performance Tuning

After an application is underway, a lot of time is spent fine-tuning its presentation. Particularly, database engines that manage noteworthy measure of exchanges experience diminished efficacy over their lifespans. The "doing business as" (DBAs) step in to drop and revamp files and clear their logs to free up storage space. Pretty much every remaining task at hand including web applications, mobile applications, big data arrangements, and line-of-business applications need some tweaking to maintain ideal performance.

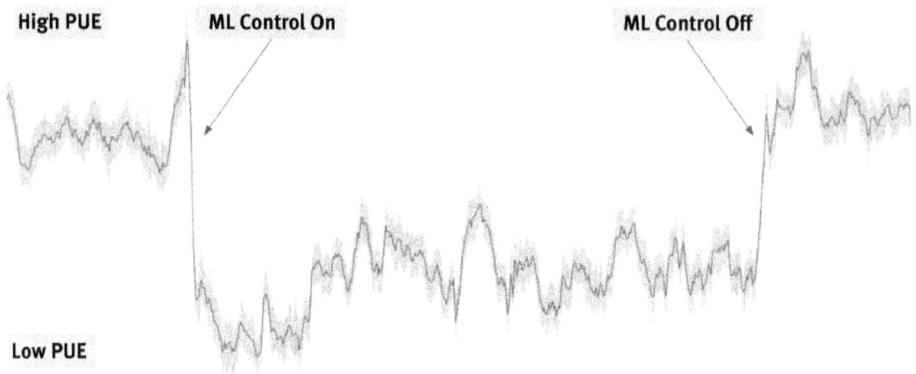

Figure 3.2: The power usage effectiveness (PUE) results balanced using the ML suggestion. Source: DeepMind; https://deepmind.com/blog/article/deepmind-ai-reduces-google-data-centre-cooling-bill-40

AI can automate most maintenance routines. By breaking down the logs and the time taken for regular assignments, for example, by preparing an inquiry or reacting to a request, the calculation can apply an exact fix to the issue. It does this by enlarging the log management by resolving the issue itself instead of raising the issue to the team. This will reduce the expense of IT support and help desks. AI will enormously affect the Level 1 and Level 2 IT support jobs. Most of the issues that are raised to them will in the future be handled by intelligent algorithms.

What are the Core Benefits of AI in ITOps?

AIOps assist data center administrators in recognizing developing issues so they can proactively address those issues – assuming the software doesn't automatically fix the issues. AIOps may also assist administrators in identifying the underlying causes of outages and execution issues.

Another significant advantage is that AIOps automates and accelerates numerous routine procedures and can further offer specialized help. This automation eases the pressure on exhausted IT offices and frees them to concentrate on more valuable work, for example, process improvement and software development.

"AIOps platforms improve IT activities through more prominent bits of knowledge by joining enormous data, AI and representation," Gartner notes in an outline of its Market Guide for AIOps Platforms. "I&O pioneers should start AIOps deployment to refine performance analysis today and enlarge to IT management and automation throughout the following two to five years."

We accept that AIOps will help change IT activities in three basic ways:

1. Give end-to-end visibility. Current ML, controlled by fine-grained IT tasks and execution data, will give IT work force and groups the strong checking capacities they need to watch the conduct and execution of utilizations and IT infrastructure across both the enterprise and the broader ecosystem, permitting them to preemptively recognize chances and approaching issues.

2. Create proof sponsored insights and recommendations. As AIOps calculations become progressively refined, IT work force will have the option to examine authentic tasks data, eliminate noise, and identify root cause issues more reliably and viably. Those insights, in turn, will empower them to make increasingly exact forecasts that lead to speedier resolve problems just as to envision and measure the plausible business effect of such issues before they happen.

3. Execute proposals automatically. In time, the calculations controlling AIOps stages may progress to the degree of consequently modifying its design services and situations. For instance, complex AIOps tools may naturally decide whether to scale new infrastructure or containers, allot much virtual ability to a venture, or turn the quantity of utilization servers up or down – and afterward make a settled upon move.

With adequate refinement, AIOps may someday have the option to computerize a critical bit of all IT tasks and observing exercises.

What is the Future Ahead for AI in ITOps?

As IT needs move past the human scale of management, IT tooling necessitates adjustment. This represents a tremendous opportunity to use AIOps to develop, advance, improve, and disrupt the current IT industry. Here are a few different ways that AIOps-empowered associations will change business in the next five years forever:

– Innovation turns out to be progressively human. Analytics and coordination empower frictionless encounters, permitting omnipresent self-service.

– The mechanization of innovation and consequently, business forms. Costs lower, speed increments decrease, and mistakes decline while opening human capital for more elevated level accomplishment.

– Venture ITOps gains DevOps nimbleness. Continuous conveyance reaches out to tasks and the business.

– Data becomes money. The tremendous abundance of undiscovered business data is promoted, releasing high esteem use cases and adaptation openings.

AI-improved automation will become more astute and progressively relevant, acquisition activity will explode, and you'll see greater development of AIOps toward the edge.

1. *The AIOps market will keep warming up.*
There's been plenty of growth in this market over the previous year, with new participants alongside a few acquisitions of new companies. Mergers and acquisitions (M&A) action will likely proceed into 2020 and beyond as bigger officeholders try to modernize their portfolios.

There's still a great deal of ground to cover similar client appropriation, and where development of AIOps is concerned. Only one out of every five associations has actualized some type of AI programming somewhere in their business, as indicated by an investigation by 451 Research.

Their research additionally shows that half of respondents have either conveyed or plan to utilize AI programming from thirty party contractors, including cloud vendors, for example, Amazon Web Services, as opposed to building their own AI and ML algorithms. Given the shortage of in-house AI skill sets and the multifaceted nature of creating AI applications, many will depend on third party seller execution methodologies to develop.

2. *AIOps will change the substance of IT computerization.*
As multifaceted nature develops in IT associations, from multicloud and programming characterized infrastructure to growing digital business activities, so will the requirement for automation – through an extraordinary computerization.

The following advancement of computerization will be more brilliant, increasingly mindful, and progressively relevant. AI and ML innovations will find hidden resources and threats, uncover patterns, filter the noise, and aid in decision-making.

AI tools will consolidate self-learning calculations so IT administrators can discover answers to issues faster and get proposals on the most effective method to advance IT execution as conditions change.

3. *AI will progressively bolster logical data ingestion and connection.*
AI tools can help diminish alert noise and address routine issues. Anticipate that future undertakings should involve the use of AI for increasingly complex assignments, for example, analyzing datasets from different cloud suppliers, hybrid environments, and edge gadgets.

These AI won't just assist with mundane IT tasks like troubleshooting, they will also be able to provide insight to support the business, for example, seeing how to improve customer experiences by optimizing digital experiences across all customer-facing technologies. Advancement begins with the business units, so it's essential to see how they and clients are creating and utilizing data.

4. *AIOps will be generally utilized on the edge.*
AIOps arrangements ordinarily run from the cloud. However, this is getting increasingly costly and languid, as data volumes and use cases develop. Accordingly,

organizations will start to convey AI tools on the edge of the system, where it's quicker and usually cheaper.

This will empower near-real-time, AI-improved checking, dispensing the travel time from the data center to the cloud service and back. These time savings will be obvious in the case of a critical incident resolution.

The best part is that executing AI on the edge won't require any new abilities. The arrangement happens consistently in the background through the cloud. Intelligent edge technology joined with the smart cloud will cement the advantages of AI to IT activities groups.

5. *Privacy considerations will develop.*

As AI on the edge develops, it's increasingly feasible for organizations to monitor desktops, tablets, and other end-client gadgets. While security groups have been doing that for a considerable length of time, IT tasks groups have normally kept their work inside the data place.

AIOps will permit IT to direct workers in augmenting the use of the applications introduced on their gadgets while conveying more clarity and control around the whole IT environment.

However, there are serious privacy protection suggestions. AIOps will apparently have the option to see everything workers are doing with their gadgets. Considering how the lines have obscured between work and individual time, this necessarily implies the possibility of accidentally collecting confidential information like personal banking accounts or medical appointments, for example.

IT pioneers, in concert with legal and HR divisions, should find harmony between observing gadgets for business steadiness and securing individual worker privacy.

6. *Vendors will finally address security.*

In shopper applications, there's been a lot of discussion in the previous year with protection, security, and morals identified with AI-upgraded gadgets, for example, Amazon's Alexa and Google Assistant.

In IT, AI is potentially a hazard. Similar calculations used to monitor systems for dubious action could also be utilized against organizations – to aid in an assault by making counterfeit records or bypassing inconsistency recognition frameworks, for example.

For AI to prevail and gain mainstream adoption, the industry should improve the security assurances in applications and discover answers for identifying AI-initiated assault techniques before they unleash potential devastation on their businesses. We should hope to see some noteworthy development in AI security from 2020 onward.

7. AIOps will get lined up with business partners.
IT associations have been working for a considerable length of time to draw nearer to business partners, trying to comprehend their needs even before they do. IT activities ought to be following a similar line of thought, and AI will assist in achieving this. In an ongoing study led by OpsRamp, 64% of IT activities pioneers said their main responsibility is to convey agile, responsive, and flexible infrastructure that can bolster quick moving business prerequisites.

IT Ops will move past ready connection into receiving more business-accommodating metrics and mapping IT metrics to explicit business services. AI will assume a job by estimating the business service sway through dissecting infrastructure metrics and binding those back to key execution markers.

8. AI will bolster DevOps rehearses.
IT activities groups are taking a gander at DevOps tools, abilities, and strategies to modernize how they work in line with business and commercial center requests. In the OpsRamp review, DevOps aptitudes bested the rundown of required capacities, as indicated by 64% of the respondents.

AI can help further DevOps rehearsals via consequent upgrades of code for execution. AI can find designs that show wasteful utilization of infrastructure assets and even subsequently make fixes. This can give a progressively steady and effective condition for a nonstop turn of events and persistent mix of (CI/CD) cycles in DevOps.

9. AI will influence work jobs in IT tasks.
Similarly, as distributed computing made a totally new arrangement of improvement and IT aptitudes, AI and ML will drive a comparative change in the way IT groups upskill. ITOps staff will have the chance to seek out data science and advancement aptitudes so they can deal with the mechanization of approaches and activities in their AI tools.

This additionally implies occupations including data section and ticket management will contract. However, there is good news: The algorithms will accomplish a greater amount of the routine and repetitive work while individuals will concentrate on increasingly vital occupations identified with overseeing and breaking down the data.

Data researchers will assume an enormous role in deciding the best proposals from AI frameworks and understanding when to abrogate the recommended activities. By 2025 over 90% of undertakings will have an automation architect to oversee and monitor automation so it develops without causing a completely new roster of difficulties and risks, as per Gartner.

10. Government interest in AI will advance development.
Foreign governments, for example, China, are investing intensely in AI. Offshore cyber-criminal groups are likely doing the same. These weights will boost government

organizations to spend more on R&D in ML and AI – to bolster their own projects for military reconnaissance and industrial espionage, among other politically important information activities.

These endeavors will influence industry, providing a strong incentive to help fill holes in security observation and mechanization.

As with any developing innovation, there is no way of knowing for sure how AIOps will be used, to what extent, or when it will see widespread adoption. In any case, one thing's certain: The requirement for savvy intelligence in IT and business will always increase. There's an excess of information, such a large number of tools and a lot of capricious change for people to deal with without risking significant productivity loss, client abandonments, and botched market chances.

In IT Ops in the coming year, AI will be one of (if not the most) significant development for positive change.

AI-upgraded devices and procedures will give IT an insight into infrastructure status and service health, the capacity to proactively comprehend and forestall issues, and the capacity to locate the likely root cause(s) and solutions to hastily help the business.

Blockchain

For a layman, blockchain innovation is something they catch wind of just when the estimation of Bitcoin makes a jump to bewildering dollar values or plunges to catastrophic lows.

In any case, blockchain covers a whole lot more than cryptocurrencies like Bitcoin. It can resolve exceptionally prickly security issues that your IT teams and security merchants have been grappling with for quite a long time – security challenges that have become meeting room issues over the previous decade since they speak to existential dangers to organizations. From an official point of view, security is no longer another person's duty. It's something each official needs to understand and give careful regard to, which is the primary reason blockchain should be on your radar screen.

What is Blockchain in ITOps?

Blockchain has presented strategies for following and managing client data. IT pioneers need to comprehend the heading of decentralized advancements – or risk falling behind.

Numerous tech sector reports notice the abuse of information and the disintegration of security. Among the unsettling newsflashes are also new terms, for example, "reconnaissance economy," where clients surrender information security for "free" services. With an end goal to battle such disintegration, legislation like the California Consumer Privacy Act give buyers the option to realize what information organizations are gathering about them and request they not sell it. Technological solutions, similar to progressions in blockchain, are less frequently talked about yet may be even more significant.

As Gartner characterizes it, "Blockchain is an extending rundown of cryptographically marked, unavoidable transactional records shared by all members in a system."

Since these time-stepped records are decentralized and promptly copied across every participating party, blockchain is exponentially harder to hack. Blockchain is additionally transparent: Anyone can find out about any transaction's history.

For organizations, the centralization of client information represents a hazard from a security and single purpose of disappointment point of view. Centralization also speaks to a limitation on new plans of action and client elements.

Blockchain – because it guarantees the unchanging nature of records and makes records recognizable without the requirement for an incorporated position – can present elective strategies for following and overseeing explicit client information protection protocols. This is particularly obvious when the expense of including information sources, and the expanded liabilities that accompany it, surpass the advantages. Considering the exponential development of client information utilization advancements, with AI and IoT being just two examples, this turns out to be amazingly useful for clients.

Also, blockchain UX/UI innovations are gaining traction. Before long, blockchain UX/UI advances will compete to establish new industry standards, much like the internet standards wars, which eventually set our present internet principles.

Gartner's view is that by 2024, clients will utilize blockchain licenses to protect about 30% of their sensitive individual information. Once there, innovations like blockchain UX/UI will profit both clients and include an incentive for undertakings.

Why are Blockchain ITOps Important?

One significant pattern that is making blockchain especially attractive is the decentralized nature of data center infrastructure. Previously, organizations had one data center where they based their security systems. Presently, edge computing is putting important organization data and resources in areas that are a lot harder to insure with conventional safety efforts.

Blockchain empowers advanced resources to be followed and secured simply like physical resources you can grasp and put behind lock and key. That is the idea, in any case. Also, it's an idea that has the potential to drastically change how organizations protect their most significant data and IT tasks.

One reason blockchain is so appropriate for a universe of circulated IT infrastructure is that it transforms a shortcoming into a quality by utilizing the open idea of the web as the establishment for securing data and resources.

In contrast to utilizing a unified security technique that attempts to keep data behind walls, blockchain is an approach to protect data that is out in the open, living in numerous areas all throughout the general population and private web. Utilizing a conveyed database structure, blockchain sets up trust between counterparties that limit access to data and tracks all entrance to that data. Considering its dispersed structure, blockchain offers a level of security not found in traditional centralized IT configurations. By disseminating and duplicating data across both the chain and a boundless number of physical servers, blockchain dispenses with the single points of failure that hackers try to pick up on for their attacks.

Perspectives on the potential effect of blockchain philosophy differ broadly, with numerous expectations and rising applications concentrated on using it to grow new applications that can convey increasingly secure transactions that accompany an unmistakable paper trail of computerized documentation. This will affect the applications that live in data centers, yet blockchain innovation will also affect the physical tasks of data centers.

The most critical job that blockchain may affect with regard to IT infrastructure is in the cloud. Since it has been created to empower use across a disseminated infrastructure, blockchain advances the extension of secure independent activities. This allows organizations to put more data, applications, and other strategic resources in the cloud as opposed to inside a central data center.

There are a couple of impediments to a blockchain-based cloud. For instance, the need to utilize exceptionally secure transmission conventions for interchanges between its distributed nodes can make blockchain more exorbitant than customary cloud tasks.

How to Use Blockchain for ITOps

Blockchain-based advances have moved away from simply supporting cryptographic forms of money. One hot region for IT Ops is smart contracts, which let you store, confirm, and execute code on a blockchain. Furthermore, various tasks now under development guarantee to supplant customary components of the computer stack, from handling to capacity to correspondences with this methodology.

Processing

Processing, one of the primary zones that blockchain disrupted, has the most full-grown ecosystem. In conventional figuring, CPUs, and graphics processing units

(GPU) handle processing logic (counting current, cloud-based distributed processing), in a joint effort with elite handling algorithms, models, and tools. For example, MapReduce, Spark, and TensorFlow.

Ethereum, Monax and Hyperledger

Ethereum altered blockchain when it permitted clients to run different types of transactions on a blockchain beside monetary transactions, and it supports a considerable range of different choices.

Ethereum presented the idea of savvy agreements made using the blockchain, opening a world of opportunities. Numerous blockchain-based undertakings today use Ethereum, or something dependent on it.

Hyperledger comprises of eight tools. Concluding which one to utilize where can be rather challenging, however a good starting point is Hyperledger Fabric, which gives foundations for identity, privacy, protection and handling, and constructs components on it. Fortunately, the whole Hyperledger venture is intended for big business clients and large-scale applications.

For instance, Ethereum runs as either an open or private blockchain, however, Hyperledger Fabric is private. It offers a choice for big business go for Hyperledger using smart contracts, or Ethereum using its own JavaScript-like language. What's more, it lets you characterize your own comprehension of "consensus" and "currency."

Monax gives SDKs to the finance, insurance, and logistics industries. Monax turned out in a similar time period as Ethereum and Hyperledger, keeping in mind that it has been overshadowed by those tasks, despite everything it contributes vigorously to upstream activities, and the undertaking's locale strives to guarantee that the innovation works with other people. For instance, it moved the core open software to Hyperledger, and the project is a member of the Enterprise Ethereum Alliance.

Alternative options to Ethereum are also emerging. Aeternity improves things by concentrating on money related applications and expelling state from the blockchain.

High-performance Computing

The decentralized idea of blockchain should make it perfect for massive-scale processing systems, however, its structure right now confines scaling. Ambitious projects, for example, Golem and iEx.ec, which try to make decentralized supercomputers or cloud computing without merchant lock-in, are aspiring tasks that are still in the beginning periods.

The TrueBit venture is endeavoring to tackle this issue by offloading agreements to specific computers in a system. There's not much detail on the project's website, however, it has distributed a TrueBit whitepaper that details how it may function.

The computing capability of blockchain relies on the accomplishment of these tasks, or projects like them. These communities say they are certain that this will occur in the following year.

Storage

Storage is a significant territory of blockchain disruption. A few offer a suitable alternative for huge scope stockpiling, although they experience the ill effects of a portion of the equivalent blockchain issues referenced previously.

Traditional computing storage falls into two camps: file and database storage. There are hard choices in the two camps, from ventures for singular work area machines to enormous scope storage activities, for example, HDFS, S3, MongoDB, and Cassandra.

File Storage

The InterPlanetary File System (IPFS) venture rides storage and communication. One of the early applications that took a gander at blockchain in another manner, IPFS is fully developed and has created a suitable environment.

While the HTTP convention downloads a single record from a single machine at once, IPFS downloads bits of a document from different decentralized machines simultaneously. It resembles torrenting, though with some differences. Take for example, Git. With features worked in for helpful file naming and strong use cases, it's a promising innovation. You can discover customer libraries for JavaScript, Python, Swift, C++, and different dialects. The venture group is making a decent attempt at utilizing IPFS as consistent as could be expected under the circumstances.

Swarm is an Ethereum segment that works in a manner similar to IPFS, however, it handles correspondence and the storage of files. Filecoin adopts an alternative strategy. Rather than offering an instrument for following transactions between blocks of spare storage around data centers and the internet, it allows you to utilize conventional capacity, yet by means of a blockchain layer that allows clients to offer space for you and tracks their use of it.

Databases

BigchainDB takes another intriguing methodology, letting a current database (MongoDB and RethinkDB) add a blockchain layer center around what they are both independently adept at. This gives you provable large-scope, large-scale storage, with the responsibility and transaction bolster that blockchain offers. This undertaking has been developed for quite a while, but is not yet available for use.

Since IPFS can peruse and compose records while databases keep in touch with them, it appeared well and good that somebody would consider utilizing IPFS as a database. OrbitDB does that. This little open-source venture hasn't seen a lot of action over the past couple of months, yet it's ideal for web projects that need simple storage space.

Communication

Two respected protocols, TCP/IP and HTTP, support most of correspondence on the web, while different protocols and models deal other niches. Although blockchain won't supplant either protocol, a few projects are endeavoring to make measures for correspondence between blockchain-based applications.

This is particularly helpful for competing associations making their own applications. However, a few individuals from the network feel this moves them away from the first intended uses of the blockchain innovation and are pushing for standard techniques, keeping blockchains mindful of one another.

Interledger Protocol

Brought by payment solution Ripple, the Interledger Protocol (ILP) intends to interface distinctive cryptocurrencies, yet not broad blockchains. It abstracts individual wallets, payment gateways and banks, and permits designers to code connectors between them.

Cosmos

For more extensive blockchains, Cosmos means to make a "web of blockchains." That's a major undertaking, and the group raised $17 million in a half-hour via an initial coin offering (ICO).

Very little details have emerged regarding how this will function, however, as indicated by the project's whitepaper, the methodology will be to present an intermediary token (an atom) that works like an exchanging system between tokens from different blockchains. This will occur by way of hubs (the principal will be the Cosmos center), while the atom considers the framework to fund itself. In ways it resembles traditional trade and interpretation systems, where you pay the middlemen for their time.

Polkadot

In a recent paper, Polkadot presented the idea of parachains. While Cosmos centers on token trade, Polkadot's methodology centers around the finish of transactions. Consider it keeping up state as you would in a distributed application.

Parachains encourage correspondence between blockchains, however, they have no capacity to settle a transaction. Polkadot is in its initial development stage.

Interplanetary Database

Interplanetary database (IPDB) expands on BigchainDB to offer something of a "system of databases." Recognizing that blockchain ventures are getting progressively concentrated, it needs to urge its clients to store data in a governance model where there is no single proprietor or caretaker. A striking explanation, yet once more technical implementation is yet to be characterized, just like the energy of private data holders.

What are the Core Benefits of Blockchain in ITOps?

The advancement of blockchain infrastructure offers a ton of potential as far as executing secure, verifiable transaction-based applications. What's more, this innovation appears to address various issues with the web. Blockchain cybersecurity frustrates hackers, lessens worries about invalid transactions while advancing productive, completely archived business forms.

Data centers are intricate frameworks, and blockchain offers a degree of transparency not yet observed with conventional infrastructure. The innovation can track, log, and store metrics about the strength of systems. Regardless of whether the data is open or private, the blockchains are transparent to allowed members, which makes confirmation simpler.

With all the discussion of blockchain infrastructure being open and decentralized, numerous associations have legitimate security concerns. It ought to be noted that in any case, blockchain has a high level of security incorporated with the protocol. Blockchain transmits information and the data is confirmed by the system and stored across a vast network, which frustrates hackers and unauthorized access. As IoT gadgets become progressively normal, blockchain data center integration might have the option to address and correct a portion of the security challenges associated with the present.

What is the Future Ahead for Blockchain in ITOps?

With the expanded security and transparency managed by blockchain infrastructure, clients will have more noteworthy trust in the insurance of their data. As transactions are recorded sequentially to shape a changeless chain, the transactions can be pretty much private, contingent upon how it's actualizing it. The "ledger" is circulated across numerous members in the system, where duplicates exist and are at the same time refreshed – each hub that takes an interest can confirm the genuine condition of the ledger and with minimal effort. It's a superior method to share data across frameworks, considering its effectiveness and precision.

Although blockchain is as of yet undeveloped as far as its potential in the commercial center, endeavors are moving toward data center coordination due to the unrivaled trust it engenders among individuals and machines, its process efficiencies for transactions, and elimination of inactivity issues known to affect traditional data center infrastructures.

Even though blockchain won't supplant the operational structure of the cloud at any point in the near future, we may see cloud suppliers utilizing blockchain in increasingly constrained yet effective manners alongside blockchain as a service (BaaS) contribution. While BaaS contributions from suppliers like IBM, Microsoft, AWS, and Google are still in their infant stages, they offer potential blockchain clients a progressively open way to fuse blockchain-based applications into their activities. Among the advantages of the BaaS model are:

– Seamless blockchain provisioning experience
– Interoperability with different stages as a service offering
– Simplified activity
– Easy to program

Blockchain is ready to have an exceptionally huge effect on how organizations protect computerized resources and convey services to clients. Does this imply IT will before long be supplanting and dealing with the present computation, storage, and communications technologies with blockchain-based advancements? Likely not immediately.

Probably the greatest issue with blockchain innovation, notwithstanding some network individuals pushing for guidelines and coordinated effort, is the quantity of tasks contending to take care of similar issues. For those innovations to become feasible, developers need to concentrate on tackling the issues that are keeping the innovation away from standard adoption.

All things considered, IT Ops professionals would do well to watch this space cautiously. When these issues are settled, you may end up considering blockchain-based choices for replacing computation, storage, or communication technology in your enterprise.

Further Reading

Artificial Intelligence

https://devops.com/a-deep-dive-into-artificial-intelligence-for-the-it-operations-aiops/
https://techbeacon.com/enterprise-it/top-10-predictions-ai-it-operations
https://www.gartner.com/smarterwithgartner/12-steps-to-excellence-in-artificial-intelligence-for-it-operations-infographic/
https://blog.syncsort.com/2019/10/big-data/the-rise-of-artificial-intelligence-for-it-operations-part-1/
https://searchitoperations.techtarget.com/definition/AIOps
https://www.bmc.com/blogs/what-is-aiops/
https://www.splunk.com/en_us/artificial-intelligence-aiops.html
https://www.cio.com/article/3393967/empowering-it-operation-teams-with-artificial-intelligence.html

https://www.bcg.com/en-in/publications/2019/artificial-intelligence-coming-information-technology-operations.aspx
https://www.forbes.com/sites/janakirammsv/2017/07/16/artificial-intelligence-is-set-to-change-the-face-of-it-operations/#2010cab01d21

Blockchain

https://techbeacon.com/security/how-blockchain-will-disrupt-traditional-computing
https://www.manufacturing.net/industry40/article/13228093/how-blockchain-can-transform-business-operations-for-manufacturers
https://techbeacon.com/security/blockchain-data-security-resource-guide-it-ops-teams
https://www.forbes.com/sites/forbesdallascouncil/2019/01/16/how-blockchain-will-shape-the-future-of-your-organizations-it-strategy/#50bb81022f0b
https://www.informationweek.com/big-data/predictions-around-blockchain-and-data-for-it-leaders-/a/d-id/1336895
https://www.vxchnge.com/blog/the-relationship-between-blockchain-and-data-centers

Aditya Kumar
Chapter 4
Human Resources

Artificial Intelligence

Most experts today agree that the adoption of artificial intelligence (AI) innovations is causing work environments to evolve rapidly. There are utilizations of AI being rolled out throughout almost every profession and industry, and human resources (HR) professions are no exception.

An ongoing study directed by Oracle and Future Workplace found that HR experts trust AI will open new doors for developing abilities and award workers with more free time, permitting HR experts to expand the responsibilities of their present jobs and in doing so, maintain a progressively vital role within their company.

Despite many HR pioneers having a keen interest in implementing AI solutions for HR tasks, in one review 81% of HR professionals nevertheless said they believe that it's difficult to stay aware and up-to-date with the pace of innovative changes at work. The sheer speed in which workplaces are changing only highlights the significance of disruption workplaces are facing. As I will explain later, it is imperative now more than ever for HR experts to comprehend the way in which AI is reshaping business.

What is AI in HR?

AI is an innovation used to carry out a responsibility that requires some degree of intelligence to achieve – it is a device trained to do what a human can do. AI is unique in relation to conventional programming, in that it has three main advantages – fast calculation, an ability to analyze information, and the ability to learn from information analyzed, which all separates AI from customary programming. Core AI advancements give higher precision and stability to ordinary procedures utilizing a calculation that integrates quality information processing with quick computation services.

AI advances offer huge potential to improve HR capacities. For example, self-service transactions, recruiting and talent acquisition, payroll, reporting, access policies and procedures, all stand to benefit from AI assistance. By integrating AI into HR organization, AI will increase the capacities for HR departments to utilize work data precisely, all for a better all-around employee experience and greater profit.

Humans and learning machines are cooperating to deliver an ever-expanding measure of HR information in the cloud, and the utilization of AI analysis offers

https://doi.org/10.1515/9783110664454-004

better avenues in executing workplace solutions and conducting routine work. The accomplishment of any association relies upon how quickly and reasonably it joins individual procedure and innovation into one effective system. AI will help to effectively computerize and automate many back-office capacities for solid HR transactions and service delivery.

The utilization of AI innovations is changing the way people complete rote, routine work forever. McKinsey's most recent estimate of AI's effect on the worldwide economy is that AI will create $13 trillion worth of worldwide economic activity by 2030. Within the HR industry, experts today are focusing on how to use AI to enhance the mix of human-led dynamic work and AI-led robotized work to create a transparent, consistent, capable, and natural workplace.

AI will have many unexpected effects when implemented in the HR industry. It is clear to see, for example, how AI will improve productivity by automating a lot of information processing tasks, yet AI may have more profound effects like increasing compassion in the workplace. Richard Coombes, pioneer of HR transformation practice at Deloitte argues that utilizing AI for recruitment eliminates the behavioral and perceptive biases that may be present during human interaction. Used in this manner, AI could have a vital role in awarding candidates and workers a level playing field when competing for jobs and promotions. This is just one way that AI will prove to be positively disruptive in the workplace.

Perhaps the most striking example we are beginning to see is the role AI has been playing in job creation and obsolescence. Just as the industrial revolution rendered many industries and jobs obsolete, while creating entirely new jobs and industries in their wake, Gartner announced in 2017 that AI will automate the jobs performed by 1.8 million individuals by 2022 making them unemployed. While the quantity of positions lost because of automation may seem alarming, it is important to take into consideration a similar report additionally referenced, detailing how AI will help make 2.3 million occupations in that same year, resulting in a net expansion of 500,000 new job openings.

A study by McKinsey in 2017 uncovered that only 5% of US occupations could be automated by AI completely, and around 60% could be semiautomated. The fact of the matter is, AI won't eliminate the need for human workforce any time soon, for better or for worse. Obviously, numerous assignments will be automated, yet a workforce prepared to adapt to the future will surely thrive.

Why is AI HR Important?

AI is ubiquitous today, and there are numerous perspectives to consider with regard to how it will affect the eventual fate of work.

"It's presently flying into pretty much every piece of software," said Josh Bersin, head and founder of Bersin by Deloitte. Considering research by Bersin by Deloitte, almost 40% of organizations are utilizing some type of AI in HR alone.

According to "Personnel Today" 38% of enterprises are presently utilizing AI in their working environment with 62% hoping to begin utilizing it this year. As stated by Bersin by Deloitte, 33% of representatives expect that their employments will be augmented using AI sooner rather than later.

Today we are progressively utilizing chatbots and remote helpers in our own lives, so it only makes sense that we now can hope to utilize them in the working environment, too. Securing new positions, answering FAQs, or getting instruction and tutoring, these are all just some examples of how utilization of AI in associations could assist us with creating an increasingly consistent, progressively adaptable. and more user-driven employee experience.

In that capacity, AI assumes a major job today in changing HR and the workforce; decreasing human biases, expanding proficiency in applicant evaluation, improving relationships with employees, improving consistency, increasing adoption of metrics, and improving working environment learning are all some of the advantages associations are experiencing today.

Jeanne Meister expressed in her article, "The Future of Work: The Intersection of Artificial Intelligence and Human Resources," how HR pioneers should start exploring different avenues regarding all aspects of AI to convey an incentive to their associations. As per Meister, HR pioneers are starting to direct AI to convey more noteworthy incentives to their associations by utilizing, for instance, chatbots for recruiting, employee services, employee development, and training.

Up until now, recruiting and talent acquisition are where AI arrangements have shined. There is a burgeoning crop of new companies and specialist coops who target the HR industry with AI-based answers for exercises, such as:

- sourcing (for instance, Textio)
- interviewing (myInterview)
- onboarding (Talla)
- training (Saberr)
- employee service centers (ServiceNow)

With regard to AI in HR, "The utilizations of AI essentially are analytics applications, where the product is utilizing history and calculations and information to be more intelligent and more brilliant after some time," according to Bersin. The most intriguing piece of people analytics is the integration of AI and human capabilities.

Interests in AI are developing exponentially. Research firm IDC predicts that the market for AI will develop from $12.5 billion out of 2017 to $126 billion by 2025, affecting all strategic approaches across pretty much every industry.

The McKinsey Research Institute referenced in its January 2017 report, "A future that works: Automation, business, and efficiency", that computerization innovations such as propelled mechanical autonomy and AI are incredible drivers of profitability and monetary development which can help make financial surpluses and increase overall societal prosperity.

As indicated by McKinsey, computerization could improve the efficiency of the worldwide economy by somewhere between the range of 0.8 and 1.4% of the worldwide GDP every year; expecting that the human work supplanted via automation rejoins the workforce in more productive roles.

Their automation analysis discovered critical varieties among different areas of the economy and among the occupations inside those segments. Considering the specialized, financial, and social variables influencing the pace and degree of automation, McKinsey evaluated that up to 30% of current work exercises could be uprooted by 2030.

At the point when the subject of AI and its effect on employments and the economy comes up, the principal focus of the conversation used to be on blue collar jobs. According to CB Insights and the State of Automation Report, there are 4.6M retail salespersons' occupations in danger in the United States alone because of AI. Something very similar may follow for 4.3M cooks and waiters, 3.8M cleaners, 2.4M movers and distribution center specialists, 1.8 M truck drivers, and 1.2M development laborers.

As indicated by CB Insights, a developing rush of AI-implanted Expert Automation and Augmentation Software (EAAS) stages will control us toward another period of AI-assisted as well as AI-improved efficiency. These EAAS stages use machine intelligence to recreate and expand human comprehension.

Not limited to blue-collar occupations, this AI-improved efficiency is beginning to threaten salaried occupations, too. What's more, it will affect the majority of the basic callings like legal counselors, HR, instructors, dealers, sales, showcasing, scientists, bookkeepers, programming designers, etc.

As much as the HR innovation scene keeps on being disturbed by AI, HR groups must discover approaches to offset these advancements with transparency. It is fundamental to ensure the execution of AI innovation is effective. AI can not be seen as a universal solution to all HR tasks and problems; it is an incredibly useful instrument and must be used as such. AI devices are dependent on the information they are provided to work viably. Because of this, effort to grasp how to use AI today will yield more profitable uses tomorrow, as more and more companies begin to rely on AI programs to deliver their HR solutions.

How to Use AI for HR?

With information at the heart of the industry, HR divisions offer a plethora of potential for AI programming applications. Datasets with potential job applicants, past applicants, and current workers all make an extremely information rich environment for

AI to yield analytics-backed bits of knowledge and insight into different HR-related procedures.

The Oracle study on cutting edge analytics in HR offices recognized zones where AI is being utilized the most among respondents (see Figure 4.1).

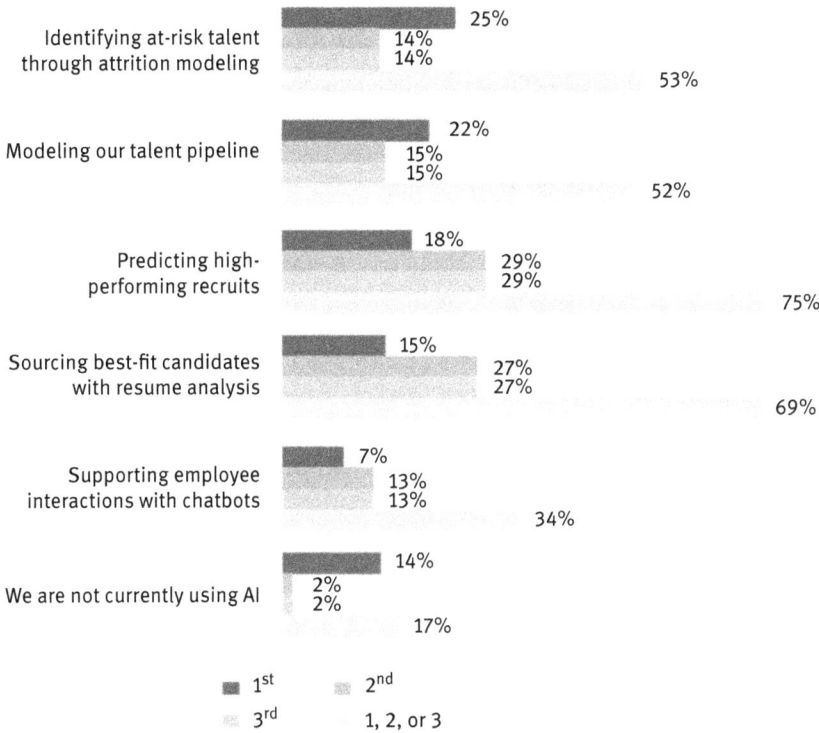

Figure 4.1: HR offices recognized zones where AI is being utilized the most among respondents. Source: Oracle/monterail.com; https://www.oracle.com/a/ocom/docs/applications/hcm/oracle-ai -in-hr-wp.pdf

The aftereffects of the analytics show that HR offices often turn to AI-fortified software to figure out which representatives are probably going to leave. In and out analysis of numerous factors, alongside AI's capacity to foresee results, may be helping recruiters curb talent attrition. Respondents additionally use AI to source the best ability through a list of qualification analysis and foresee which of the applicants can possibly produce the most important yield for the organization.

Recruitment and Onboarding

While numerous associations are now incorporating AI innovation into their enlisting endeavors, most by far of associations are definitely not. Truth be told, Deloitte's 2019 Global Human Capital Trends review found that a solitary 6% of respondents accepted that they had the top tier enrollment forms in innovation, while 81% accepted their association's procedures were standard or below standard. Hence, there are huge opportunities for experts to adjust their procedures and receive the rewards of utilizing this trendsetting innovation.

During the recruitment procedure, AI can be utilized to the advantage of both the employing organization as well as its job applicants. For instance, AI innovation can smooth out application forms by structuring easier to understand application forms that a job applicant is more likely to finish, successfully decreasing the quantity of surrendered applications.

While this methodology has made the job of the HR division in enrollment a lot simpler, AI also takes into consideration less complex and increasingly important applications on the candidate's end, which has been shown to improve application completion rates.

Moreover, AI has assumed a significant role in competitor rediscovery. By maintaining a database of past candidates, AI innovation can examine the current pool of candidates and distinguish those that would be a solid match for new jobs as they open. Instead of using time and resources searching for new talent, HR experts can utilize this innovation to recognize qualified representatives expediently and more effectively than any other time in recent history.

Once hiring managers have discovered the best fit for their open positions, the onboarding procedure starts. With the assistance of AI, this procedure doesn't need to be confined to standard business hours – an enormous improvement over onboarding procedures of the past.

Rather, AI innovation allows recently recruited employees to use HR support at any time of day and in any area through the utilization of chatbots and remote help applications. This change not only gives representatives the capacity to experience the onboarding procedure at their own pace, it also lessens the regulatory weight and consistently brings about faster integration.

Internal Mobility and Employee Retention

Notwithstanding upgrades to the recruitment procedure, HR experts can also use AI to support internal mobility and employee retention.

Through customized input reviews and employee recognition systems, HR offices can precisely measure worker commitment and employment fulfillment. This is an invaluable tool in helping understand the general needs of representatives.

In an ongoing report from the Human Resources Professional Association, some AI programming can assess key points of employee achievement to distinguish those that ought to be advanced, accordingly driving inner mobility. Doing so can essentially decrease talent acquisition costs, bolster employee retention rates, and maintain a strong corporate community culture.

This innovation isn't constrained to recognizing chances to advance from inside, in any case; it can also foresee who in a group is intending to quit. Having this information as soon as possible allows HR experts to deploy retention efforts before demoralized or disinterested workers commit to leaving, which can greatly diminish worker turnover rates.

Automation of Administrative Tasks

One of the key advantages of utilizing AI in different HR departments is in automating low worth, effectively repeatable managerial tasks. This gives HR experts more opportunities to add to strategic planning at the organizational level. This empowers the HR office to turn into a strategic business partner within their organizations.

Smart technologies can computerize procedures, for example, the administration of benefits, prescreening candidates, planning meetings, and that's just the beginning. Although every one of these capacities is imperative to the general achievement of an association, completing the errands involved with executing such procedures is by and large tedious, and the burden of these obligations frequently implies that HR experts have less time to add to serving their workers in progressively effective manners.

Tasking AI programming with automating repetitive errands can lift this burden. For example, an examination by eightfold found that HR workforces who used AI programming performed managerial assignments 19% more successfully than divisions that didn't utilize such innovation. With the time that is spared, HR experts can give more vitality to strategic planning at the organizational level.

Personalized Experience

The impact of AI is most felt when securing talent. The screening of prospective candidates, recording and maintaining the database, automating interview schedules, communicating something specific, answering job seekers' queries and other fundamental HR tasks all stand to benefit from the application of AI.

The outcomes are critical, quantifiable, and quick. It diminishes the recruiting time and increases efficiency for HR experts. The team is left with more time for higher-esteem work like sourcing, enrollment advertising, employee engagement, and employing managers.

For example, the Job Intelligence Maestro (Jim) for DBS Talent Acquisition Team reduced the screening time from 32 minutes to 8 minutes for every applicant.

AI-upheld programs acquaint the new representative with the work profile, fresh recruit data like reporting authority, team members, task assignments, administrative tasks, policies, and practically all direct data through an application or PC on his/her first day.

Workforce Management Decisions

Other HR job roles (aside from enrollment) where AI is making an effect incorporate HR system and employee management, analyzing organization approaches and practices, overseeing payrolls, automating workforces, investigating corporate compliance, litigation strategy, analyzing success, and other related projects. The more technical-minded HR workforce can promptly apply innovation to HR capacities, learning and advancement applications to greatly improve the information processing, and planning capabilities of their company's HR department.

Smart People Analytics

An employee's performance generates large tracts of information that can be used to evaluate their overall ability and value added to the company. By keeping track of the representative's various exercises like perusing emails, ventures, and different errands for a concise period, it can identify exceptional workers and report accordingly to the organization's HR department. This allows the association to effectively employ engagement and retention strategies for workers who provide the most value to the company.

What are the Core Benefits of AI in HR?

AI has smoothed out numerous HR forms. These refined computer programs exceed expectations at analyzing data, arranging, and adjusting information categories in manners that equate or surpass human ability. In contrast to individuals who can become worn out or exhausted, or bring oblivious biases into their choices, AI programs are quick, consistent, and productive.

AI is progressively being utilized to automate numerous HR procedures, and it shows. A study from McKinsey ventures found that AI will definitely change business, regardless of the industry: "AI might convey extra monetary yield of around $13 trillion by 2030, boosting worldwide GDP by about 1.2 percent a year." Keeping this fact in mind, let us examine seven different ways AI are expected to or already are improving the effectiveness of HR departments around the world.

AI Can Sift through Thousands of Applications Faster

Void positions can debilitate your workforce and hurt organization resolve. So, it's critical to rapidly fill positions – while still trying to find the right, and ideally the best person for the job.

Analyzing a deluge of incoming resumes for a competitive post is a challenging assignment that is inclined to result in most applications not receiving the full attention they warrant, lest the application processing takes up too much of HRs time. AI can spare HR divisions as much as 23 hours of work per recruit by examining incoming applications and utilizing calculations to survey and assess the candidates' understanding, training, and aptitudes.

It Increases Retention Rates and Productivity by Helping You Hiring More Qualified Candidates

In addition to the fact that AI speeds up the candidate selection process and gives priceless analysis, it also utilizes that information to help match candidates to the right jobs. AI calculations can distinguish the traits of successful employees and search for applicants with comparative attributes for certain occupations.

It Reduces Hiring Bias

Despite discrimination in recruiting being immoral and illegal in most nations, HR faculty sometimes allow personal biases and prejudices to affect the employing procedure knowingly or unknowingly, even when conscious efforts to be impartial are made. AI, however, analyzes without passion or prejudice, and can ignore data in regard to a candidate's age, race, and sexual orientation. It also doesn't start with any inclinations in favor or against certain geographic regions, colleges, or institutions. Utilizing AI can reduce unfair recruiting predispositions and help make a socially inclusive work environment.

It Streamlines Employee Onboarding

Fresh recruits normally have numerous inquiries in regard to benefits, paid time off, and company policies. AI chatbots can answer these repetitive requests, opening HR faculties to deal with undertakings like training and office visits. AI can also help with recently recruited employee desk work, helping representatives get the chance to settle into work faster.

It Helps Employers Craft Job Descriptions

Present AI programming can assist scouts with creating the ideal expected set of responsibilities. Projects like Textio perceive gender bias in ads, helping recruiters choose contextually neutral language. Moreover, by contrasting the language in a promotion and past advertisements that have functioned admirably, AI programming can enable the essayist to create the right content to attract the ideal candidate.

It Improves Employee Engagement and Builds Better Relationships

AI's uses go past employing. From planning meetings to training workers, the present AI innovation smooths out basic business procedures and improves the efficiency of all HR work functions.

It Helps You Save Time

This extra efficiency enables recruiters and HR divisions to use this spare time to pursue more productive endeavors with undivided attention. HR chiefs who don't utilize any automation for assignments such as payroll, applicant tracking, training, job postings, and more, state they lose on average 14 hours a week finishing these errands manually. If your association doesn't utilize AI programming to automate even a few parts of HR, you could be losing time and cash.

What is the Future Ahead for AI in HR?

The fate of HR is both AI and human as HR pioneers focus on enhancing the integration of human and computerized work. This is driving another need for HR: one that requires pioneers and groups to build up a familiarity with AI while they rethink how HR may become even more personal, human, and natural in the workplace.

1. *AI Plus Human Intelligence Enhances the Candidate Experience*
When it comes to talent acquisition, organizations can observe critical, quantifiable, and prompt outcomes in the entire employment process. Less time spent to employ new and more suitable workers expands productivity for recruiters, and conveys an improved candidate experience that is consistent, reliable, and natural.

One organization that has capitalized on AI- assisted recruitment is DBS Bank. The DBS Talent Acquisition group made Jim, a virtual enrollment bot fueled by AI. Jim is used to direct candidate screening for those applying to be wealth planning managers, a high-volume work in the consumer bank, shortlisting the many suitable candidates based on quantifiable qualities.

2. Interestingly Human Skills Will Grow in Importance

The interest in human aptitudes and skills will continue to develop, as per the Future of Jobs Report from the World Economic Forum. The World Economic Forum expects that 75 million current employments will be displaced as AI assumes control over progressively routine parts of work. This will be offset by 133 million new openings, in job roles requiring enthusiasm and specialized intelligence, similar to innovation plan and programming. In this manner we should observe over the next decade many repetitive and boring roles or job functions rendered obsolete, so human workers may pursue more important, challenging, and interesting problems and functions.

3. AI Won't Take Away Jobs but Help Workers Do Jobs Better

As Gartner estimates that AI will make a significant net gain in employment opportunities, the spotlight for 2021 will be in concluding how to best utilize AI to assist laborers with carrying out their responsibilities better. PwC estimates 20% of administrators in US organizations with AI activities report that they will roll out AI across their business this year and anticipate that AI planning should both involve a reconsideration of employments and work forms to develop greater benefits and generate more income.

For HR pioneers, we see this already happening. Oracle and Future Workplace directed research with 600 HR pioneers entitled AI at Work, to research where AI was being utilized in the working environment to reimagine candidate and employee experience.

4. New Openings Will Be Created Using AI

Making new openings as AI turned out to be progressively far reaching inside organizations had been an immense challenge for C-suite pioneers in 2019. The Center for the Future of Work at Cognizant Technology Solutions handled this issue with two reports, 21 Jobs for the Future and 21 More Jobs for the Future of Work. These occupations have been sorted out from low tech to cutting edge over the 10-year skyline from 2019 to 2029.

5. An AI Ready Workforce Will be Critical to an Organization's Future

Now that we are in 2021 – with AI moving from buyers' lives into the working environment – upskilling non-AI laborers to figure out how to function with AI is increasingly significant. Building up an AI prepared workforce includes five key activities:

- Firstly, distinguish the business's issues and opportunities, to explain how utilizing AI begins by gathering information on the present condition of the issues and opportunities. This is also the appropriate time to set the key performance indicators (KPI) you need to affect with AI.
- Fabricate a practical cross group of key partners to advise them the business advantages of utilizing AI to tackle key business issues.
- Execute learning opportunities for key employment jobs affected in HR by AI (e.g., those in recruiting, new hire onboarding, and corporate learning).
- Distinguish new openings and abilities required as AI is utilized in the working environment.
- Change performance management and development skills required in HR jobs to incorporate a basic comprehension of how to utilize AI across the worker life cycle.

6. *Ability-Based Hiring Gains Traction*

In 2018, Future Workplace facilitated an abilities-based recruiting hackathon where we asked, for what reason weren't more organizations embracing aptitudes-based employment to enlarge the talent pool? based recruiting is characterized as the act of setting explicit aptitudes and competency prerequisites for an occupation as opposed to depending exclusively on candidates' qualifications. Today, more FORTUNE 1000 firms are going on record as employing applicants without an advanced education as a necessity.

Abilities-based recruiting may begin by changing a set of working responsibilities and removing a degree prerequisite, yet it requires moving outlooks on where and how an organization sources ability. What's required is to change the outlooks of hiring managers and business pioneers to source in new manners and methods. These better approaches to source nonconventional competitors run from boot camps, coding schools, MOOC's, technical secondary schools like P-TECH (a joint secondary school certificate and partner degree in STEM), job training led at public venues, secondary schools, or even supporting a broad hackathon. Despite your industry, receiving an abilities-based recruiting approach requires teaching business partners, recognizing benefits and hindrances of broadening the ability pool, and building up a system for the two aptitudes-based recruiting just as instructive and learning pathways to upskill an increasingly diverse employee population.

7. *Workers Will Trade Money for Meaning at Work*

The experience of meaningful work is an individual one, as Gallup reports an ordinary worker is chipping away 47 hours out of each week with one out of five working over 60 hours every week. With so much of their life spent working, workers are placing greater importance on looking for meaningful work, a working environment that adjusts to their qualities and a steady and solid work culture.

An ongoing report entitled Meaning and Purpose at Work reviewed 2,285 American experts across 26 enterprises to discover how significant "having importance" was to workers in their respective careers.

When asked if they would rather have more salary or a more meaningful career, workers said they'd be eager to forego 23% of their whole future lifetime income if it meant they could enjoy work that was consistently important to them. This implies building more prominent significance at work is a fundamental prerequisite to a stable and healthy workforce, neglected at great short-term and long-term detriment. Representatives who discover significance at work are more joyful, increasingly productive and dedicated, and are much less prone to absenteeism.

8. Augmented Reality is Transforming Corporate Training
A developing number of heads of worldwide learning and development are directing virtual reality (VR) to train representatives. What's more, the most fascinating cases involve utilizing virtual reality for compliance training. Verizon is utilizing augmented reality to train senior supervisors on protocol if there is a store burglary.

AI exceed expectations at undertakings that depend on data processing and pattern recognition, completing these functions faster and more effectively than human beings can, making it an important tool in automating numerous parts of HR work functions. It can not be emphasized enough that the "human" part of HR shouldn't be disregarded. From settling on the final recruiting choices to finding inventive approaches to keep workers connected and content, HR executives know their workers and their association in manners AI programming can't replicate. AI simply is a device that can give HR colleagues more opportunity to become more acquainted with workers, shape organization culture, and address issues that crop up by providing HR workers with more useful information to act on.

Additionally, innovations are only as useful if people are willing to embrace these innovations. HR staff can facilitate the progress to AI by arguing to representatives how utilizing AI in HR can help almost everybody in the working environment, increasing productivity, happiness, and profit.

Blockchain

The endurance of a business relies upon the feasibility of its workforce. Yet to assemble a genuinely profitable group of employees, an association needs to oversee two basic procedures well. The first is the onboarding of new talent, followed by its ongoing support for ideal productivity and development.

Recruiting and sustaining required operational capability is the primary obligation of HR management, obviously a fundamental division in any association.

Citing Forbes Human Resources Council, an enrollment association for senior-level HR administrators from various enterprises stated, "If workers are the soul of an association, the human resources division is its central sensory system."

Organizations and associations burn through billions of dollars every year on HR and related exercises. There have been many experiments and innovations in how to improve HR effectiveness, with a great deal of accomplishment. Most associations currently depend on expanding IT frameworks to oversee everything about their workforce. Be that as it may, there is still more improvement achievable.

What is Blockchain in HR?

Blockchain innovation is maybe most popular for its job in defending the cryptocurrency infrastructure (e.g., Bitcoin), making budgetary transactions secure without the requirement for a bank or a go between. However, the innovation is moving toward an arrival in the HR space, which will definitely change the way that HR experts handle a lot of delicate employee data and convey different HR forms.

As blockchain innovation turns out to be more standard and open, all individuals from the HR division – from recruiters to the senior authority – will probably discover it disrupting their everyday work processes. The recruitment procedure, tapping talent pools, running record verifications, confirming business history, connecting with provisional laborers with smart contracts, onboarding, keeping up employee data, keeping up employees' very own data, dealing with monetary transactions, and overseeing finance frameworks, all stand to be improved with the application of blockchain technology. It can even streamline cross-border payments via atomization of constant trade rates and other purview parameters, which hold suggestions for organizations that recruit and work comprehensively.

One of the main difficulties HR experts face is understanding the essentials of what blockchain is and how it improves HR capacities. Basically, a blockchain is an appropriated computerized open record used to monitor records. The term block is basically another word for record. A blockchain, at its center, is just a chain of records. Blockchain is extraordinary and unique in comparison to other recordkeeping frameworks since it depends on an appropriated record, which means the chain of records is stored across a large network of independent computers. This decentralizes and scrambles the data, protecting and securing it.

The extreme level of security makes the blockchain innovation a decent counterpart for the HR business, which is frequently tasked with overseeing a lot of sensitive data about an organization and its employees.

Regardless of the considerable number of ways blockchain innovation might disturb HR management, HR groups need not be alarmed. There is still some time to prepare for the coming blockchain revolution – and the innovation has a solid reputation of achievement in the enterprises it has contacted up until now. For instance, banks would now be able to decrease infrastructure cost by 30% through block-chain arrangements. This is accomplished by scrambling a large number of capacity focuses, none of which contain a complete name or a record number.

While only 0.5% of the worldwide populace is at present utilizing blockchain innovation, the interest is rising, and it is expected that 80% of the populace will be engaged with blockchain innovation in some capacity within the next 10 years. For HR groups, the standard selection of blockchain could open worth and advantage for bosses and employees alike, beginning with the capacity of recruiting chiefs to place the perfect individuals in vacant occupations.

To show how it could chip away at the two sides of the business relationship, blockchain can empower people to keep up, secure, and offer controlled access to a complete blockchain-driven advanced ID that incorporates basic personal data for use by bosses. This could incorporate information regarding instruction, aptitudes, proficiencies, and accomplishments. Through this advanced ID, people would have the option to transform their certifications into genuine incentives for promotion and career development, while managers can identify the most suitable employees for the job through data-driven analysis.

If its achievement in banking and supply chain is any sign, blockchain is ready to enhance the ways in which we manage human capital in various limits.

Why is Blockchain HR Important?

There is much work involved in screening any recruitment procedure. Before short-listing of candidates even begins, HR administrators need the candidate data to be correct and verified so that there are no fake resumes or fraudulent applications ar-riving at the framework, lest unqualified or hostile candidates gain employment.

To guarantee that candidate data is right, HR administrators can utilize a block-chain database to get the qualification data and confirm it utilizing the Distributed Ledger Technology.

Resumes can even turn into a thing of the past as HR directors essentially gain access to candidate data in an industry-wide database and afterward, track the ad-vancement of the candidate during their education and profession. Furthermore, having industry-wide blockchain databases additionally guarantees that every can-didate is assessed for the achievements that they have managed without looking through various data stores or numerous such databases.

At the end of the day, discovering whether a specific candidate is who they pro-fess to be is made simpler, more transparent, and with more integrity. In this way, blockchain is best utilized for automating and smoothing out the recruitment frame-works in associations that lessen time spent analyzing, increasing accuracy, and helping HR management staff to increase overall efficacy. Obviously, overreliance on innovation has its own disadvantages and thus, HR chiefs must have access to the most trustworthy records containing the data, and not trust any single database indiscriminately or uncritically. Nevertheless, blockchain greatly eases the burden of much personnel auditing.

Another key benefit of utilizing blockchain is in the domain of the so-called gig economy or the part-time work segment in associations. Utilizing blockchain, HR chiefs can guarantee that every single connected datum, for example, the quantity of hours worked or the assignments finished is exact, correct, and linked perfectly to wages paid. By connecting the wages and the payouts to the former, timely payments can be made without the HR supervisors having to oversee every one of the records for the gig workers.

Without a doubt, the development of blockchain is corresponding to the development of the gig economy. In addition, smart contracts can be drawn up wherein minute details and profound volumes of data can be kept up for every gig worker. HR administrators can also utilize a similar Industry database to confirm whether such part timers are verified and compensated accordingly. What's more, there is no requirement for elaborate verification frameworks for finance, detailing, reviewing, and consistence.

Along these lines, every one of the exercises in the HR management esteem chain turns out to be progressively productive with the utilization of blockchain innovation lessening workloads and guaranteeing that associations can get efficiencies from the economies of scale.

Blockchain is an innovation that will lead to imaginative and effective enhancements over current HR procedures, with its emphasis on streamlining each errand in the HR management esteem chain.

Additionally, reporting and archive management is simple as all the HR staff needs to do is to pull out important data from the records from one database as needed, effortlessly. Additionally, legal auditing and compliance as a rule requires the most precise and complete data collection of all relevant business information. Blockchain and its undeniable advantages in this regard can guarantee that such administrative record keeping is made simpler, more reliable, and more secure.

For example, whether recording or providing details regarding dashboards, an automated HR scorecard can provide a real time reporting framework to provide the best possible record keeping.

Lastly, utilizing the blend of blockchain, AI, and analytics, HR managers can be prescient in foreseeing patterns identified with HR management. They can fill in vacant positions in a timelier fashion as these technologies diminish the time taken significantly, while not compromising the authenticity and reliability of data. They also confer advantages in scaling up rapidly, which means that there is potential for drawing from an even more extensive candidate pool just as there is a more profound data store to draw from. With every one of these focal points, businesses insiders anticipate that it is a matter of time before most, if not all, associations receive blockchain for HR management.

How to Use Blockchain for HR

Blockchain is disrupting a significant number of the ventures that HR divisions work nearby to oversee human capital. For instance, beside blockchain's predominance in the financial business, Forbes has distinguished the healthcare industry as one of the top enterprises liable to be disrupted. As indicated by Bitfortune, 55% of healthcare applications will receive blockchain for business deployment by 2025. HR divisions will therefore need to be on the forefront of the developing healthcare landscape – including the usage of blockchain – so they can keep on being an expert on conveying healthcare plans and wellbeing projects to employees.

In any case, the utilization of blockchain will be something HR experts should know about for association purposes. Since the HR office is the guardian of such a large amount of the data that is integral or personal to employees' lives and how an organization works, blockchain innovation will be integrated into the HR framework through a huge number of utilization cases – lending transparency and trust to the whole system.

Fortify Security for Sensitive Personal and Monetary Data

HR groups are entrusted with leading absolutely the most volume of budgetary transactions for most associations, taking care of things such as sensitive employee data related with pay, healthcare, money, banking, disciplinary records, execution records, expense reimbursement, etc.

The entirety of the data a HR office retains presents a danger of being misused and, as more organizations face data breaches, it is of the utmost extreme significance that protective measures are set up to forestall fraud, misuse and maintain security. In the face of increasing cybersecurity crime, blockchain innovation is being commended as an answer to this problem.

Blockchain's distinct advantage for HR is characterized by its security capacities. Already blockchain has demonstrated itself to be viable for risk management and software security, such that even aviation and defense giant Lockheed Martin is utilizing it.

Actualizing blockchain implementation can help impede both internal misuse and external hacks of sensitive employee records. Access to the blockchain is constrained and controlled and even those with access to records, can not unilaterally make changes to the record. This curtails both internal fraud and external hacks of sensitive employee records.

With the ascent of the Internet of Things (IoT) in HR, there is developing concern of hackers frequently gaining access by deliberately misusing shortcomings in edge devices. The caution and safeguards applied to PCs are frequently dismissed while guaranteeing the security of IoT gadgets, leaving associations helpless against hacks. Blockchain offers solid assurances against data alteration by locking access to IoT devices and closing undermined devices inside the IoT network if a security breach is suspected.

Blockchain serves to viably decentralize data as a key point of resistance against hacks and misrepresentation. Data is a piece of an organization's money in the computerized age. It is quickly becoming one of the most prized resources an organization has. If you store all your jewelry, money, and different assets in a single area of your home, what occurs if a criminal enters your home and discovers this area? Since blockchain spreads data across an enormous system of computer storage spaces, it resembles putting your most significant possessions across a huge number of areas to mitigate your risk of being seriously affected or wiped out by a single attack.

Improve Recruiting Processes, Verification of Job Qualifications and Background Checks

Regardless of whether we call it lying, exaggerating, or embellishing your work history, we acknowledge that occasionally what you see on a candidate's CV isn't generally what you're getting. A reported 75% of HR directors have recognized a lie on a CV. With about 20% of recruiting directors also reporting they go through under 30 seconds looking at a CV, it is difficult to realize what number of fabrications go undetected.

Fortunately, blockchain can offer trust in the veracity of its data. In current recruitment frameworks, it is hard to decide the precision of a potential employee's work and training history. Indeed, even the most prepared recruiters can be misdirected by a candidate's purported business history and education qualifications.

Generally, HR administrators have depended upon CVs, which candidates can adjust and adorn with embellishments. While LinkedIn and reference calls can be utilized to check some data, these strategies just give a superficial layer of confirmation. Moreover, these simple procedures can also be time-consuming and inaccurate.

HR experts agree, leading a conventional record verification system can be challenging and costly. It can also put a huge burden on candidates, requiring various administrative hurdles to be crossed. Blockchain can decrease the work and cost presently associated with background checking.

Even though blockchain can't ensure all mistakes or misrepresentations will be recognized, it can successfully decrease incidents. It additionally gives bosses the most precise depiction of a candidate's accreditations and background.

The advantage of blockchain is also given to candidates as certainty, permitting them to apply to jobs that they realize they are equipped for. It additionally mitigates the worry that different candidates may be advancing beyond them by applying to a similar activity with false resumes and qualifications. This transparency makes everything fair for all candidates.

Streamline Payroll, Contractor Payments and Vendor Tracking

One of the most widely recognized use cases for blockchain HR includes an organization's biggest cost and the procedure that employees welcome the most: payroll. Blockchain can supplant a considerable sum of the manual errands required in current payroll frameworks. Blockchain also offers "smart contract" arrangements that permit an organization to computerize and secure payments to temporary workers and merchants.

Worldwide organizations specifically could appreciate benefits with blockchain in regard to providing a cross-border payroll to employees in overseas jurisdictions. Blockchain naturally filters through exchange rates and liaises with delegate banks so employees can be paid rapidly – and at a lower cost to managers.

Through smart contracts, a few associations are utilizing blockchain to pay out employees, temporary workers, and merchants. Actually, it is accounted for that 45% of early adopters of blockchain are now executing smart contracts inside their associations.

A smart contract works out in code a lot of parameters utilizing articulations and logic functions in "if this, then that" (IFTTT) language. These contracts can be planned so that, when placed in motion, the payment procedure is made completely reliant on these coded conditions. It is additionally made irreversible unless the terms of a contract should be rewritten.

At the point when a specific number of hours of work have been finished (this would be a potential "if this" variable), the smart contract subsequently pays the employee, temporary worker, or vendor the correct payment (a "then that" variable) by sending the credited bit via remotely executable code. This code is connected to an instruction from the company's bank account to the contractor's bank account, which at last initiates the payment transfer.

HR would not have to contact their organization's bank or do a monthly payment run. Rather, the transparent, constant blockchain records help track invoices and encourage conveyance, charging and detailing of transactions. There is also no need to wait for the usual payroll processing time.

The smart contracts work as an assurance that work is finished, and that the payment will make it to the employee, contractual worker or seller in an appropriate and convenient manner.

Automate Taxes and Mitigate the Strain of Audits

Taxation assumes a basic job in the life of a business or a person. For HR experts, continually adapting to expense laws and guidelines across purviews guarantee they frequently have their hands full. Payroll taxes are then just further confounded by different components like rewards, commissions, extra time pay, back pay, aggregated sick time pay, HR costs, etc.

Blockchain's excellent capacity to record and update employee tax arrangements naturally offers direct benefits to HR offices. By streamlining taxation processes, blockchain-fueled stages will set a new standard for HR offices around the world.

Whilst no business is happy to receive an external audit, it nevertheless happens. Audits are intimidating to such an extent that it has really suppressed innumerable organizations that only feel comfortable maintaining physical record frameworks, despite the time, vitality, and cash they require to appropriately upkeep.

Whenever presented for audit, having blockchain innovation as it is presently set up is analogous to having a life preserver thrown out to you while you're battling to remain above water in stormy weather. The blockchain makes it simpler for a business to continue an audit since it can safely impart its records to regulators in near real-time. The time and cost spent for document collection is decreased radically. Moreover, the blockchain's cryptographic hashes and source verification fabricate a solid hindrance against document manipulation and fraud.

Enhance Employee Experience with Better Access to Benefit Packages and a Dynamic Expense Reimbursement System

HR and employees alike will come to value blockchain's capacity to provide quick and easy access to benefits packages. When employers outline the terms of employment preceding recruiting, it is HR's obligation to maintain the conditions in the agreement. The conventional model requires manual execution of arrangements that may affect an employee's benefits package, running risks of mistakes or preventing proper delivery of benefits.

Setting these terms via a blockchain contract allows HR to effortlessly deliver these benefits. For instance, if an organization traces that an employee's healthcare benefits are due to kick in after a 90-day waiting period, the blockchain innovation can be built to actualize those advantages at the allotted time. Once more, this is coded through the equivalent IFTTT language that oversees smart contracts.

Aside from healthcare benefits, Blockchain can conceivably offer an increasingly robust way to deal with pay scales by applying defined salary increments for distinguished aptitudes or key capacities that are considered significant to the organization. They can also oversee performance-based bonus awards to employees in an increasingly quantifiable, data-driven way.

Blockchain develops the employee experience even in the domain of expense reimbursement. In its present arrangement, reimbursing employees can be tedious. For employees, they are regularly compelled to wait that paperwork to go through and checks to clear. For HR, it can also exhaust time and vitality.

Blockchain is improving the expense reimbursement scene by permitting associations to make their own organization currency. In building up an individualized cryptocurrency unique to their organization, associations will diminish uses related with the present expense reimbursement processes: ending handling charges, representing universal exchange rates, lessening in-house HR staff, etc. This additionally provides corporate portability, with organizations currently being able to handily repay between different locales.

With current reimbursement frameworks, there is a progressing issue of conflict resolution among managers and employees about what ought to be redressed, what ought not, how, when, etc. Blockchain-led solutions guarantee transparency, with all organization financed transactions connected into the blockchain arrangement. This offers for both managers and employees a transparent and simple dispute resolution framework, allowing both sides to reach agreeable compensation and conditions.

As we can see, although at first developed in the cryptocurrency business, blockchain is stretching out into all aspects of work. There are numerous potential uses for blockchain innovation, which could disrupt recruiting, finance, tax assessment, benefits administration, data storage, and so much more. Despite current difficulties in cost and adaptability, the case for blockchain HR solutions is solid.

Advancing transparency and trust in organization forms are two needs for HR experts as they manage human capital and face a serious recruiting scene. While the specialized presentation of blockchain innovation and its capacity to scramble and offer laser sharp precision are difficult to refute, blockchain's prosperity will rely upon how well it can establish trust and transparency into an association's tasks, an endeavor for which it is well-equipped to handle.

What are the Core Benefits of Blockchain in HR?

Blockchain isn't a magic wand for every problem, however, its mundane functions can do a great deal more to make the career of an HR administrator simpler and objective in judgement.

Make it Simple to Demonstrate Identity

The first benefit, and perhaps the most important for the time it saves, is in streamlining the workflow of HR management. Take, for example, the initial phase in the recruiting procedure. Using blockchain verification offers an easy way for HR management to authenticate the qualifications and capabilities of individual applicants, via their own blockchain identity record.

Blockchain applications like Civic consider the free confirmation of carefully designed identity records that one can present to potential businesses. As a major aspect of the application, a candidate could offer the HR division access to their externally confirmed identity on the blockchain by utilizing a unique private key only they could have.

Make it Simple to Proof Qualifications

Counterfeit scholastic and professional certificates are something businesses around the globe need to pay attention to. A portion of the certifications are intricately designed, such that it takes expert attention to identify whether they are real or not.

Most commonly, the simplest way to verify if a document is genuine is to contact the awarding institution to affirm the legitimacy of an issued award. However, this takes time, and it has not been unheard of for fake institutions to be issuing illegitimate certifications, too!

With the blockchain, institutions have a simple and less exorbitant approach to distributing or confirming the authentications they issue over the web. Critically, outsider elements like the administration can vouch for the authenticity of the records, even without a physical copy. Likewise, the reports are available to HR with a private key a candidate gives. Furthermore, a business can verify a certificate issued anywhere on the planet, without having to go through the lengthy process of contacting the awarding institution through their communication channels.

Encourage Employee Commitment through Smart Contract

With blockchain, it is simple for the HR office to automate the greater part of the communication between itself, the fund office, the employee, and different offices through smart contracts.

Specifically, it is trivial to computerize payments, so HR doesn't have to mediate. For instance, a smart contract application can discharge payment to an employee when predefined conditions are met, such as meeting an appropriately clocked time or meeting a sales quota.

Improve Privacy, Cut Expenses, and Secure Employee Data

The innovation gives more control, privacy, and security for data. When recorded, data becomes immutable. It can't be controlled or altered by anybody to suit personal agendas.

It also provides a viable and safe alternative for an HR department considering going paperless, and that essentially cuts the expenses of running the office. This is particularly significant for private ventures that don't have great budget plans to spend for HR services.

What is the Future Ahead for Blockchain in HR?

Things being as they are, where will all this lead us to?

As with most innovations, innovative turn of events – and their selection – require some investment to be profitably used. The execution of blockchain-based answers for addressing a portion of the previously mentioned HR challenges won't occur without any forethought, it's probably going to be a steady procedure of improvement and development.

The main wave of adoption will probably arrive in the form of blockchain-based candidate checks, a clear use case. Real-time employee payments could be another, and we may also enjoy less spam as we deal with our own professional profiles via blockchain applications.

The second wave of blockchain-at-work innovation could be about better talent markets, greater visibility of work, employees and matches. It could also involve more trust in the marketplace.

The third wave could include pondering the nature of the association itself. If we get a bigger fluid workforce that could be called upon for ventures that would mean fewer permanent individuals and long-term job contracts. So perhaps we'll have increasingly self-sufficient associations and spotlight on networks of groups, with a whole host of dynamic workers competing for short-term contract work.

Further Reading

Artificial Intelligence

https://www.hrexchangenetwork.com/hr-tech/articles/ai-in-hr
https://poseidon01.ssrn.com/delivery.php?ID=
06609706710210608308900601309603012406104506608403806610909801401109311410412207409300205003212506109905406610812002511512606805308100702104512709010707008002803003500205211406802511510412507207700508710908609412000712306406710710311111702308200311901&EXT=pdf
https://www.cmswire.com/digital-workplace/7-ways-artificial-intelligence-is-reinventing-human-resources/
https://www.hrtechnologist.com/articles/digital-transformation/the-beginners-guide-to-ai-in-hr/
https://www.northeastern.edu/graduate/blog/artificial-intelligence-in-human-resource-management/
https://www.forbes.com/sites/jeannemeister/2019/01/08/ten-hr-trends-in-the-age-of-artificial-intelligence/#61653acc3219

https://medium.com/@albertchristopherr/use-of-artificial-intelligence-in-human-resource-
    management-ddb4e4de9c6e
https://talentculture.com/seven-reasons-ai-will-take-hr-one-reason-wont/
https://www.monterail.com/blog/ai-transforming-hr
https://www.aithority.com/ait-featured-posts/5-ways-artificial-intelligence-is-reinventing-hr-
    technology/
https://www.ey.com/Publication/vwLUAssets/EY-the-new-age-artificial-intelligence-for-human-
    resource-opportunities-and-functions/$FILE/EY-the-new-age-artificial-intelligence-for-human-
    resource-opportunities-and-functions.pdf

Blockchain

https://www.gartner.com/smarterwithgartner/5-ways-blockchain-will-affect-hr/
https://www.hrtechnologist.com/articles/hr-compliance/5-ways-blockchain-technology-can-
    revolutionize-human-resource-management/
https://voice-on-growth.mercer.com/en/articles/innovation/blockchain-for-human-resources.html
https://blog.cake.hr/blockchain-in-hr-8-ways-blockchain-will-impact-the-hr-function/
https://www.digitalhrtech.com/blockchain-hr-challenges-applications-future-of-work/
https://www.asiablockchainreview.com/how-can-blockchain-benefit-human-resource-
    management/
https://blog.namely.com/blockchain-human-resource-management
https://www.hrdive.com/news/blockchain-what-is-it-and-how-is-hr-using-it/513229/
https://www.pwc.co.uk/issues/futuretax/assets/blockchain-can%20impact-hr.pdf
https://www.managementstudyguide.com/how-blockchain-can-help-hr-managers-in-efficient-
    management.htm

Tom James and Aditya Kumar
Chapter 5
Contact Centers

Artificial Intelligence

Artificial Intelligence (AI) is set to radically alter the value of contact centers. The vast sums of data generated at a contact center is a great resource AI can utilize to identify the best information focuses, client needs, and change the way organizations collaborate with their clients. Already there has been enormous enthusiasm for utilizing AI-based virtual operators that in principle, would be indistinct from a genuine individual. In 2018 at GoogleNext, there were numerous showings of individuals requesting pizza and finishing different exercises through a virtual specialist. This simple interaction between people, services, and AI are a prelude to the future of contact centers.

What are AI in Contact Centers?

Organizations measure the clients' fulfillment by analyzing superficial data assembled from the contact center. This information may incorporate more specific elements of the call. For example, how much time an agent spent on a call or visit with a specific client, whether the issue was settled on the main call, and what was the criticism of the client (if any) upon the conclusion of that discussion.

One thing that escapes the notice of such recording efforts, however, is how much effort the call required from the client's end of things. Any part of protocol or procedure that may raise the barrier of effort for the client is difficult to estimate, but studies by Dr. Skyler Place show that small things like clients needing to repeat their name and complaint number at whatever point they are changed to another rep is incredibly frustrating. Additionally, any language boundaries subvert successful correspondence. Perhaps the greatest gap in client-side information gathering, is determining whether the client is even fulfilled or not in any great detail.

In this way, AI helps the rep by continuously investigating the tone of the client, the beat of the language, and the demeanor of the guest. AI measures pause, interferences, tones, dynamicity, and the intrigue level of the client just as it does for the operator. "A decent AI framework performs three undertakings: client information assortment, investigating the setting of the discussion and inferencing likewise," says Jafar Adibi, head of data science at Talkdesk.

Perhaps the greatest change to shake the economy lately has been the ascent of AI, and this pattern has escaped from the universe of contract centers and client

https://doi.org/10.1515/9783110664454-005

services. The phrase "Back in My Day" is thrown around a ton in internet-based forums and platforms, yet as Facebook wars rage on among millennials and baby boomers, they feature a portion of the nuances of (and occasionally complete changes to) social, political, and financial change in recent decades. While individuals of all ages have mixed sentiments about AI's impact on their lives, there is proof that AI's role in like-mannered occupations is already essential to business prosperity.

Human Empathy + Robotic Ingenuity = Better Customer Service

One business handle that has been intensely affected by the ascent of AI is the contact center. Utilizing AI to enhance the treatment of redundant assignments is presently an intrinsically vital application in contact centers, doing everything from steering calls and emails to the correct specialist to taking care of and preparing installments evermore safely.

Although a human touch is still usually of great importance for ideal client encounters, AI and automation help to avoid blunders in like-manner routine errands. These sorts of enhancements are welcome in regions where clients are disappointed by human mistakes, as appeared in an ongoing review done by the Institute of Customer. Savvy organizations are currently understanding that the response to client support difficulties isn't exclusively in better training for human operators or hiring more human operators to deal with high volumes of support requests, but in automating administrations intelligently, to create progressively productive outcomes with predictable and standardized results.

AI in Contact Centers

The client experience (CX) will without a doubt be improved with an understanding of the accommodating impact of AI. Some are already unknowingly enjoying the benefits of AI assistance. The advanced shopping experience right now works hand in hand with AI, with 75% of US buyers who shopped online having connected with some type of AI, from computerized installment procedures to chatbots intended to help discover the item that the client is searching for rapidly. These procedures incorporate consistency with a procedure, which provides an alternative for most human intervention, while forwarding increasingly complex circumstances to human overseers. The end result makes a CX that comprehensively fulfills all client needs, using a collaborative approach between AI and human work.

A study done by Gartner gauged that 85% of all CX would act self-managed by 2020. In view of this, it is basic to have a fit workforce in the contact center that can support complex needs, that additionally grasps the requirement for a mix of AI and computerization to support the less complex difficulties. For these simpler-to-address issues, software engineers have started to actualize forms intended to make human-robot cooperation a normal and ordinary part of the workplace. A few of the ways in which AI is turning out to be advantageous to CX is:

Sentiment Analysis: Sorting assessments and feelings dependent on keywords so client collaborations can be intuitively dealt with.

Machine Learning: The capacity for machines to learn without the assistance of software engineers. Janelle Shane, with a PhD from UC San Diego, stood out as truly newsworthy with her blog that called attention to the battles that machines at times have with learning human complexities: everything from making paint shading names to making titles for romance books. In any case, AI have made ready for snappier and increasingly effective identification of security breaches and other legitimately significant client issues.

Natural Language Processing: Natural language handling is only one more manner by which PCs can attempt to comprehend the mind-boggling language and feelings of human clients through multimodal means.

Why are AI Contact Centers Important?

Offering top notch client support is key with regard to finding new clients, retaining existing ones, and making a devoted client base that will utilize your business again and again.

A business can have a prevalent assistance or item, yet on the off chance that it's not offering an encounter that its clients are enchanted with, it could soon end up losing income.

Benefiting as much as possible from innovations, for example, AI and chatbots, is an imperative to truly thrive.

Any business that has or still utilizes the customary call center will know about its issues. Regardless of how much training a delegate is given, it's close to unthinkable for them to fulfill every single one of the ever-changing needs of the customer.

Regardless of whether the delegate is waiting while they are attempting to connect with the fitting division or looking through one of the numerous CRMs they have before them, the experience can be a moderate and regularly baffling one for the client.

Every year $62 billion is lost through poor client assistance, as indicated by PWC's Consumer Intelligence Series. Progresses in innovation have changed the game, at last offering an opportunity to close this gap. This is the place AI becomes possibly the most important factor. As indicated by the PWC investigation, AI can help plug that spill by going well beyond what humans can do. AI is not limited to being utilized to bring down client exertion, it's also a progressively proficient approach to guide the purchaser to the data they need.

Some 60% of purchasers concurred that AI instruments can decrease the time it takes to find a solution that is tailored to their inclinations, while 38% said AI can offer a "better one-than one customized understanding."

As client exertion is at the center of attention, there is a great deal you can do to convey easy encounters by structuring administrations for your clients that are clearer and more useful – including exploiting the most recent AI tools.

Numerous client assistance associations presently remember a proportion of client exertion for their subsequent reviews and surveys, regardless of whether it is Customer Effort Score (CES), Net Promoter Score (NPS), or Customer Satisfaction Score (CSAT).

Twenty- to thirty-year-olds are turning into the most significant clients for the business, making up the biggest demographic segment of present-day purchasers. This well-informed segment requests easy encounters – snappy, smooth, and frequently at the last possible second. How would you convey high worth, elite client care that will leave clients, and specifically twenty- to thirty-year-olds, saying "that was easy . . . "?

Through AI obviously. AI engages client care operators to offer a consistent assistance service and makes the experience your clients have with your organization essentially simpler, increasingly productive, and even more charming.

Here are some ways that AI can diminish client exertion and help take care of issues:

Looking for help: AI allows clients to remain inside their picked strategy for collaboration. For example, online networking, email, or course calls can easily be assigned to the most ideal asset.

Waiting: AI diminishes wait times considerably by either offering virtual help through chatbots or immediately interfacing clients to a live individual as required.

Explaining: AI saves clients time by clarifying data, details, and other information. AI is intended to "learn" from the information about every client and either work straightforwardly with them to take care of issues or present the fundamental details to a live specialist.

DIY: AI has fundamentally evolved the way self-administration operates. Other than chatbots that can computerize many the most well-known back-and-forths that go on among organizations and their clients, the innovation can powerfully locate the most important and explicit details to assist clients with settling their own issues.

Proactive: AI diminishes client exertion by envisioning what they may require before they need it, and offering substance or devices to proactively moderate traps they could experience with an item or administration.

Readiness: The information gathered through AI can be utilized to find out what client exertion resembles across a specific geographic area, size of the record, clients who bought a particular item or different sections. AI can help create systems that could legitimately bring down the general normal of CES scores.

How to Use AI for Contact Centers

Replacing Interactive Voice Response Processes

An interactive voice response (IVR) has a lot of shortsighted predefined rules that it follows in a deterministic way. A model may be a "sales" rule that transfers the caller to the sales department.

Interestingly, AI that incorporates regions like natural language processing and machine learning procedures can comprehend explanations, rather than merely giving the client various decisions to act on.

Likewise, with IVR a predefined input gives a predefined yield. With AI, a predefined information set may give a totally extraordinary yield, contingent upon what the framework has realized through probability calculations.

AI ought to also improve the caller experience in the long run by reducing miscommunication caused by many current automated call services, for example, the regularly baffling "press 1 for sales" or "press 2 for client assistance," trailed by a line that adversely impacts current contact center communications.

Capturing Data From Customer Interactions

Both AI voice operators and chatbots can catch a great deal of granular information around every client cooperation, which can be utilized by analytics engines to help enhance the call center procedure.

AI devices like sentiment analysis can also help accelerate this procedure by rapidly spotting patterns like outrage or disappointment within a large data set, at a pace reliably faster than a human guide.

However, the thought of AI totally supplanting a human contact center group is yet a far-off prospect, particularly considering the perspectives of numerous clients toward AI in client assistance. For instance, most individuals have expressed the view that there ought to consistently be the choice to move to a live counsel in the contact center.

Navigating Customers Around the Company Website

Staff shortages are a typical issue, especially in bigger multichannel contact centers where advisors are often time-stretched, and few are multiskilled. AI can be valuable while handling this issue.

Remote helpers, for instance, can start by guiding clients to the right piece of the site or FAQ. On the off chance that the right hand can't answer a solicitation, they just direct the client to a live talk advisor.

What's more, with AI innovation, the more it gets utilized, the more it learns. This iterative process of self-improvement means the AI is continuously increasing its capacity for refinement. This capacity makes it perfect for managing ordinary IT forms like password resets.

Managing Big Data

Contact centers regularly collect huge measures of client information. Clients are certainly mindful of this and have generally expected improved client assistance as a byproduct of giving bountiful measures of individual data for organizations to utilize.

One dissatisfaction that clients regularly face is rehashing their details on different events, or they may get an odd proposal from an organization that is totally irrelevant to them. At the point when these things occur, disappointment begins to set in.

To handle this, robotic process automation (RPA) assists with taking out repetitive client and representative exertion by catching, analyzing, cross-referencing, and sharing data across stages and channels; all while the entirety of this avoids being intrusive.

Predicting Customer Behavior

AI will discover new patterns in client conduct, which once recognized will be invaluable in the initial phases of any client event. Interaction analytics tools as of now can do this, however, the expansion of AI will quickly distinguish proof and imply that there is less requirement for human mediation.

Given this early knowledge, call center supervisors will be able to brief counsels with the goal of handling the rising client needs and desires successfully. This could prompt retaining clients who may have been going to leave or up-selling to clients who are searching for data about another similar product or service.

The capacity to spot slants in client information will also empower call center chiefs to demonstrate best practices and anticipate the results or the outcomes for a specific strategy.

By utilizing AI along these lines, an association could see benefits in asset arranging, sales and promoting campaign planning, and attain an increasingly precise voice of the customer (VoC).

Removing Humans from Skills-based Routing Tasks

Recognizable procedures like estimating and abilities-based steering will in the future turn out to be progressively automated and will require less (if any) human assistance.

Organizations that accomplish self-learning algorithms by means of AI will gain an upper hand since they'll be taking full advantage of their ocean of information. Because of that, frameworks that are right now administered-based will push toward "intellectual" frameworks that take into consideration increasingly insightful expectations and responses.

This will assist with improving the CX by improving the way contact centers both foresee and react to requests. It will also imply that consultants can play to their qualities on an increasingly nonstop and reliable premise.

Improving Self-service

The main areas where AI will be utilized in the contact center are in advances to self-service capabilities of everyday requests and basic communications.

Nonetheless, for AI to genuinely satisfy its latent capacity, complex semantic handling needs must be met to cause individuals to feel like they are really addressing a human being, and frameworks should be completely incorporated to limit the blemishes in its usage.

For instance, if a client profile is not complete, this may confine the capacity of AI to manage interactions effectively.

To permit AI to mechanize precise reactions and serve customers most successfully, it must have the correct data and information.

Whenever done effectively, implementing AI in contact centers can guarantee that enquiries are managed proficiently, while improving precision and administration levels.

Communicating with Customers via Robots

In contrast to their human partners, robots are reliable, dependable, and consistently available. They are capable of unceasingly practicing at interfacing with self-administration applications and keenly scanning for data, to help settle inquiries rapidly.

Robots can be an extraordinary resource in the contact center, whenever actualized well, liberating clients from multifaceted problems and diminishing expenses by constraining the requirement for human cooperation.

Be that as it may, achieving harmony between the human and robot workforce is of paramount importance. Don't simply consider AI enabling self-administration, additionally consider how it can engage advisors, by giving them more opportunity to establish rapport and affinity with clients on the telephone.

Monitoring Advisor Performance

One kind of AI, which is incredible from a quality outlook, is real-time speech analytics (RTSA).

The solution analyses advisor and client discourse to give live criticism to consultants, group pioneers, and quality assurance groups about what is being said, and examine how it is being said. It additionally monitors stress levels, discourse clearness and content adherence, all while the call is in progress.

This innovation also has the capacity of tuning into the substance of the call and searching for the missing data the counsel may provide for the client.

Identifying Call Types and Passing Contacts to Relevant Channels

When accepting calls, AI can be utilized to help distinguish the kind of incoming call request, with the goal that it very well may be given to the applicable station, be that human association or chatbot.

AI can also furnish contact center guides with valuable foundation data on the client or the idea of an enquiry by means of a single desktop view, so they can close the call rapidly and successfully.

To put it plainly, implementation of AI will require organizations to reevaluate the way that they cooperate with their most important resource – their clients.

Future accomplishment for organizations will be to a certain extent reliant on how they sort out their client collaborations and their eagerness to put resources into their contact center group, who are progressively managing increasingly complex client interactions.

Predicting Customer Needs

RPA tools can use machine learning engines and big data to anticipate client needs, so the chatbot may speak with them proactively.

By analyzing, interpreting, and seeing high volumes of client requests, the arrangement could bolster up-selling or cross-selling of different items or administrations, while the RPA robots could auto-fill the application structure to save the client time.

As the innovations develop, it will become simpler and more financially savvy to make conversational interfaces for clients to communicate with chatbots in an increasingly natural manner.

Automating Responses to Customer Complaints

Combining process automating technology with optical character acknowledgment (OCR) enables the automization of increasingly complex business forms.

A typical test confronting numerous undertakings today is the capacity to comprehend unstructured information, such as client complaints and requests, precisely and productively.

This mix of AI can resolve many of these issues, including:
- Client letters, emails, and web structures, which are ingested into the framework as scanned pictures (through OCR usefulness).
- The framework has the capacities to comprehend the purpose of the enquiry and concentrate all the applicable details from the substance. At that point it delivers and sends a prescribed client reaction over to the human employee. The employee has the option to alter the content before sending it over to the client.
- The organized information is received by an RPA robot for checking information and enhancement (adding extra pertinent data to the case as required).

The refreshed information is then transferred to the client.

What are the Core Benefits of AI in Contact Centers?

AI is the best thing that has ever happened to call centers in recent history.

Not only has AI improved client experience, but it has also additionally enabled call centers to screen the nature of calls easily.

Unfortunately, most organizations shockingly don't have an appropriate foundation for a contact center incorporated with AI. Nevertheless, you don't need to stress in light of the fact that there are numerous organizations, for example, the OracleCMS Australian Contact Center that offer call center administrations at reasonable rates.

Here is a guide on a portion of the advantages you gain from implementing AI in call centers.

Gathering Data from Conversations

AI-empowered chatbots and the virtual-advisors can accumulate discrete information for every client, allowing the merchants to place this information into analytical engines to produce useful knowledge. Moreover, you can divide the bits of knowledge with the assistance of AI analysis. This will identify even abstract notions like the outrage or level of conflict indicated in the tone of a specific client. Call center companies are already seeing the benefits; as per the Deloitte Digital's

Global Contact Center Survey (May 2019), 13% of contact centers are already utilizing AI-empowered virtual consultants or chatbots, 59% are on pilot testing, with only 28% having no arrangement to switch.

With the widespread adoption of AI chatbots, it is interesting to note that clients are hesitant to see AI chatbots completely supplant human operators. Nine out of 10 clients suggested that there ought to always be a choice to change to a human guide. Along these lines, it is still unlikely AI chatbots or virtual reps will replace their human counterparts completely in the near future.

Capacity to Predict Customer Behavior

After the sentimental analysis of the client-operator communication, supervisors will have the option to foresee client conduct in the initial periods of future interactions. AI will accelerate cooperation using logical tools. These tools will provide exact and precise knowledge that operators can utilize quickly. With this, the chief will have the option to forecast up and coming downturns. The administrator will brief guides and thus be able to tackle the dissatisfied clients who may have been about to abandon their interest in the company's services or products.

Also, AI incorporation will empower supervisors to foresee the results of a specific system or model of practices. Along these lines, the association will see another increase in efficient resource allocation, sales and marketing, and voice of clients.

Auto-answering Customer Complaints

Merchants are confronting another chaos of unstructured information when it comes to client queries and complaints. Without a doubt, the administration of this indistinct information requires a major allotment of resources and time. By examining how the amalgamation of AI and OCR resolves this issue, we can see how AI will improve the CX at reduced costs:

- First, scanning (intensive OCR office) of all the requests and complaints takes place, followed by this information being incorporated into the framework.
- AI on your framework holds the capacity to get a handle on the tone of the content. The framework will then "conclude" how to react to a specific client.
- The human group will review and forward the reaction to the client, sparing time and resources.
- The organized information will also subsequently be stored in the framework for additional treatment or future use.

AI Helps to Improve Team Communications

By filling in as a virtual assistant, directing the most significant and ideal representative to the client concern they are best equipped to deal with, AI diminishes the hold time and the exchange time. This improvement to the CX is also not just limited to linking representatives to clients, but also representatives to their colleagues. By improving and creating consultant networks, helping to form regular channels of communication between team members, AI can help build teams of interdependent experts, who can understand and aid their colleagues with client concerns.

Hence, AI is sufficiently poised to make daily communications intelligent, smarter, smoother, and simpler to break down. The benefits to clients will be palpable, when they encounter an opportunistic, reactive administration that has the solutions they need paired with a charming discussion. In addition, collaboration tools additionally use AI while interconnecting all reps to one another. As before, they may act as a virtual assistant, discovering important data and topic focuses.

Checking Representative's Performance

An ongoing discourse analyzing expert is reaching centers and is already a valuable auxiliary helper. It aids with tone assessment, context, and intention comprehension of both speakers on the call. In this way the experiences, drawn with the assistance of this tool, will expound the discourse goals, outrage level, worry in talks, and the lucidity of the discussion. This information will be utilized further by the team leaders, advisors, and manager to formulate a proper methodology for achieving the highest client satisfaction.

Finally, the AI-empowered framework will have the option to tune in to the discussion and think about what is absent. At that point, the framework will procure missing data on screen before the consultant to advise to the client.

Perceiving Customer and Call Types

The most significant favorable position of the AI is to perceive the approaching call and direct it to the pertinent chatbot or a human counselor. Also, the AI framework will give vital foundation data, client's history, nature of the request, and the fitting conceivable arrangement of that request by means of a single window on the PC screen.

In this way, organizations need to reexamine the way they currently work. In the future, the greater part of the organizations will anticipate the contact center as a ROI rather than a cost. Likewise, the organization's notoriety will rely more upon the strategy with which they will settle their clients' interests as client cooperation is getting increasingly mind boggling with time.

Determining Customer Needs

With the assistance of big data and AI frameworks, companies will have the option to anticipate client requests. In this way, the AI counsels or chatbots will collaborate with those clients proactively. Consequently, by analyzing, understanding, and accepting AI tools, all this will assist the client with finding the correct item or administration service. In addition, the AI-empowered chatbots will autofill the structure to spare the client's time.

Be that as it may, with the gradual technological advancement, it will be simpler and financially savvy to suggest the usage of AI counselors for increasingly natural conversations.

Robots Dealing with Customers

Robots are effective at scanning for answers to the clients' interests and are increasingly solid in their general execution. They are consistently available and can provide authoritative answers in every topic. In this way, a contact center with AI-empowered tools or services will be equipped to rapidly provide precise and advantageous data. By providing consistent answers and results, AI incorporated robots diminish the unpredictability, disarray, and reaction time of all queries. This frees the human task group to spend their time resolving issues of crucial concern. Maintaining a human-AI balance is the way to progress for a contact center; other than encouraging clients, AI robots can also help human counsels to collaborate with clients successfully.

Staff Cost Saving

Contact center staff recruiting and training is an exorbitant and costly procedure. Another representative sets aside significant effort to become familiar with the ropes. In the interim period, the burden of work is shifted to the current operators. This additional strain hinders the performance of even the most experienced staff.

In addition, turnover rate in the contact center is notoriously high: practically 45%. That is the reason a contact center needs to run HR exercises continuously. AI-empowered chatbots can resolve this issue and greatly reduce company HR expenses, by filling the human guide gap and permitting reps to concentrate on other fundamental exercises.

Client Experiences Enhanced Personalization

Another significant favorable position that sellers can snatch by utilizing AI is that it provides the client an increasingly customized understanding of the site. AI-empowered frameworks do this dependent on recently gathered client information and the general inclinations of the client. Thus, AI will empower the client to have a continuously customized experience, helping them to understand wider ranges of things from items to the site maps. Eventually, it will improve the consumer's loyalty and increase the reps' performance with tasks at hand.

After some time the client will feel more affinity with that specific helper. Along these lines, the change rate will be expanded, and additionally the reiteration rate will see significant improvement.

What is the Future Ahead for AI in Contact Centers?

Perhaps in 20 years we'll have commonplace, streaming voice discussions with AI operators in contact centers. Our short-term prospects, however, are a promising start; the primary development being that the job of AI in the contact center during the coming decade will be far less noticeable for the end client. It will draw on various information sources to anticipate customer and company needs in a background role, handle communications on its own where conceivable, and give in-call support where required.

Humans will in any case still be there when the information or common sense shows they do a better job. So, the fate of AI in the contact center is not one where people are made wholly obsolete, but one where programming tools make humans progressively more effective; basically, in the same way they have for the last 60 years.

Blockchain

Envision this situation: an aircraft traveler brings in a request to make changes to their flight agenda. It's the second time they've called; the first run through, an error was made which was only just seen by the traveler after getting another email confirmation. Realizing who was accountable for the error will decide who is culpable for any of the expenses related to any subsequent change, making a record of the initial interaction critical to avoid a potential dispute that pits traveler and operator in a "he said, she said" situation.

Can a customary database break the case? It can come extremely close, yet it is still inclined to permit errors. Blockchain innovation, however, gives unquestionable transaction following. In this specific situation, a blockchain-sponsored contact center could record each progression the operator took when they rolled out the alteration, and even give a record of the transaction to the client post-call. Any specialist could then effectively pull up the data on their screen and realize what unfolded without tuning in to an account of the discussion.

Blockchain thus turns into a safety net that goes about as a record of truth for the two gatherings since it can't be altered or erased. This sort of transparency promises to reshape client care – and client trust.

What is Blockchain in Contact Centers?

Blockchain innovation could change the way organizations market to and retain their clients in radical ways.

For example, by utilizing blockchain innovation, organizations may set up a customer retention-as-a-service arrangement. Since the data can't be changed or erased, the use-reward path or chain is lasting, open, and transparent.

Take Incent, for example, a reliability program manufactured utilizing blockchain. Incent utilizes blockchain innovation to make tokens that all the traders who utilize their system may use.

Shippers can offer these tokens to their clients as remunerations, with the token trade taking place swiftly. The tokens can be exchanged through either the client's cell phone or internet browser. In view of this omnichannel experience, clients can move, sell, or trade their tokens on open commercial centers for other dedicated tokens or fiat cash.

With most promotion of blockchain technology focusing on cryptocurrency, the worth and use of the basic innovation – the blockchain – is frequently lost in all the clamor. The two ideas are regularly conflated, which cheapens the significant discussions that business chiefs ought to have about the job blockchain can play in smoothing out their business, improving CX, and conveying primary concern development.

Associations like Amazon, Comcast, CVS Health, IBM, Mastercard, and UBS are all currently utilizing the blockchain innovation space, giving them an arrangement of trust as pioneering implementers. The following advancement in client commitment will be driven by blockchain; what better place to strengthen trust and client connections than in the contact center and CX condition?

Why is Blockchain Contact Centers Important?

"From a CX point of view, it is going to totally change how a merchant or business communicates with its clients," states Steve Weston, managing partner of SK Weston and Co., situated in Washington DC. "Blockchain innovation gives both the client and the contact center specialist they connect with more control, on the grounds that the stage contains all the applicable data they need, and in an encoded and secure way."

Weston adds that the capacity to disseminate information to outsiders also improves the procedure, chiefly because it takes out the need to lead research and source data from various sources. This viably conveys instantaneous access to precise customer data.

"The CX advantage is the capacity to give prompt criticism or answers to the client that are right and applicable at the first run through of asking, which discredits the requirement for call backs and tedious confirmations."

Nobody is truly discussing blockchain in the CX or contact center space, and that may be a slip-up. "Contact centers are centered around AI or RPA usage right now which, when joined with blockchain, give them an inventive, driving edge," says Shelli Ryan, principal of the CX Blockchain Institute and CEO of Ad Hoc. "The issue is that if contact centers – particularly BPO service suppliers – aren't likewise showcase prepared for blockchain in 2020 they will be abandoned. Inward contact center groups might just execute blockchain themselves, leaving BPOs in obscurity."

How to Use Blockchain for Contact Centers

Quicker, Relevant Interactions

Prompt access to significant client data and experiences diminishes friction and time waste, which is an amazing advantage for the cutting-edge contact center as administrators hope to fulfill advancing buyer commitment needs.

Shorter first-call goal times improves client care, while access to data can shape important notions of commitment that are logically relevant across channels. Blockchain innovation changes how data is stored and accessed. Thus, by radically cutting transaction or connection time, the customer center can essentially help build a business' CSAT.

This upgraded service conveyance additionally creates important client connections that entrench loyalty and drive repeat business. This is the next advancement in improving the customer experience that will disrupt contact center & business process outsourcing operations. BPO service suppliers have a window of opportunity to lead from the front and initiate blockchain usage and arrangements in customer experience situations that will deliberately situate them as prime industry reformers.

Real-world Applications

To comprehend the role blockchain more readily can play inside explicit business verticals, for instance how BPO suppliers or customer experience offices can reform their client support conveyance, let's take a look at the real-world applications of blockchain.

The healthcare sector, which is presumably the most intricate to service among verticals today, could fundamentally improve work functions like claims processing from medical aid providers and insurers, which is an infamously mind-boggling and arduous procedure today.

The underwriting procedure necessitates that operators experience various frameworks to initially stop the case and afterward meet the consistence and managerial prerequisites to get endorsement and lastly, influence payment.

"This multifaceted nature makes it hard to redistribute these service solicitations to BPO suppliers, and it is difficult to offload to self-service channels given the present prerequisites. Be that as it may, I accept blockchain will totally change this dynamic since everything could be put away in one area. This makes chances to redistribute the procedure to an omnichannel-empowered contact center, or even engage clients through self-service channels."

Diminishing Contact Center Expenses

While the potential advantages are clear, contact center administrators must consider various factors before actualizing blockchain innovation.

Most importantly, it changes the caliber of specialist that administrators can utilize in the contact center condition, which requires a total upgrade of their recruiting system. Operators could possibly get to a more extensive pool of potential operators on the grounds that by expanding the procedure, the innovation adequately brings down the base expertise and competency requirements.

With access to more profound and precise client data, specialists would also require less preparatory work. Most importantly blockchain can generally decrease specialist costs, while simultaneously diminishing the recruiting procedure, as the advantages would be significantly more prominent in omnichannel conditions.

Upgrade Omnichannel Capacities

Research led by Knowledge Executive in 2019 with worldwide customer experience administrators and chiefs shows that blockchain is quickly being embraced in the banking, telecom, human services, and retail enterprises.

"Service conveyance consistency and personalization across web visit and email stays a significant test for administrators, however blockchain can adequately address these issues," says Mark Angus, CEO, Researcher and Strategist of Knowledge Executive.

In the retail business, blockchain can abbreviate sales and bolster demands by promptly giving whole transaction, service, guarantee, and conduct data to operators. Hierarchical storehouses and service issues in banks – which frequently have distinctive item houses, detached contact centers, and dissimilar CRM frameworks – can be circumvented with blockchain.

The way blockchain opens these capacities lies in blockchain's capacity to strip out unpredictability through the way data is checked, safely stored, and accessed. This removes the need for interfacing with various frameworks and can tear down the information silos that presently exist in numerous applications and heritage back-end frameworks.

With increasingly powerful omnichannel abilities, contact centers can push for more cooperation in these stages, which provides extra operational efficiencies and can further upgrade the customer experience and build consumer loyalty.

Thus, hope to see more assets apportioned to omnichannel capacities, particularly as administrators can computerize more connections through AI-empowered bots when the blockchain innovation is adequately applied.

This guarantees that the more unremarkable and essential client requests can be off-loaded from specialists onto an automated framework to decrease operation times, increase productive communication volumes, and boost operator efficiency.

Shifting Operational Model

It is expected in the near future that blockchain will drive a move in a contact center's working model. It's a convincing offer for contact center administrators, who are feeling the squeeze to diminish working expenses while expanding service conveyance and returns as CEOs today are intensely focused on the primary concern to convey benefits and investor esteem.

Blockchain can address those concerns simultaneously. Organizations need to see this innovation as a critical market disruptor. Those that don't grasp it will be left behind by rivals who have gained a critical competitive advantage, be it through improved margins, better general delivery, or both.

What are the Core Benefits of Blockchain in Contact Centers?

Clients increasingly depend on different clients and strangers to look for client assistance, for example, structuring (on the web) networks and counseling online assets. Nonetheless, client care is still the dominating "goal" for clients and the contact center, and the key drive behind the will to discover backing and data to illuminate key issues.

Tragically, contact centers don't generally get/guarantee the consideration they merit and frequently posit that it's difficult to put forth a case for better client service and improved client centricity. In even worse cases for some, C-level executives, contact centers (and different business-basic activities, e.g., IT) are viewed as a necessary evil or cost, instead of the fundamental driver of substantial business and client esteem they truly ought to be.

All things considered, for some reason we think little of the client care role and additionally the contact center. One reason, albeit far from the most significant one, is that the CX is guaranteed by marketing.

Indeed, the CX is regularly delegated to a branding and marketing setting these days, as opposed to one of genuine service and business/client esteem creation. Furthermore, that is not a decent development in what ought to be a coordinated effort (regardless of whether contact centers also have a great deal of work to do themselves, to assume a progressively significant role in client experience).

CX and service is increasingly utilized by advertisers in the branding context. Have you ever perused the center brand slogans of numerous business as of late? They're exceptionally indistinguishable. "We serve our clients." "We offer extraordinary client encounters." "We're nimble and adjust to our client's needs." Innovative. Tuning in. Mindful. Present day. Transparent. Legitimate. Open. The platitudes go on and on. As ideal as it is to remind ourselves, we truly need to be client driven, every one of those referenced qualities are not differentiators with regard to client associations and observations. Serving clients, being light-footed, sincere, and focused on client encounters are not simply values, imagined by brand advertisers in their detached ivory towers. They are the extremely fundamental activities and attributes clients today expect and merit.

CX is also frequently utilized in a showcasing setting without associating with the remainder of the business in an all-encompassing manner, or is mixed up as sheer personalization and change streamlining. Offering further empty talk to the CX and client assistance is additionally marketing related advertising, one which regularly occurs in a setting of PR battles, monologues, advanced apparatuses, and sincere goals. It's acceptable when showcasing constructs decent apparatuses and services clients can utilize. They can be exceptionally applicable and lead to incredible encounters. Moreover, the developing interests in social analytics, marketing automation, content personalization, etc., aren't generally done so as to improve the client experience. They're done to get more reach and transformations. Change streamlining is centered on the CX and brings about better client encounters. As a general rule it's about demonstrating better outcomes and higher ROI to the C-suite.

A common maxim among advertisers is: "it costs multiple times more to get a client than to hold one." The full truth is more complex than that, but it is still an important thing to understand. Bain and Company once said that it costs six times or more to get another client than to hold one. In almost every case, however, the company gains so much more value on client-oriented customer service than through marketing outreach.

What is the Future Ahead for Blockchain in Contact Centers?

"Blockchain is generally valuable in ventures where there is a requirement for perceivability of start to finish data and where there is a requirement for trust," says Chris Trew, a blockchain master and the originator of blockchain-development platform Stratis.

Trew as of now observes the innovation being utilized in the healthcare industry. For instance, when health records are moved between the contact center and patient, or specialist and contact center – blockchain allows the sender and the beneficiary to ensure that the archives received are indeed the originals by contrasting the blockchain properties of the two documents.

Blockchain's encryption offering is perfect for making sure a wide range of secret records are legitimate. How much it will be utilized in client assistance is up for debate. Tamar sees increasingly broad adoption of the innovation in a couple of years, however, Trew says it doesn't bode well to utilize blockchain in enterprises where transparency and immutability are not huge priorities.

Until further notice, it is making advances in how finance and healthcare brands convey and handle client care with the speediest effects being felt in contact centers serving the human services and fintech enterprises.

Olickal of Chain Advisors, then, is hopeful about blockchain's potential for disruption. "Blockchain changes the whole way we consider trust," he says. "For example, on the off chance that you and I settled on an understanding that I would accomplish something, and I didn't finish, you would host to go to a third party to arbitrate the dispute."

"Be that as it may, in the blockchain condition," Olickal proceeds, "we would now be able to program those understandings and the worth will be moved with no partiality. [With blockchain technology], there is a chance to change the manner in which we take a look at trust."

Further Reading

Artificial Intelligence

https://www.talkdesk.com/blog/ai-for-contact-centers-how-artificial-intelligence-is-transforming-contact-centers/
https://www.vonage.com/resources/articles/artificial-intelligence-contact-center/

https://www.callcentrehelper.com/12-top-uses-of-artificial-intelligence-in-the-contact-centre-123361.htm
https://www.cio.com/article/3353641/practical-ai-in-the-contact-center-starts-with-agent-assistance.html
https://www.techrepublic.com/article/how-artificial-intelligence-is-taking-call-centers-to-the-next-level/
https://customerthink.com/a-reality-check-about-ai-in-contact-centers/
https://www.aithority.com/guest-authors/10-ways-artificial-intelligence-transforming-the-contact-centers/
https://insights.datamark.net/the-role-of-artificial-intelligence-in-modern-contact-centers/
https://www.advantagecall.com/customer-service-and-ai-advantage-communications
https://www.bmmagazine.co.uk/business/the-benefits-of-artificial-intelligence-in-contact-centres/

Blockchain

https://www.star2star.com/insights/blog/call-center-trends
https://www.cmswire.com/information-management/how-to-use-blockchain-technology-to-retain-more-customers/
https://www.cxblockchain.org/8-reasons-why-blockchain-should-be-number-1-in-your-cx-strategy/
https://www.telusinternational.com/articles/future-customer-experience-blockchain
https://www.i-scoop.eu/customer-experience/customer-experience-contact-center-challenge/
https://www.ttec.com/articles/how-blockchain-will-upend-customer-experience
https://fmlink.com/articles/jll-digital-technology-contact-center-future/

Tom James and Aditya Kumar

Chapter 6
Building Maintenance

Artificial Intelligence

Artificial intelligence (AI) is the new business trendy innovation. It's difficult to go even a couple of hours without hearing the term – from ads on TV, to bulletins, and obviously throughout the workday. Despite its apparent ubiquity, what does AI truly mean? What effect will AI have on working structures today and in the future?

The Brookings Institution finds AI is one of the most misjudged terms among business pioneers. Citing specialists who have examined AI, the Brookings article says that "AI by and large is thought to allude to 'machines that react to stimulation consistent with traditional reactions from humans, given the human limit with regards to examination, judgment, and expectation.'"

A significant number of the AI items in facility management are programming based, and, as the Brookings article puts it: "'settle on choices which regularly require [a] human degree of mastery' and assist individuals with envisioning issues or manage astoundingly up." This thought mirrors the objective of economically available items that make structures increasingly effective and operationally solid.

What is AI in Building Maintenance?

Understanding AI is both an intricate and straightforward procedure. It's fundamentally all math that is utilized to break down data and settle on choices dependent on characterized factors and favored results. AI in facilities management (FM) implies wiping out uncertainty and letting PCs do the thinking, saving time for facilities managers, however, in what manner will this influence the business throughout the next few years?

AI in FM expands the capacity of facilities managers to supervise and review details influencing everyday activities. Utilizing self-optimizing frameworks, controlled by the internet of things (IoT), AI in FM liberates time for colleagues. As it is, they can concentrate more on serving clients and enhancing experiences. Also, AI in FM is already beginning to see widespread implementation, yet facilities managers may not be aware such innovation is already being utilized – because its use is being seen in an increasingly typical and mundane fashion.

For instance, it is no longer an uncommon sight to see self-vacuuming and self-mopping gadgets utilize AI to map out a floor, clean the floor, and come back to a docking station. FM is becoming ever more brilliant in its scope and function, and

https://doi.org/10.1515/9783110664454-006

clients expect on-request service. This applies to corporate real estate (CRE) suppliers, private property chiefs, cafés, and retailers, too. If something breaks down, clients or occupants need prompt answers. Luckily, AI can recognize these issues when they happen, yet the greatest value is obtained when utilizing noteworthy and continuous information to distinguish relationships between current operational execution and potential breakdowns, distinguishing the requirement for repair or substitution before a glitch happens. As explained by Nick Barker by means of Combined Selection Group Ltd., this improves reaction times by up to 97%!

Why is AI Building Maintenance Important?

AI is already commonplace in modern households with smart home items like Nest, Alexa, and smart household tools like vacuums; it won't be long until occupants will anticipate a similar involvement in their work environment. The IoT advancements that power the smart office offer an assortment of potential advantages for facility managers. Thus, innovation usage will move the business to procure new abilities and skills in fields like cybersecurity. Effective associations are meeting this challenge by expanding cooperation among activities and IT groups, so the two groups see each other's needs and capacities.

Expanding on this pattern, we are now observing uses of voice control interfaces for energy managers, property managers, and tenants along the lines of Google Home and Alexa. Instead of depending on a visual dashboard, soon a property manager could ask Alexa to list the leases coming up for reestablishment one year from now, or a maintenance specialist could arrange new parts without interfering with hands-on work.

The presence of intelligent assistants and augmented reality displays will change the central practices of numerous facility activities and errands, from lessening time spent on rounds and readings to record keeping, or even completely automating control of building energy systems to help balance local grid demand. Operations groups may adopt different strategies to deal with these difficulties; for example, by including new aptitudes, executing certain assignments remotely versus on location, and drawing in various types of specialist organization accomplices to fill capability gaps. Lastly, humans will settle on basic business choices, outfitted with the available intelligence to do so more quickly and effectively.

On the operations side, there is an open door with respect to neural system models – PC calculations that impersonate the natural capacity of humans and creatures to process data – to foresee the seriousness of issues from a mix of content and photos entered on work orders. They could also be utilized to investigate pictures from cameras that are pointed at basic or key observed factors as well as photographs of equipment over time to anticipate when maintenance ought to be finished.

While this innovation isn't used at this point, there is huge potential for AI to play a critical role in examination and analysis, utilizing numerical and discrete information, combined with full scale information (e.g., photos and content) to help manufacture AI based neural systems, as opposed to the "conventional" AI presently utilized inside the field of information science.

In order to take into account the effect inhabitants have inside their structures, property/building administrators are beginning to search for approaches to use AI as a method for expanding tenant commitment and streamlining the tenant's understanding of their own effects on the building, such as their energy footprint. These endeavors require an astute mix of new, IT-based arrangements with existing operational innovation framework.

While integrating inventive advances into more parts of our lives is exciting, there will be difficulties that must be tended to before the full potential for AI may be realized here. With the expansion of interconnected advances, cybersecurity concerns – truly not the territory of facility operations teams – are brought to the forefront. Truth be told, in Veolia's latest FM benchmark study, 92% of respondent's evaluated cybersecurity as a top factor molding FM system throughout the following two years.

The developing interest for system and application security combined with the interest from occupants to have control of the state of their space has prompted a more focused agreement on the planned integration of structure frameworks into one system. A typical, holistic system encourages information sharing and adaptability; through coordinated effort among IT and operations groups associations will have the option to deploy solutions that work for clients and while still meeting cybersecurity requirements.

How to Use AI for Building Maintenance

AI's uses in building maintenance extend beyond self-cleaning vacuums and espresso preparing robots. It's being applied to advancements and structures throughout the workspace, molding and improving routine procedures in manners that are regularly imperceptible to the casual eye. "Smart" buildings, for instance, are being developed with AI advancements incorporated from the start, giving insightful AI oversight on atmosphere control, security, cleaning, maintenance, lighting, and parking.

The potential advantages of incorporating AI into business capacities is huge, as indicated by the specialists, who imagine trillions being infused into worldwide economies. The fundamental basis for these value increases is that the incorporated efficiency gained from robotization – that is, machines accomplishing the work or humans – or augmentation with machines helping the current work power with their occupations in extraordinary ways, increases the work productivity we can achieve with less energy expended.

These advantages align perfectly with our human objectives, for example, conserving resources, reducing wasted time, and bringing down the expense of tasks, all three objectives that anybody in FM is exceptionally well-acquainted with. This is particularly important for those managing large-scale, multibuilding activities where the consequences of waste and inefficiency can increase at an alarming rate.

The good news for FMs is that AI works by empowering machines and systems to secure gains with certainty, preparing a lot of information and changing in accordance with new developments by perceiving the outcomes of the situation it observes. As opposed to manually finishing dull, tedious assignments, for example, like managing work orders, arranging preventative maintenance, and analyzing work project spending trends FM programming with AI capacities can automate these tasks, doing errands with practically no human intercession required. Subsequently, supervisors will profit by speedier processes, monitored vitality and resources, diminished expenses, and a smoothed-out work process that is proactive versus reactive.

Let's take a closer look at four progressive uses of AI coming to fruition across the FM business today.

Foresee Faults and Schedule Preventative Maintenance

As indicated by the International Society of Automation, $647 billion is lost every year to machine downtime. Regardless of whether this is brought about by evolving season demand, extended use or gradual obsolescence, tools and hardware are inclined to inevitable shortcomings and when deficiencies occur, they can cost your business cash in multiple ways.

AI-empowered FM programming can anticipate and even forestall breakdowns by analyzing and deciphering verifiable information on past resource failures, administrations, and work necessities, and utilizing this data to consequently make work arrangements and direct them to the appropriate vendors.

AI tech is handily incorporated with IoT systems that monitor device and appliance health and usefulness utilizing learned benchmarks of "typical" and "strange" information and yield. At whatever point an "anomalous" result is recorded, AI innovation can identify the issue, estimate the time and cost to fix it, and schedule qualified labor for the task. Invoicing additionally turns out to be increasingly effective as planned work orders are consequently opened, closed, endorsed, and paid properly by analyzing bell curve data from past requests of a comparable degree.

One case of AI-empowered FM programming that can aid in these undertakings, among others, is ServiceChannel's Decision Engine. The Decision Engine utilizes prescriptive examination to assist FMs in making smart information-driven choices while choosing contractual workers, surveying recommendations, and booking maintenance. With AI-empowered automated maintenance and breakdown identification, little FM groups can oversee hundreds (or even larger quantities, as scale allows) of buildings and resources with significantly decreased machine downtime. This in turn, diminishes waste and spares resources, time and energy for FMs to concentrate on far more significant issues.

Decrease Energy Expenditure

Percentagewise, organizations commonly burn through more cash on energy resources – warming, cooling, ventilation, power, and water – than pretty much any other classification of building management. All things considered, energy costs make up about 19% of all out uses for the average business facility in the United States, as per the National Grid. Plainly put, it's a classification that merits serious management consideration, both on the grounds of cost-cutting and ecological mindfulness.

While there are several different ways to diminish energy utilization across facilities, AI provides a hands-off answer for reducing significant energy drains, commonly found in items like HVAC, refrigeration, and power. Utilizing predictive analytics, AI-empowered techs can monitor and more efficiently manage energy use, for example, by turning down the heating/cooling of a building during times of idleness, dependent on recorded utilization designs (found from cutting edge models of a specific building's warm qualities or IoT sensors that distinguish pedestrian activity).

The Nest indoor regulator fills in as an extraordinary case of AI tech that is now available (since 2011, truth be told). As promoted on the brand's site, this AI-controlled indoor regulator "realizes what temperature you like and fabricates a timetable around yours." Independent investigations have indicated that the Nest indoor regulator spares its private clients between 10–12% on warming bills and up to 15% on cooling. While right now it is just available for business use in little buildings and workplaces, the potential for investment funds in these conditions is likely much higher.

Beyond real-time monitoring, AI tech (in blend with IoT and remote management dashboards) can also locate energy leaks and operational inefficiencies, for example, in inadequately fitted HVAC pipes or a defective electrical transformer. In any event, anticipating when these leaks are destined to occur can allow AI to locate problems before they cost buildings any money. This allows FM groups to reliably arrange and plan around energy expenses and facility inhabitance with the fullest picture available.

Recognize Security Risks

AI is bringing progressive abilities to physical security at business facilities. Security is a critical need for most FM groups, yet it's not commonly prioritized. As surveillance systems become more intricate and the volume of security-related information expands, AI can help fill in the gaps left between manual auditing and management.

Access control, CCTV surveillance, intrusion recognition, package screening, and weapon discovery are only a couple of instances of typical information driven security innovation in FM. While providing intrinsically valuable utility and information, these applications can be upgraded and made much smarter with the addition of AI and machine learning.

One persuasive startup, Aegis AI, has created AI-fueled programming that can identify when an individual in video film is carrying a firearm. This exceptional layer of situational mindfulness gives tremendous value to a facility security program, particularly with the expansion of emergency alarms and specialist on call notice.

Another youthful yet rapidly developing organization, IC Realtime, recently presented an application and web stage named "Ella" that utilizes AI to investigate CCTV film and categorize its analyses under labels and keywords, for example, "red vehicle," "dark hoodie," etc.

These kinds of AI-empowered innovations are immensely encouraging to any business with huge facilities or retail sites. Traditional surveillance systems require a group of security work forces checking various screens continuously; the broader the observation, the more individuals are required to oversee it – an expensive venture that is not immune to human error, attention spans, or limits of exhaustion. AI is a ground-breaking arrangement, fit for handling enormous amounts of visual information without exhaustion, capable of quickly focusing on subtle threats or details. Shoplifting, the delivery of a suspicious package, or a concealed firearm can be searched for by an AI 24/7, with a level of consistency and accuracy that would not be possible to replicate under human watch.

Smarter Reporting and Analytics

A far-reaching investigation program is basic to any FM group's prosperity. Utilizing the bits of knowledge gathered by analyzing facility information, directors can improve facility intelligence, settle on the best-supported plan of action, and plan vital activities – all while observing spending plans and long-term objectives.

Today, AI is disrupting the traditional analytics model. In the past decades, facilities information has been arranged physically and choices have been made dependent on an expert's "gut feeling." AI is currently computerizing these procedures to produce faster, reliable information, dependent on a far-reaching audit of recorded information. By expelling the potential for human biases and error, AI-empowered FM programming can more effectively separate capital and operational expenses, improve consistency, and upgrade demand forecasting.

Another advantage of AI in FM investigation has to do with consistency: with AI-empowered programming, even an inexperienced worker is equipped with all the information they need to make smart decisions on resource management. Prescriptive examination supported by years, or even decades of facility information can reveal the recommended options and propose the most appropriate, financially savvy course of action. This occurs with next to zero manual research being required.

The customized experiences provided by an AI-controlled investigation will at last permit your business to reduce expenses, forestall breakdowns, and keep both customers and employees satisfied.

What are the Core Benefits of AI in Building Maintenance?

AI gives extra insight into, and command over ecological and facility controls, yet it can also enable your group to appreciate more advantages. For example, AI can open new revenue streams, by diminishing energy use to make a net-zero energy area, viably doubling capital arranging capacity. By improving forecasting and predictability capabilities, AI enhances preventative maintenance planning. Through better consistency, facilities managers can easily separate capital and operational costs, lessening general facility expenses.

On the off chance that something goes wrong, automated reporting and self-optimization can identify potential problems when they occur – and use this knowledge to predict future problems before they occur. AI intelligence empowers mechanized detailing and formation of work orders, including the entering of information into a computerized maintenance management system (CMMS), which when coordinated appropriately increases the predictive capabilities of FMs yet further.

All this analysis of facility conditions and functions also has the incredibly vital benefit of being able to identify hazards to inhabitants. Workplace hazards, fires, or even poor light, air, and water quality can bring about awkward work conditions at best, and injury, medical issues, or loss of life at worse. AI can identify these dangers in a similar fashion as they would recognize potential gear breakdowns, offering valuable advice on how to keep the workplace a safe and healthy environment.

Lastly, one of the most significant advantages AI offers is its ability to integrate with current and future systems. Already AI can integrate with virtually any connected system via the IoT. This advantage is the most significant; the IoT utilizes robotized frameworks to report data. Dwelling in cloud-based advances, IoT-associated frameworks can coordinate with more frameworks and increase potential investment funds.

What is the Future Ahead for AI in Building Maintenance?

The future looks bright for information driven building activities. These arrangements can spare time while operating a building and convey better results for inhabitants. One trouble with understanding AI in buildings is the way that it very well may be applied in a myriad assortment of ways. There is a scope of reasonable use cases. The broadness of the innovation occasionally causes confusion regarding what AI can really be expected to do for the average facility manager. Here is an assortment of utilization cases that facility administrators might be keen on applying in their own buildings, as examples of some of the innovative changes to come:

1. Energy monitoring and estimation and confirmation (M&V). M&V is an extraordinary example of AI, since it takes what can be an extremely mind-boggling set of computations (making a building's exhibition model) and computes them. At that point, new factors, similar to climate and inhabitance, can be utilized to give energy consumption estimates utilizing a similar model. With enough information to observe the correlations between energy, climate and inhabitance, a precise model can be utilized to determine one of these factors if the others are available. Because of M&V, climate and inhabitance analysis can be utilized to appraise energy use under a preretrofit situation, which can be contrasted with the real energy utilization after the retrofit. The difference between real and anticipated energy is an appealingly precise approach to increase energy reserve funds (contrasted with seeing energy charges when the retrofit has been made).

2. Demand management – before or behind the meter. Understanding current energy demand is critical for providing a quality framework. Utilities need to know how much power they'll have to use and try as much as possible to avoid costly overuse or redundant use of energy. More information on energy utilization and the qualities that drive that utilization (e.g., climate and inhabitance) can convert into better forecasts about how the matrix will carry on. With this information, it's conceivable to decrease energy demand, save cash, and improve network quality.

3. Central air control. Understanding the exhibition of subsystems, as HVAC, is significant. In the summer, cooling requests in an office can be the difference between setting another costly demand peak or maintaining a strategic distance from a hefty charge. AI can provide cost investment funds by precooling a building in the early mornings depending on schedule/meeting and notable inhabitance information. The building's HVAC framework would promptly begin at the beginning of the day, when energy is more affordable, and start cooling space for the day ahead, all without human oversight. Also, if a building has utilized a precooling methodology before, AI may help improve future precooling endeavors. As the Google data center model proposes, there are huge open doors for investment funds by utilizing AI.

4. Equipment predictive analysis. Information pulled from complex machines found in buildings, similar to chillers and boilers, can be overpowering to facility administrators. In any case, when these information streams are broken down by a product arrangement, patterns may show up. This analysis may demonstrate a high probability of failure in the near term, in view of the condition of the equipment and reasonable estimates regarding how it is utilized (e.g., anticipated working occasions). The extra understanding, which may enable a facility team plan

upcoming maintenance, can lessen unforeseen equipment blackouts, add consistency to the financial plan, and keep tenants agreeable.

5. Space planning. As more workplaces move to open arrangement plans and increasingly adaptable game plans, there is a risk of room shortages and overbooking, particularly at high demand occasions. Today, as indicated by CBRE, around 40% of rooms are vacant. Offering a lot of room isn't an issue for tenants, however, it is expensive for the proprietors and administrators. With the advent of indoor space sensors, it is possible now to predict demand at various occasions – both when arranging another open office and everyday management. AI helps by pulling in the information from these space sensors and providing estimates of occupancy, in addition to data that can assist with settling potential issues.

6. Foresee facility cleaning needs. Custodial staff routinely clean completely unoccupied spaces just as much as heavily used spaces. This calendar-based methodology is suitable for occupied spaces that are frequently utilized. Be that as it may, even with greater adaptability in how tenants connect with spaces, a few spaces will tend to be utilized more than others. There is an opportunity for spaces to be cleaned as is needed, considering actual use. Today, this cleaning timetable might be founded on sensors that track occupancy, yet AI can assist with anticipating cleaning requests and even create a calendar for specialist co-ops. The Edge in Amsterdam has just begun moving toward this path, as it gives information to custodial staff on use in specific spaces, so staff can design their exercises dependent on condition. This information-driven way to deal with a customary assistance is particularly attractive in real estate, where the physical space remains the core of the business. In addition, AI can improve continuously by consequently requesting different materials and items for the workplace space, in view of genuine and anticipated occupancy patterns.

7. Well-being and security. Numerous business buildings spend a lot of cash on the indoor security of their workplaces. There is a scope of AI applications identified with well-being and security, however, many are still in their infancy. For instance, rather than utilizing a key card for determining access, one startup is utilizing facial acknowledgment. Well-being and security use cases may raise a few inquiries regarding protection, which is one explanation as to why they may not be seen in as much regular use as different applications yet.

Notwithstanding use case, AI applications in buildings may also drive more youthful representatives to enter the business. Facility management is experiencing an ability deficiency: The average worker is 51 years of age. More youthful workers regularly search for places that offer current innovation, and AI arrangements could provide this critical aspect to buildings. The facility management industry has not been wholly successful at drawing in youthful ability early. In any case, AI advances may expel a portion of the managerial assignments and make the business an interesting career path for skilled young workers.

There has been some worry that AI may cause mass job redundancies, and FM is no exception. With the ability deficiency in facility management, this appears to be an incredibly unlikely prospect. Also, running a building will consistently require some degree of human oversight. The most probable impact of AI is that AI arrangements will essentially change certain parts of certain occupations. The positions aren't lost, however, they are going to change.

These worries fit into the greater subject of the AI appropriation cycle. *Chicago Booth Review* distributed an article on AI appropriation and profitability development. The article noticed that improvement is probably going to follow a J-bend, a time of low profitability development, trailed by a time of high development. This is usual when an innovation is embraced and might be because of the time it takes for endeavors and enterprises to figure out how to best use these new abilities. The article refers to specialists who accept that the AI appropriation cycle will be long and flighty. For all intents and purposes, for facility administrators, this implies there is a lot of time to obtain AI innovation, and no compelling reason to surge. Yet, it additionally implies that organizations ought to put resources into training and appropriation to guarantee that representatives utilize these arrangements successfully.

Pushing ahead, AI is probably going to be an important factor affecting the activity and occupancy of buildings. Even though it might require some investment for buildings to completely embrace this innovation, the long-term advantages will far exceed the short-term costs. Be that as it may, the way to this point is uncertain. Facility administrators ought to instruct themselves on the capacities that AI can convey while additionally thinking about how the innovation could help with explicit issues in their buildings. AI has the propensity to be unreasonably advertised as a panacea, however, past this publicity, there are genuine opportunities for greatly improving building management.

Blockchain

Blockchain innovation is among one of the most disruptive forces of the decade. Its capacity to record, empower, and secure colossal quantities and kinds of transactions brings up a fascinating issue: Can the equivalent conveyed record innovation that powers bitcoin additionally empower superior execution of vital tasks in a completely different setting like construction? With issues including the management of huge groups of temporary workers, subcontractors, and a plentiful array of building codes, safety guidelines, and measures? "Progressively, we are pondering when and where we have to contend and what would we be able to share and work together on," said David Bowcott, worldwide executive of development, advancement, and knowledge in Aon's worldwide development and infrastructure gathering. Utilizing blockchain to automate the contractual processes and administrative work supporting these perplexing activities could save money, free up valuable resources, and accelerate project delivery.

What is Blockchain in Building Maintenance?

Blockchain innovation enables disseminated, encrypted, and secure logging of digital transactions. It is the fundamental innovation of Bitcoin and different cryptocurrencies. Blockchain is relied upon to alter figuring in a few zones, especially where centralization was unnatural and protection was significant. In this chapter, we present research on where and how this innovation could be valuable in the construction business. The work depends on the investigations as of this writing into open issues that exist in construction process management. These are then the present-day abilities of blockchain.

We are spurred by the way that construction ventures include a unique gathering of a few organizations. We study how much the connections among them are progressive or shared and note that especially in data concentrated stages, centralization of data management was fundamental because of technological limitations on information transmission. When utilizing blockchain innovation, correspondence designs among members demonstrate a distributed nature of connections. In such condition, blockchain can give a dependable infrastructure to data management during all building life-cycle stages. Regardless of whether building information management (BIM) is utilized, which assumes a centralized building information model, there is a role for blockchain to manage data on who did what and when and subsequently provide a premise to any legitimate contentions that may happen. On the building site blockchain can improve the unwavering quality and reliability of development logbooks, works performed, and material quantities recorded. In the facility maintenance stage, blockchain's principal potential is the safe stockpiling of sensor data, which is sensitive security information.

We infer that blockchain gives answers for some present issues in development data management. In any case, all things considered, it will be incorporated with conventional IT infrastructure on which construction applications are fabricated, instead of utilized legitimately by creators of construction related programming. It can possibly make construction processes less incorporated, which opens requirements for planning how to move toward that path.

FM incorporates resource management, space management, IoT management, administrative/consistence adherence, and purchasing and billing issuance. Assets management requires observing, issue identification, and the utilization of IoT for recognizing conditions and activating occasions. FM includes following work orders, planning upkeep, doing preventive management, and furthermore following resource statuses through equipment guarantees, life cycle evaluations, agreements, and contracts. Data management of facilities should now be possible utilizing a blockchain rather than a database. Blockchain is a distributed computerized record that records data, which is open and shared by numerous nodes, each one verifying the authenticity of the record being updated. The excellent utility of blockchain is that this decentralized mode of recordkeeping gives transparency in data being taken care of, simplifying cooperation between qualifying parties. Since FM includes issuance of agreements and contracts, smart contracts can be conveyed to gives a transparent and quicker approach to make transactions since they too can be automated in a blockchain network.

Why is Blockchain Building Maintenance Important?

The commercial real estate (CRE) industry seems to invest heavily in keeping a few parts of its activities mystery. For example, comparable lease rental rates, property costs and valuations, can all be kept confidential to preserve a potential upper hand or advantage in potential dealings. Be that as it may, privileged insights are difficult to keep – and may not be wanted – in the present hyperconnected and digitized world. Because of increasing consumer interest for transparency, innovation headways, and the disintermediation by new companies, construction companies are step by step making a portion of this data open. Therefore, property-related data is progressively accessible in digital and paper form. This notwithstanding, a huge portion of the digitized data is facilitated on disparate systems, which obfuscates transparency and effectiveness, and results in a higher rate of mistakes that also allows the potential for fraud.

Blockchain innovation – a digitized, distributed ledger that permanently records and offers data – could empower the CRE business to address these wasteful aspects and errors. As per a 2015 World Economic Forum overview of 800 officials, data, and interchanges innovation division specialists, 57.9% of the respondents accept that 10% of the worldwide GDP data will be transferred by blockchain innovation by 2025.

Industry players presently realize that blockchain-based smart contracts can assume a significant role in CRE, possibly changing center CRE activities, such as property transactions (buying, dealing, financing, renting, and management). After some time, blockchain selection will have a more extensive effect, as it provides great benefit to open utility services, for example, in waste, water, energy charging, and data-driven city management.

It offers multiple benefits for those with stringent requirements for data sharing and database integrity. Those who require a common database – basic for renting, buying, and deal transactions – stand to benefit from a blockchain-assisted database. Multiple entities, including proprietors, occupants, administrators, loan specialists, financial specialists, and service suppliers, can modify such a database – executing and managing real estate properties as they engage in deals with one another.

What marks this common blockchain database as unique in comparison to a centralized database, is that the blockchain database can provide a level of trust that doesn't exist elsewhere for first-time parties. Commonly, members in renting, buying, and deal transactions are new to one another and could be over-cautious and may even have data sharing concerns. Nonetheless, blockchain can help diminish this hazard through computerized personalities and increasingly transparent record saving frameworks for real estate titles, privilege, liens, financing, and tenure.

Lastly, blockchain offers an opportunity for disintermediation – confided in middle people, for example, title organizations can be disintermediated through blockchain, because of the expanded security and transparency in title management and auto-affirmation by government land registries. This security can even be extended to the formation of smart contracts, where already today some real estate transactions are carried out by the automatic completion of certain actions based on conditional clauses in a blockchain-supported contract. For example, the determination of a buy deal transaction could be reliant on loan approvals or title clearances.

How to Use Blockchain for Building Maintenance

Enterprises are at the forefront of technological advancement and utilizations of innovation have had the option to make their operations leaner, accordingly lessening cost overheads and expanding productivity. Blockchain has seen a remarkable amount of publicity and the advancement of this innovation has even been touted as a new technological revolution. It will disrupt whole enterprises and expand new efficiencies that will usher us into another period of financial transparency, operational proficiency, and digital security.

Blockchain innovation is a machine approved chronicle process and considers recording transactions in a digital ledger, dispersed across a few machines in a system. The various transactions, or blocks, are connected to each other utilizing cryptographic keys, or hashes. The key terms here are "ledger" and "transaction," which show the essential usefulness of the innovation. For an exceedingly long time, organizations have conveyed some type of private ledger for accounting and holding budgetary data that is utilized to make pay articulations and monetary record reports among different capacities. As blockchain innovation executes a dispersed digital ledger over numerous machines, it very well may be applied anywhere an account ledger is utilized and transactions are occurring.

The innovation can be applied to progressively broad use cases anywhere records should be kept as it allows for an unprecedented level of security, immutability (i.e., the subtleties and contents of which can't be changed as it is scrambled, put away, and dispersed on gadgets across the system), and traceability. Given that smart contracts (self-executing directions, conditions, and results modified into the blockchain) can also be actualized, the uses and applications of blockchain are continually being tested to see what more it can achieve.

The uses of blockchain broaden well past the finance and financial services enterprises. Organizations giving blockchain infrastructure as a service, for example, IBM and SAP have made coalitions to create blockchains with enterprises in customer items, telecom, retail, pharmaceuticals, logistics, horticulture, aviation, modern hardware, energy, and public services businesses. Different partnerships, for example, Microsoft and Kodak have additionally made promises to put resources into blockchain. We had a customer ask us an inquiry once "For what reason do you not use Blockchain to store building data?" Collecting interim data from many focuses per building every moment would not be the best use case for blockchain, as there is no chain of occasions to follow. For this situation, utilizing a private blockchain to sign in data focuses from buildings would not be appropriate given that records would need to be refreshed and accord would need to be set up more than 300,000 times each day.

Nevertheless, property management and real estate is an industry that can profit enormously from blockchain. Starting now, we still can't seem to see a blockchain consortium of real estate and property management firms. Utilizing this innovation for tenant billing, equipment warranties, and indoor occupancy tracking have all been proposed and there is a decent case for each one of them. A blockchain empowered tenant billing framework would take out a great deal of the paper pushing and authoritative expenses. Utilizing on-board sensors to screen equipment performance for the motivations behind guarantee could be an incredible approach to expand the certainty of building administrators in buying hardware and getting discounts when it doesn't perform as per expectations. Tracking indoor occupancy for guarantees may raise a few protection issues, however, it may also eventually offer some incentive as it will assist in making digital characters and would permit a building to provide food and services directly to its occupants.

Here are some different ways facility management and the real estate industry can profit by the blockchain innovation.

Regularly Scheduled Service and Maintenance Contracts

All kinds of hardware in a building consistently needs support and adjusting whether it is HVAC hardware, for example, boilers, chillers, mechanical gear, for example, siphons and fans or electrical gear such shift gears and move switches. Diverse hardware may have separate prerequisites, for example, how frequently it should be serviced. Utilizing a private blockchain to monitor standard support and service visits from contractors would provide diagnostic capability and accountability to building maintenance and support. A procedure of executing smart contracts to discharge installment once work has been confirmed as finished can be created to deal with and record transactions of the work in question. For most HVAC and electrical gear companies, once the onboard smart interfaces, sensors and controls checking for ordinary upkeep and overhauling work completion have confirmed the job is done, smart contracts can be triggered to consequently release payment, record, and update the blockchain.

Small Purchase Orders (Contracts Under $5,000)

In buildings where a BAS is introduced, the HVAC gear is modified to work a specific way. With time, the successions of activity require changes or refreshes and these progressions don't cost in excess of a couple hundred or thousand dollars. Arrangement of activity changes or small equipment establishments/substitutions in small contracts are very exact and direct, not at all like bigger contracts where the extent of work can be very perplexing. Numerous property management firms don't give purchase orders to their contractors for such modest quantities. A portion of customers just email their contractors and ask them to invoice the expense from the work. This procedure, or scarcity in that department, causes issues when the work is finished and should be returned to sometime in the not-too-distant future. Property managers and contractors resort to more seasoned correspondence for details and a considerable amount of time is needlessly squandered. Much of the time, there is no official record for this sort of work and if property supervisors or activities staff leave or switch employments, the data is lost. If BAS data is being gathered by an examination stage, AI can be utilized to confirm little groupings of activity changes. A procedure of executing smart contracts on a private undertaking blockchain would be perfect for the arrival of payment once AI has confirmed that the work is finished. Having a record on a private blockchain would give a total record of work done. It is imperative to bring up that numerous liberties have been taken with our hypotheses in this model, for example, making assumptions on investigation stages, organized, grouped data and AI calculations. Effective adoption of these advancements in buildings frameworks is inconsistent or essentially nonexistent in regard to AI. Be that as it may, it shows the capability of what is conceivable by applying a mix of these innovations and the efficiencies and advantages to be gained are readily apparent.

Large Contracts (Contracts Over $5,000)

For bigger contracts for capital use activities, such as significant hardware updates and huge establishments, utilizing smart contracts would not be feasible because of the multifaceted nature of the work. Yet recording the transactions to sellers and contractors in a private blockchain will permit property management firms to achieve more noteworthy transparency for record keeping purposes and would give traceability when more seller invoices and contracts need to be examined. This provides the whole transaction history with unparalleled security and transparency.

Energy Trading

Detailed examinations into energy exchanging have been performed by PWC, the global network of consultants, and the thought has been investigated by numerous service organizations. Buildings that produce energy through sustainable methods can take care of overabundant or scarce periods of energy in the network. Smart meters are utilized to compute power creation and utilization. Any power exchanged to different customers alongside the transaction can be followed utilizing blockchain.

Despite the clear benefits blockchain innovation presents, it is still for the most part hypothetical as wide-scale reception of this technology is still in its early stages. The pace at which associations have focused on embracing it is, however, growing rapidly, and as an ever-increasing number of associations adapt, the advantages will eventually be realized. Blockchain vows to serve a few the basic building blocks of the New Deal for buildings by giving a recognizable digital impression to demonstrate truth-based investigation and service transparency to advance fruitful connections between building proprietors and merchants. It is fundamentally important that facility management and real estate industry specialists everywhere have a genuine look at how blockchain innovation can serve their interests.

What are the Core Benefits of Blockchain in Building Maintenance?

Specifically, what makes blockchain significant for facility directors is that it offers a streamlined approach to store and access secure data. Blockchain has the capacity to work as a conveyed, single wellspring of shared truth. It can possibly turn into the top arrangement of record for all transactions. As indicated by an ongoing article in IFMA's *Facility Management Journal*, if this somehow managed to occur, "the economy will experience an extreme move as new, blockchain-based, sources of influence and control develop. Blockchain can possibly change the manner in which facilities are managed, going from work order tracking to preventive maintenance to life cycle assessments."

The fundamental advantage that blockchain offers facilities managers is digital trust. Blockchain works as a cloud-based, changeless, digital ledger of exercises between parties. The term cloud-based implies that it doesn't live inside your association's private server, or some other organization's private server. The permanence of this ledger implies that it exists as a perpetual record of exercises between parties.

For the facility management industry, this innovation has applications for recording property transfers, resource digitization, HVAC framework exercises, tenant occupancy of cubicles, and security access. Blockchain additionally may possibly help oversee IoT connected gadgets and smart buildings with sustainable power sources, for example, solar-based gadgets. For instance, if a facility is in a two-way energy communication with the grid, blockchain can make it progressively secure and simpler to build up a digital record of energy-in and energy-out transactions.

The advantages of applying blockchain abilities in FM revolve around upgrades made to processes requiring tracking exercises, point-by-point gear and flexibility needs. For example, blockchain in FM empowers real-time visibility and security of FM exercises. This incorporates utilizing blockchain innovation to follow contractual commitments of occupants and field service sellers.

Blockchain will also guarantee administrative adherence. Such upgrades can adequately have the additional advantage of expanding qualification for charge findings or energy-related credits, liberating capital for different employments.

It may very well be private or open, ideal for security activities in FM. Blockchain could be open or private, so it can significantly build responsibility and security of data in FM.

Commonly, blockchain innovation is versatile, setting off another passage in every transaction or utilization of data. Since FM health facilities may also lessen the danger of cross-contamination, hospital-acquired infections, and even decrease the danger of malpractice all the while.

What is the Future Ahead for Blockchain in Building Maintenance?

Blockchain innovation will probably be a future driving force for transparency, effectiveness, and cost investment funds for building proprietors and occupiers by eliminating many current wasteful aspects in key procedures.

Working environment and FM organizations and industry members assessing an update or redesign of their present frameworks ought to have blockchain on their radar as its evident value can provide huge incentives to the business. While across the board execution of blockchain is as of yet far off, it is wise to put time and energy into assessing and exploring the manners by which this energizing innovation could and will eventually be actualized.

Obviously, it is essential to keep up to date regarding implementing emerging technologies, mastery and expertise in a moving objective. While blockchain might still be on the road to widespread adoption, it already has profound potential to positively benefit the future of facility management activities. The time to plan is now!

Further Reading

Artificial Intelligence

http://blog.qsifacilities.com/artificial-intelligence-in-facilities-management
https://www.facilitiesnet.com/facilitiesmanagement/article/7-Ways-Artificial-Intelligence-Is-the-Future-of-FM--18497
https://www.facilitiesnet.com/facilitiesmanagement/article/How-Artificial-Intelligence-is-Reshaping-Facilities-Management--18496
https://servicechannel.com/blog/4-applications-ai-facilities-management/
https://www.servicefutures.com/how-can-ai-optimise-facilities-management
https://www.imnovation-hub.com/digital-transformation/artificial-intelligence-and-facility-management/
https://emerj.com/ai-sector-overviews/ai-building-automation-current-applications/
https://www.softwebsolutions.com/resources/AI-the-future-of-smart-facility-management.html
http://blog.veolianorthamerica.com/the-future-of-ai-in-facility-management

Blockchain

https://www.pbctoday.co.uk/news/bim-news/facility-management-blockchain/49965/
https://newdeal.blog/uses-of-blockchain-in-facility-management-53e3f76d62ca
https://hbr.org/2019/07/how-blockchain-will-change-construction
https://www.intellis.io/blog/what-are-the-benefits-of-blockchain-for-facilities-managers-in-2020
https://medium.com/coinmonks/blockchain-in-facilities-management-refocusing-on-the-office-experience-7e9efbe9ab29
https://www.sciencedirect.com/science/article/pii/S187770581733179X
https://papers.ssrn.com/sol3/papers.cfm?abstract_id=3487409
https://www.aurecongroup.com/markets/property/buildings-of-the-future/easy-life-complex-technology/blockchain-impact
http://blog.qsifacilities.com/blockchain-in-facilities-management
https://www2.deloitte.com/us/en/pages/financial-services/articles/blockchain-in-commercial-real-estate.html

Tom James and Kiren Chong-James

Chapter 7
Manufacturing

Artificial Intelligence

Artificial intelligence (AI)-driven machines are laying the groundwork for a simpler future by yielding many advantages – offering new opportunities, improving production efficiencies, and bringing machine collaboration closer to human cooperation. For a huge assortment of businesses, whether it is gaming, banking, retail, private, or public, AI will see even more integration into the fundamental practices of each industry. Manufacturing is no exception, and AI will be pivotal in the coming revolution of industrial automation.

Expertise shortages, complexity in decision-making, issues related to integration and over-burdening quantities of data, utilizing AI in manufacturing plants empowers organizations to totally change their procedures to resolve all these issues and more.

What is AI in Manufacturing?

What's the first thing that you think of when you think about a manufacturing unit? An automated production unit? Or an ungainly modern space with many laborers under one rooftop? With the progression in the innovations, AI, and internet of things (IoT), centered on improving the procedures of manufacturing ventures and assisting with boosting profitability and efficiencies, there is a smart factory revolution that is changing the way we conduct industrial activity through industrial automation and information analysis.

Manufacturers regularly consider AI an intricate and costly affair. Despite these impressions, AI and IoT devices improve different sectors of manufacturing and make your business increasingly capable by broadening human abilities. The robotics market is developing at a remarkable rate and computerization is dictating the way laborers work in the creation lines to more profitable ends. To this end, AI is likely to cause a tremendous jump in manufacturing output, efficiency, eco-friendliness, and personal satisfaction for workers in the future.

Current inquiries show that 58 percent of manufacturers are interested in AI technology, yet only 12% of respondents are actualizing it. Organizations are in a race to grasp advanced innovations like AI in manufacturing. These advancements are basic drivers that empower Industry and will at last engage manufacturing to keep on being the foundation of the worldwide economy.

https://doi.org/10.1515/9783110664454-007

Grasping digital technologies, similar to AI, empowers manufacturers to fulfill the ever-changing needs of their clients. We are seeing expanded client requests for fast pivots on designs, materials, bundling, packaging, and production volume in the electronics goods market. In certain instances, these necessities can put a strain on resources – affecting item quality as well as productivity. Digital innovations give the edge that makers need to develop and adjust to these quick evolving requests.

Why is AI Manufacturing Important?

AI and machine learning in particular is the new, incredible asset for expanding utilization of added substances and vitality in pretty much every industrial procedure. Today, conventional manufacturing organizations are effectively starting to execute machine-learning models to cut expenses.

Although most industrial procedures have been studied in detail for a considerable length of time, the latest advancement in the region of AI, specifically machine learning, has opened new frontiers for additional improvement. Because of the uncertainty intrinsic to complex procedures, innovators need to utilize an exorbitant number of resources to cover any deviation in procedure.

AI lets us create a model that considers information originating from various sources: starting from material creation, the nature of crude or raw materials, and readings from several sensors. The trained model precisely predicts parameters of the last item, and dependent on this forecast computes accurate measures of added substances expected to be required to accomplish the mentioned parameters for every particular batch.

IoT and AI have been a piece of the manufacturing business now for quite a while, with a ton of manufacturing units and industrial facilities receiving these innovations improve production. Such advances have been altering large scale manufacturing of merchandise and boosting the yield of various businesses.

Human workforces may be restricted by the limits of human biology, as even if staff individuals work in shifts, it is difficult to maintain 24/7 productivity. Here machines offer an obvious advantage, in that their consistency guarantees quicker and constant production of merchandise. AI-driven robots can work 24-hours every day and help to drive operational productivity. AI can decrease the manufacturing labor use, improve the efficiency, and reduce maintenance issues.

IoT can accumulate information from numerous machines to convey constant streams of information analysis, bringing about ideal execution and the completion of outstanding tasks at hand. This also allows merchandise to be tracked for purpose of order tracking and logistics management, and maintenance issues or focuses can be anticipated.

Advanced data analysis enables the manufacturers and partners to recognize the variables that may cause failure or breakdown so they can take proper activities and measures to resolve them. With cutting edge information experiences and real-time tracking, machinery maintenance can be planned before any issue emerges. This will assist with reducing the danger of expensive downtimes, too.

How to Use AI for Manufacturing?

The Manufacturer's Annual Manufacturing Report in 2018 found that 92% of senior manufacturing officials accept that "Smart Factory" digital technologies, including AI, will enable them to expand their profitability and empower staff to work more astutely. In any case, there is a huge gap between ambitions and execution: Forrester says that 58% of business and innovation experts are examining AI arrangements, yet only 12% are effectively utilizing them.

Accenture and Frontier Economics gauge that by 2035, AI-controlled advances could expand work profitability by up to 40% across 16 enterprises, including manufacturing. In a similar paper, the creators claim that AI could add an extra 3.8 trillion dollars gross value added (GVA) in 2035 to the manufacturing segment, which is an expansion of practically 45% contrasted to business as usual.

Andrew Ng, the fellow benefactor of Google Brain and Coursera, says:

> AI will perform manufacturing, quality control, shorten design time, and reduce materials waste, improve production reuse, perform predictive maintenance, and more.

And he's right. AI is changing manufacturing in many ways – – these are only a few glimpses of what's to come.

Quality Checks

Some defects in items are too small to be seen with the unaided eye, regardless of whether the overseer is extremely experienced. Nonetheless, machines can be furnished with cameras more delicate than our eyes – and thanks to that, recognize even the littlest imperfections. Machine learning and oversight allows machines to "see" the items on the production line and recognize any flaws. The subsequent stage may be sending the photos of said blemishes to a human overseer – yet it is anything but necessary anymore to have this human component, the procedure can be completely mechanized. Landing.ai, an organization established by Andrew Ng, offers a mechanized visual examination device to discover even minute imperfections in items. The framework perceives defects, marks them, and sends alarm flags that the item is defective.

Prediction of Failure Modes

Do you know the tale about Abraham Wald and the missing shot openings? This is the true story of a splendid analyst. During World War II, he was asked by the Royal Air Force to choose where to add armor to their aircraft. You don't want your planes to be destroyed and your pilots injured, nor do you want to add too much armor and thus slow your planes down. The British analyzed and disassembled planes that returned to Britain from bombing raids and found that most damage was around the fuselage region of the aircraft. Using common sense, they thought to reinforce the fuselage. Wald suggested that these planes didn't include the planes that never made it home. What's more, Wald was just searching for the "missing openings" – those around the motor. On the off chance that a plane was shot there, it never returned. Furthermore, despite the harm around the fuselage, such damage wasn't preventing the planes from coming home to Britain. That is where endurance inclination occurs – we select information to think about and ignore other vital pieces, often because of an absence of its perceivability. This can prompt bogus ends and red herrings.

This bogus thinking can affect items and procedures, as well. Products can fail in an assortment of ways, independent of the visual assessment. An item that looks impeccable may at present separate not long after its first use. An item that looks defective may even now carry out its responsibilities very well. The way we watch items and blemishes is one-sided and numerous things might be not quite the same as they appear. With huge measures of information on how items are tried and how they perform, AI can distinguish the regions that should be given more consideration in tests.

Predictive Maintenance

Predictive maintenance allows organizations to anticipate when machines need maintenance with high precision, rather than speculating or performing preventive maintenance. Predictive maintenance forestalls unplanned downtime by utilizing machine learning. Innovations, like sensors and progressed investigation implanted in manufacturing gear empower maintenance by reacting to alarms and settling machine issues. A passage from Deloitte's *The digital edge in life sciences: The business case for digital supply networks* report explains how IoT adds to predictive maintenance:

A case for the utilization of IoT and machine learning can be seen in the predictive maintenance of machines utilized for manufacturing titanium inserts. Titanium's hardness requires devices with jewel tips to cut it. The degree of bluntness in the precious stone tips, and when to hone them, has been hard to quantify because of a wide range of factors that influence it. The utilization of vibration or sound sensors and torque screens can help evaluate the condition of the machinery, as dull tips move and sound in an unexpected way.

Predictive maintenance is now utilized by various manufacturers, including LG and Siemens. Roland Busch, Siemens AG CTO, says:

By analyzing the information, our AI frameworks can reach inferences in regard to a machine's condition and distinguish abnormalities to make predictive maintenance conceivable.

Examinations led by Oneserve in the UK shows that 3% of every single working day are lost yearly because of broken machinery, and the effect of machine vacation was estimated to cost UK manufacturers more than 180 billion pounds per year. Predictive maintenance then presents a viable way to forestall misfortune.

Generative Plan

Generative planning is a procedure that includes a program creating various yields to meet determined measures. Creators or architects input structure objectives and parameters, for example, materials, manufacturing techniques, and cost constraints into generative plan programming to investigate structure choices. The arrangement uses machine learning in procedures to gain from every emphasis what works and what doesn't. We should examine this model from Autodesk (see Figure 7.1).

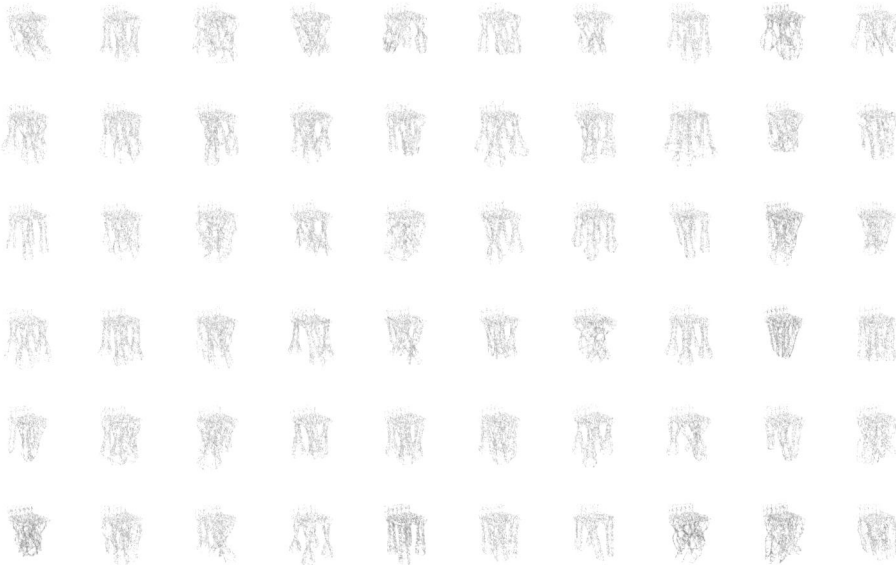

Figure 7.1: Generative plan of a parametric chair.
Source: Autodesk; https://adsknews.autodesk.com/stories/future-things-get-made-harnessing-power-artificial-intelligence-next-frontier-design/384_generative

Figure 7.1 delineates a generative plan of a parametric chair. The calculation finds innumerable different ways of structuring a straightforward thing – for example, a chair. You need to enter the parameters: four legs, raised seat, weight prerequisites, negligible materials, etc. At that point, the calculation produces an assortment of alternatives. The product isn't there to supplant humans, however. It's another case of AI being an expansion to human work. As depicted via Autodesk:

Computational structure doesn't supplant human inventiveness – the program aids and quickens the procedure, removing the constraints inherent in planning and assisting the creative mind.

Generative structure is an approach to investigate thoughts that couldn't reasonably be investigated by any human individual in a work setting – simply consider how much time it would take an average individual to come up with a hundred distinct approaches to plan a chair. AI can do it in the blink of an eye, allowing the human designer to browse a wide scope of alternatives. Computerized changes like that can alter the way an organization conveys an incentive to the clients and improves the effectiveness of procedures.

Advanced Twins

An advanced twin is the virtual portrayal of a manufacturing plant, product, or service. The portrayal coordinates the physical properties of its true partner through the utilization of sensors, cameras, and other information assortment techniques. In an article for *Forbes*, Bernard Marr expounds on advanced twins:

This pairing of the virtual and physical universes allows analysis of information and checking of frameworks to take off issues before they even happen, prevent downtime, grow new chances, and even arrange for the future by utilizing reenactments.

To make advanced twins work, the first thing you need to do is coordinate smart segments that assemble information about the constant condition, status, or position of physical things. The parts are associated with a cloud-based framework that get all the information and processes it. This innovation is already utilized by NASA, one of the most prominent associations embracing the innovation. They required an answer that would permit them to work, maintain and repair frameworks that were not in their physical vicinity. John Vickers, NASA's driving manufacturing master and chief of NASA's National Center for Advanced Manufacturing says:

A definitive vision for the advanced twin is to make, test, and fabricate our hardware in a virtual situation. When we get it to where it performs to our requirements, when it perfectly simulates our actual processes, at that point the physical form needs to tie back to its computerized twin. This can be done through sensors, so the advanced twin contains all the data we could have by investigating the physical form.

Environmental Effect

The assembling processes of an assortment of items, including gadgets, involves significant harm to the Earth. Extraction of nickel, cobalt, and graphite for lithium-particle batteries, expanded production of plastic, tremendous energy utilization, e-waste – just to give some examples, all lead to significant environmental damage and disruption. Jahda Swanborough, a worldwide expert in environmental conservation and lead at the World Economic Forum claims that AI could change manufacturing by diminishing its ecological effect. AI can bolster new emerging eco-accommodating materials and help streamline energy productivity – Google as of now already utilizes AI to do that in its server farms.

Making Use of Data

As a rule, there's an entire assortment of approaches to utilize enormous sums of information in manufacturing. Manufacturers gather huge measures of information identified with activities, forms, and different issues – and this information paired with cutting edge investigation can provide important bits of knowledge to improve the business. Supply chain management, risk management, expectations on sales volume, item quality maintenance, forecast of review issues – these are only a few of the instances where enormous sums of information can be utilized to the advantage of manufacturers. This sort of AI application can reveal bits of knowledge that were before inaccessible.

Price Forecasts

To make items, you first need to buy the necessary resources. The problem is the costs of raw materials can fluctuate wildly. For instance, if you purchase stainless steel, its cost is influenced by an assortment of elements, including the listings of the Metal Exchange or the costs of different components, some of them not recorded on the metal trade. With the fast changes in costs, sometimes it might be difficult to evaluate when it's the best and most ideal time to purchase resources. Knowing the costs of resources is also important for organizations to gauge the cost of their item when it's prepared to leave the production line. This is the case for materials like stainless steel: the costs can fluctuate, contingent upon the present listings, for example, of nickel or the cost of ferrochrome. The framework can give exact value suggestions on account of dynamic estimating that is utilized by online business organizations like Amazon, where the machine learning calculations break down recorded information to consistently offer optimum cost appraisals.

Robotics

It's not surprising that a huge portion of manufacturing occupations are performed by robots. Despite this, ordinary industrial robots require explicit instruction to complete the errands they were made for. The customary robots currently should be furnished with a fixed system of collecting parts, yet AI-fueled robots can decipher CAD models, which takes out the need to program their developments and procedures. In 2017, Siemens built up a two-armed robot that can fabricate items without being preprogrammed with instructions.

Customer Service

When you think of customer service, what industries come to mind? Accommodation, retail, banking? They manage clients frequently, so client support is a significant piece of their business. In manufacturing, nonetheless, the significance of client support is regularly disregarded, which is a mistake as lost clients can mean a huge number of dollars lost in missed sales. AI arrangements can dissect the practices of clients to distinguish designs and foresee future results. Watching real clients' practices allows organizations to answer their requirements with a greater probability of success. In 2018, Nokia divulged the most recent rendition of its Cognitive Analytics for Customer Insight programming, giving incredible new capacities to specialist organizations, businesses, IT and building associations, allowing them to reliably convey a customized client experience. This product allows specialist organizations to rapidly distinguish issues and organize enhancements.

What are the Core Benefits of AI in Manufacturing?

AI is assisting manufacturing by providing several key core advantages over manually programmed manufacturing methods, such as in coordinated automation or continuous production with automatic maintenance. Repeating exercises, restructuring production models, rising capabilities, building computerization arrangements, reducing human error, and conveying unrivaled degrees of value confirmation are just some of the key benefits AI provide for the future of manufacturing.

For example, while humans are compelled to work in three shifts to guarantee consistent production, AI-maintained machines are fit to work every minute of every day in the production line. Organizations can extend as far as production capacities permit and fulfill the significant needs of clients around the world.

AI can also help reduce workplace accident occurrences at manufacturing plants, as steps toward AI-led manufacturing imply fewer human assets needed to do hazardous and excessively arduous work. As robots supplant humans and perform typical and unsafe exercises, the quality of working environments will go up and accidents will diminish across the board.

As this dangerous manual work is rendered increasingly obsolete, with AI assuming control over the manufacturing plant, mechanizing exhausting and conventional human errands, laborers will get the chance to concentrate on challenging and creative undertakings. While AI deals with unskilled work, humans can concentrate on driving development and steering their business to the cutting-edge limits – retraining themselves to perform high-skill occupations.

This comes with great ROI, since despite the initial capital cost of bringing AI into the manufacturing business, the benefits provided by astute machines dealing consistently and continuously with everyday exercises, significantly lowers working expenses.

Included Benefits of AI

AI and industrial automation have progressed significantly in the ongoing years. Improvement in machine learning procedures, progress in sensors and in this manner, the development of processing power has helped produce a shiny new age of robots. AI encourages machines to assemble and separate information, recognize designs, learn and adjust to new things or situations through machine intelligence, learning and discourse acknowledgment. Utilizing AI, manufacturers will have the option to:
- Make quick, information-oriented choices
- Encourage improved production results
- Advance procedure adequacy
- Limit operational expenses
- Encourage superior scalability
- Encourage product development

Additionally, as AI becomes adept at understanding regular language and interpreting it, this will allow workers and managers to communicate with software more easily. For instance, software users are regularly inclined to search for things as opposed to exploring a complex menu. AI allows the product to grasp the client's aims that make the framework accessible, which leads to great yield and less blunders.

What is the Future Ahead for AI in Manufacturing?

AI is a game-changing innovation for any industry. As the innovation develops and costs drop, AI is increasingly available for organizations as a viable commercial investment. In manufacturing, it tends to excel at making things, improving designs, and cutting costs. The manufacturing business has consistently been anxious to grasp innovations – and doing so effectively. Presently with AI reception, they can make quick, information driven choices, advance manufacturing forms, limit operational expenses, and improve the way they serve their clients. This doesn't imply that manufacturing will be taken over by the machines – AI is currently an auxiliary modifier to human work, and nothing can be a substitute for human intelligence and the capacity to react to unforeseen changes.

AI will affect manufacturing in ways we have not yet envisioned. In any case, we are already able to take a gander at some increasingly recognizable models emerging.

The improvement in computer visualization has for some time been utilized for quality control by identifying item defects continuously. Be that as it may, since manufacturing produces more data than any other time in recent memory, coupled with the fact that plant administrators would prefer not to pay representatives to enter data – AI with computer visualization can justify how data gets captured. An assembly line laborer ought to have the option to draw from raw materials reserves off the shelf and have the stock transaction made, naturally dependent on a camera watching the procedure. This will be the regular UI, simply completing the job needing to be done without having to examine or add things into a framework.

One more thing AI will affect is with the IoT. IoT will give an approach to convey supplies and administrations to clients who may not even be aware that they are required. Furthermore, IoT can send in-depth telemetry back to makers and wholesalers to investigate quality and elements that may drive failures. To sum things up, IoT is an internal wave of data that AI can use to reason over and advance. This will encourage expanded generative structure forms where items are reconsidered in manners progressively like development.

Some important statistical information of AI in different sectors:
- By 2035 AI innovations are expected to grow in production by 40% or more. (see Figures 7.2, 7.3 and 7.4)
- AI will help the financial development a normal of 1.7% across 16 businesses by 2035. (see Figures 7.2 and 7.3)

Figure 7.3 illustrates the growth forecast with AI as a new element of production.

AI's proponents claim that the innovation is just a developmental type of mechanization, an anticipated aftereffect of the Fourth Industrial Revolution. AI might be effective at making things, improving them, and making them less expensive. Be that as it may, there is no trade for human inventiveness in managing the unexpected changes in tastes and requests – or in concluding whether to make things by any means.

The effect of AI on industrial growth
Real annual GVA growth by 2035(%)

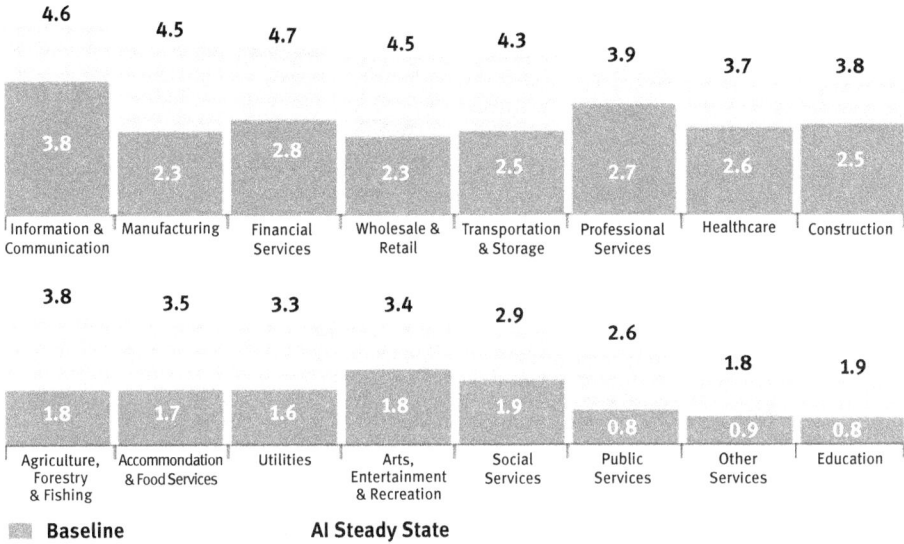

Figure 7.2: The effect of AI on industrial growth.
Source: plantautomation-technology.com; https://www.plantautomation-technology.com/articles/the-future-of-artificial-intelligence-in-manufacturingmanufacturing-industries

The effect of AI on the growth of different industries

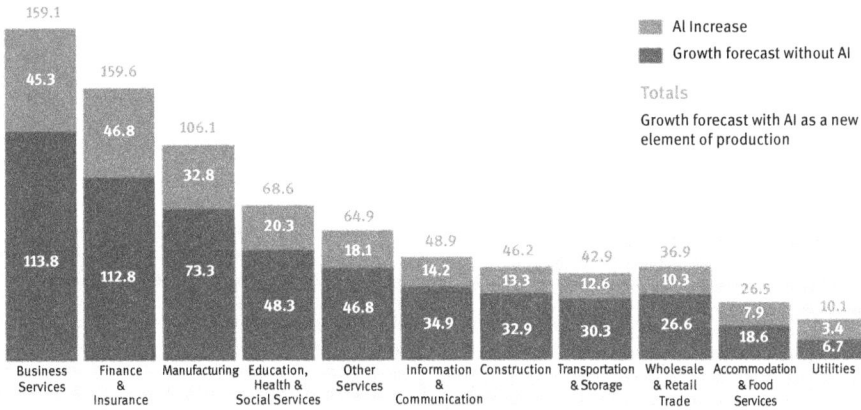

Figure 7.3: The effect of AI on the growth of different industries.
Source: plantautomation-technology.com; https://www.plantautomation-technology.com/articles/the-future-of-artificial-intelligence-in-manufacturingmanufacturing-industries

Great Value Added in 2035 (Manufacturing)

Total GVA AI steady state:
US$ 12,173 bilion

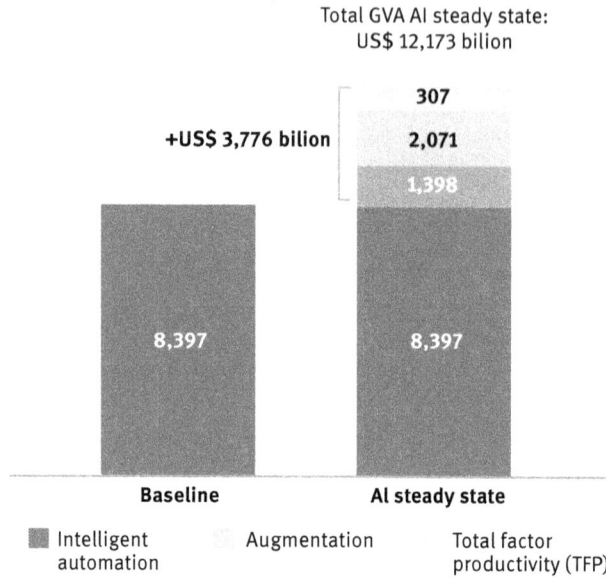

Figure 7.4: Gross value added in 2035 with respect to the manufacturing sector.
Source: plantautomation-technology.com; https://www.plantautomation-technology.com/articles/
the-future-of-artificial-intelligence-in-manufacturingmanufacturing-industries

Blockchain

Blockchain innovation can fundamentally change organizations across different segments. Numerous enterprises like healthcare, training, supply chain, retail, and numerous different areas are experiencing a change under the blockchain impact. In this chapter I will feature how blockchain is changing the manufacturing business.

Manufacturing harbors one of the most productive uses of blockchain. You can pick any zone of manufacturing, and discover blockchain's application in that very field.

Regardless of whether it is via suppliers, shop floor activities, acquirement, strategic sourcing, or anything pertaining to manufacturing, blockchain can trigger totally superior approaches for conducting the manufacturing business.

We realize that supply chains shape the base of each manufacturing industry and blockchain can be an impetus to help add some grace to the chain framework. With the mediation of blockchain innovation, the entire supply will turn out to be increasingly effective. Along these lines, blockchain can ensure an increase in the item quality, product tracking, and with this, the producer will have the option to satisfy the need of the client on schedule and furthermore guarantee that the highest quality item is conveyed to the client.

What is Blockchain in Manufacturing?

Transparency inside a supply chain is intrinsic to the manufacturing industry, and blockchain can convey that in spades. With blockchain, transparency is expanded across each region of manufacturing whether it is from providers, key sourcing, and acquirement, to shop floor activities including machine-level observing and service.

A viable and productive supply chain is a basic part of manufacturing. Nevertheless, with supply chains working across different associations, states, and even nations, it can be challenging to achieve transparency in each moving part. Exacerbating the situation, there is frequently no uniform standard technique for recording, putting away, and trading data.

This is where blockchain becomes possibly the most important factor. Blockchain can assemble better, more brilliant, and progressively secure supply chains, always following an item's excursion. No longer do people inside a supply chain need to guess when materials dispatched out, who took care of them, and when they'll show up; the trail is evaluated with constant transparency and is always recorded as blocks in a chain.

"Numerous manufacturers are extremely amped up for blockchain's potential capacity to confirm merchandise traveling through the manufacturing supply chain," says Greg Cline, head of research for the Aberdeen Group's manufacturing, product innovation, and engineering practices division. "The profoundly transactional and frequently multi-step nature of business process services implies that the potential utilizations of blockchain in manufacturing are noteworthy."

Why is Blockchain Manufacturing Important?

One of the key drivers of the worldwide economy is the manufacturing business. As indicated by the World Bank, this industry itself represents about 17% of the worldwide GDP. Shockingly, the business has consistently been tormented with a few issues including quality control and inefficiency. Aside from this, intricate and detached supply chains have permitted phony and fake items to advance into the market, prompting lost buyer trust and brand notoriety for organizations. Likewise, expanding client desires are putting more weight on manufacturers for conveying quality items at nominal costs.

Blockchain, a dispersed database can possibly drastically change the manufacturing business by offering transparency across each part of manufacturing. Directly from sourcing, obtainment, and vendor quality to activities, such as machine-level checking, blockchain can prepare us for a totally new plan of action. Blockchain can be utilized by manufacturing organizations for smoothing out their supply chains that compensate for their business establishment. The distributed ledger architecture of this flexible innovation can assist organizations with improving provider request precision, the nature of an item, trace the origin, and track the journey of items across the supply chain. This will assist manufacturers with guaranteeing speedier turnaround time, increasing item quality and sales volumes.

When it comes to tracking, following the real root of a section (utilized for manufacturing an item) directly from the point of production through to the retail section is troublesome and bulky. This is on the grounds that it incorporates numerous procedures – making specialized documentation, getting industry confirmations and timestamps and quality checks all necessary – without factoring in any potential human error incurred along the way. An IoT controlled blockchain-based framework helps in resource provenance, and in this way improves transparency for the members of the value chain. The data accumulated from the IoT sensors (when incorporated into the blockchain), also guarantees that no holes in resource requisition has occurred as development of merchandise across the supply chain is permanently recorded on blockchain.

Another significant benefit of utilizing blockchain in manufacturing is that not at all like the current supply chain ecosystem, which is directed by data experts for the confirmation of records, blockchain gives a decentralized stage where data can be acquired by each member of the supply chain. Since authenticity is demonstrated, and data gets permanently recorded as an item moves across the supply chain, mediators could be dispensed with as they increase complexity, incite deferrals, and increase costs.

In the financing of invoices, blockchain offers significant benefits here, too. Invoices have over time become a significant part of expanded supply chain money costs because of the dangers related to and the persistence required to lessen the expenses. This fundamentally occurs because of an absence of transparency among the members of the supply chain including makers, providers, backup plans, account suppliers, etc. Blockchain can be utilized for tokenization of solicitations, which forestalls numerous financing issues as well as guaranteed cost reserve funds. This happens because each receipt that is circulated across the system is timestamped with hashes and is given a unique identifier.

More funds can be acquired by eliminating the inefficient obtainment of items. This inefficiency can occur because of complex supply chain forms that open an association to dangers and undesirable costs. With a Blockchain fueled arrangement set up, manufacturing organizations can smooth out and computerize their supply chain, which accelerates the request and handling of installment for improved income and gainfulness.

One more issue that torments the present business ecosystem is the absence of transparency in preparation of payments. Likewise, the nearness of numerous gatherings engaged with confirming and sending payment brings about postponed installment to manufacturers. Blockchains' keen agreement usefulness automates the payment procedure along these lines guaranteeing speedier and ensured income to the manufacturing providers.

How to Use Blockchain for Manufacturing

The manufacturing industry is a noteworthy component of worldwide GDP, and that is especially evident in America. Manufacturers were answerable for $2.33 trillion to the United States, what could be compared to 11.7% of the country's monetary yield. Moreover, 1 dollar in manufacturing yield contributes generally $1.89 to business development in related divisions. Also, with 12.75 million employments sustained by the US manufacturing segment, it is noteworthy all by itself for keeping business and the national economy humming along.

In the same way as other areas, however, manufacturing's apparent health isn't really demonstrative of future achievement. As indicated by Deloitte, the business will call for 3.5 million new openings throughout the following decade to sustain its development direction, however, roughly 2 million won't be filled because of an absence of talent in the workforce. Supply chains become perpetually confused and trapped as the economy keeps on globalizing, and an absence of aptitudes in the division will just make dealing with those supply chains an undeniably costly and headache-inducing task.

On the off chance that representatives aren't thrown a bone and skillful substitutions don't keep on emerging, this will without a doubt become one of the main concerns regarding the future of manufacturing. This is the reason some are anticipating the blockchain as an answer for streamlining supply chain management and ideally maintaining production levels, if not making more noteworthy productivity than businesses achieve today.

Supply Chain Management/Auditing

Seventy-eight percent of supply chain directors stress over supply chain disturbances, and uneasiness can be especially high in manufacturing, a division which has an outsized dependence on raw materials. It's easy to understand why they are nervous; somewhere in the range of 2014 and 2017, supply chain waste and misuse extortion chance spiked from 25.2% to 35%. For the third year out of four, Deloitte announced that purchaser and industrial item experts detailed the highest level of supply chain maltreatment of any industry, with 39% of respondents revealing at any rate one instance of extortion in the earlier year.

Manufacturers have focused on innovation, including blockchain, to limit supply chain interruption and suppress their supply chain-related anxiety. By 2020, an expected 60% of significant manufacturers will be dependent on computerized stages, which will be answerable for supporting capacities that are directly accountable for 30% of their income. Also, by 2021 a variety of new advancements will be inserted in the manufacturing segment, with 20% of the top manufacturers relying upon a mix of AI, IoT, psychological frameworks, and the blockchain. Trust assumes too huge a role in manufacturing supply chains, yet blockchain could change all of this. Organizations are attempting to consolidate frameworks through which all members on a supply chain add to and update a solitary record. These frameworks will permit manufacturers to curtail item misfortunes and give an extraordinary proportion of provenance to the individuals who they pass the completed item along to. It will also assume a significant job in administrative consistence, which has increased in significance since the advent of the Drug Supply Chain Security Act and the Food Safety Modernization Act.

Sharing and Compensating 3D Printing Designs

Additive manufacturing, otherwise called 3D printing, still can't seem to achieve mainstream appropriation, however, business prospects are going the right way. A little more than 500,000 work area 3D printers have been sold so far in 2018, with these side interest level machines filling in as a sign that more individuals are trying things out with additive manufacturing. This speaks to 52% year-over-year development, a pace more prominent than the 38% development recorded in 2017. Considering present conditions, 1.5 million 3D printers will be sold in 2020, however, these patterns will fluctuate in general.

All things considered, despite everything, the business faces a few obstacles. At the present time, 28% of additive manufacturers use the innovation to hasten product development, while just 16% utilize 3D printing to offer customized products. This speaks to a huge, missed opportunity, as the potential commercial center for low-level additive manufacturers to structure and make exclusive plans could be significant. Another issue close by is the treatment of 3D-printed weapons. They are an intriguing issue, spurned by the disclosure that 1,000 individuals downloaded plans for 3D-printed AR-15s when they were made available by an organization called Defense Distributed.

The capacity to give a protected stage whereupon 3D-printing plans and guidelines could be bought or shared between parties for nothing or at a truly moderate cost – with a proportion of vital oversight as a precursor – is one of the blockchain's guarantees for the innovation. Such a commercial center would provide 3D manufacturing originators a paying crowd to sell their structures as well. Since the blockchain has demonstrated a solid match for taking care of budgetary transactions, it would be fit for putting away immutable, irreplicable structures, also encouraging the real deal and execution of those plans.

Lowering Barriers to Entry for Smaller Manufacturers

Reestablished love for the American manufacturing area has opened new doors for smaller manufacturers to gain a beneficial and dependable balance in the local market. The United States' Purchasing Managers Index (PMI), a composite file brought about by J.P. Morgan that gauges the quality of the manufacturing sector, hit a seven-year high that was set in December 2017. As indicated by CNBC, there were 327,000 new openings made in the manufacturing sector between July 2017 and July 2018, the most in any year since April 1995.

Those new openings were a manifestation of more prominent yield by manufacturers, who totaled $6 trillion in net yield a year ago. Eighteen thousand employments were included in September, a milestone that opens doors for people and new organizations. Manufacturers, buying associations, providers, and procurement brokers, all in all make up the stray pieces keeping the wider manufacturing industry chugging along, and inefficiencies in these areas, alongside the recently discovered yield recovery, imply that there are splits that trendsetters can fill, exploiting a solid business atmosphere.

Using the blockchain is one approach to make an incentive for a business trying to make their name in manufacturing. An announced 58% of manufacturing organizations used blockchain innovation in 2017. The individuals who use it astutely – regardless of whether it is in supply chain, order tracking, maintenance, somewhere else, or the entirety of the above mentioned – may gain the upper hand they need to surpass the big dogs of the manufacturing business.

Ensuring the Validity of Transactions/Reducing Systemic Failures

Manufacturing isn't resistant to data breaches, and these breaches take numerous structures. Under Armor, one of the biggest athletic attire manufacturers on Earth, reported in May that its MyFitnessPal application had been penetrated by unknown groups, acquiring usernames, emails, and the passwords of up to 150 million clients. Under Armor shares dropped by 3.8% therefore, and a claim was recorded against the organization in June.

This is only one case of an industry-wide, and even cross-industry pattern toward data hacking. Manufacturing, so dependent upon supply chains, might be especially vulnerable, as 39% of officials overviewed as a feature of a Deloitte evaluation announced being the victims of data breaches in the past a year. Of that 39%, 38% detailed losing between $1 million and $10 million; the programmers are going for the most significant stores of data and hitting them hard. The most widely recognized types of data taken from manufacturers is close to home, personal data (32%), organization privileged insights/restrictive data (30%), and individual qualifications (24%).

The magnificence of the blockchain is that it requires the endorsement of all gatherings in a single chain to favor data changes to the record. While this may sound lumbering and cumbersome, it is the mainstay of blockchain security, as it spreads the potential vulnerabilities from a single passageway across the whole system. Since manufacturing requires close consistent correspondence among providers, and a single data breach could compromise the activities of each gathering, this degree of security could prevent extortion, avoiding both minor and disastrous frameworks failures.

Improving Trust in Products through Public Data

As indicated by one estimate, the expense of extortion (all inclusive) in the manufacturing sector is $3.7 trillion, however, that figure could rise as hackers get increasingly skilled and sophisticated. As indicated by a similar report, the average expense of extortion for singular manufacturers is $194,000, which would qualify as a noteworthy hit to any organization's income sheet. Corruption, which artificially drives up the expense of working, was an issue for almost half of the manufacturers reviewed. Billing scams, also the aftereffect of poor or ineffectual oversight and bookkeeping frameworks, influenced about 33% of those surveyed.

Extortion in the assembling and shipment of food and consumable items is especially ruinous, and can result in health risks for consumers, even death. In America, one organization that scours worldwide supply chains for proof of extortion collaborates with examples of misrepresentation in about 70% of the cases investigated. In China, that figure is nearer to 100%.

Manufacturers are exposed to broad parts-certification procedures, and there's no reason why shoppers shouldn't be made privy to such data. The blockchain's decentralized record innovation could permit this data to be shared, yet not traded off or modified. This data regarding supply chain provenance could be accessed very quickly, which is important when an item is as delicate as food or as expensive as a supply of raw materials from abroad. Eventually, manufacturers could set up their credibility as dependable, ethical providers of products and services, thus gathering more grounded client faithfulness.

Authentication of IoT Devices in Manufacturing

The IoT – the many associated gadgets and sensors that permit big data to be gathered – is affecting most enterprises, and manufacturing is far from a special case. Indeed, manufacturers depend more intensely than most on using calculated data to lower inefficiency and raise benefits. This is represented by the way that, somewhere between 2016 and 2017, IoT arranged associations in manufacturing developed by 84%; the second-place growth industry, energy, saw just a 41% expansion.

IDC has anticipated that by 2019, 75% of enormous manufacturers will have refreshed their activities with IoT gadgets to alleviate hazards and accelerate the time it takes to offer items for sale to the public. That is a great figure, particularly considering Verizon's finding that some 73% of all administrators are at present looking into or sending IoT arrangements. Again, these figures uncover how disproportionately critical the IoT is and will keep on being in the manufacturing area.

Similar to the case with any IoT arrangement, the integrity of data being gathered is as significant as the way that the data is being gathered. Providing a safe system by which IoT gadgets can be validated, observed, and through which data can be safely passed along and quickly shared is the essential use case convergence of blockchain tech and the IoT for manufacturing.

Better Tracking of Maintenance Work

"Downtime" in manufacturing, which is frequently because of maintenance issues, is a troublesome expense to ascertain. Truth be told, over 80% of organizations can't determine the genuine true downtime cost (TDC) viably. Unplanned downtime, which is the classification frequently credited to hardware failure, is significantly more exorbitant than foreseen personal time. As per an Aberdeen Research report, 82% of manufacturing organizations have encountered some type of spontaneous personal time in recent years, with that wrinkle in tasks costing as much as $260,000 every hour.

For manufacturers depending upon more established hardware, these work interferences can be increasingly successive and even more expensive to tackle. Truth be told, the maintenance cost distinction between two moderately new production plants fabricated just 10 years separated could be as much as 100%. Also, with numerous assessments anticipating American manufacturing segments (such as the car business) decreasing sooner rather than later, segments truly can't stand to invest significant energy and cash on obsolete maintenance frameworks.

The blockchain gives an interoperable, single-source record that all gatherings (expecting they are taking an interest) on a supply chain can counsel to accomplish continuous updates. Consider when you request a pizza and Domino's gives ongoing updates regarding the request's status. Take this idea and apply it to manufacturing maintenance updates, and you have a framework that is better prepared to distinguish and monitor maintenance progress, eventually utilizing that data to uncover inefficient contractual workers as well as procedures.

Securing Critical Data/Logs

In one year, 87% of manufacturing organizations were influenced by a type of misrepresentation, to a more prominent extent than any other industry division. Vendor or procurement fraud represented 23% of those cases. A later study found that a much higher extent of manufacturers – 91% – had encountered extortion, a sign that the issue not going to solve itself; it's deteriorating.

As per Kroll, which conducted the latter study, a total absence of worldwide oversight over Latin American providers to the worldwide vehicle industry had produced critical liabilities regarding extortion. For another situation, professional sports jerseys were being falsified so well in China that the fake item was indistinct from the genuine one. This instance of stock misrepresentation is one case of a predominant pattern that damages trust in manufacturers and cheats purchasers and providers out of their well-deserved dollars. Absence of oversight, poor recordkeeping frameworks, and different defects in the business' infrastructure came in around $3.7 trillion in losses to the worldwide manufacturing division yearly, incorporating $120,000 in median losses to US manufacturers.

Considering how helpless the manufacturing segment is to extortion, the execution of blockchain innovation to make a permanent, carefully designed record for individuals throughout the manufacturing supply chain will save boundless investment funds.

Local, Direct-to-consumer Platforms

The system of manufacturers and the engineers who they depend upon to give basic parts is densely populated, and most of manufacturing-related entities are small in stature. Of 251,774 firms inside the manufacturing segment in 2015, all except 3,813 were considered "little." And keeping in mind that huge temporary workers take on a corresponding, and frequently excessively enormous, portion of manufacturing supply gets, the individuals who are searching out neighborhood or specific mechanics require clever frameworks to explore their choices.

Regardless of whether a business is attempting to locate the most qualified machine search for each part they require, or is just attempting to locate the best incentive for singular parts across a variety of a few potential providers, the blockchain is permitting engineers and manufacturers to interface on a progressively effective, far reaching system. Startups have tailored the blockchain as a stage that matches manufacturers and organizations to parts providers, permitting buyers to review a few statements and pick the machine shop that best accommodates their financial plan. Production progress can be evaluated continuously, and smart contracts guarantee that no cash is moved until all the prerequisites of the agreement are satisfied.

Production Part Approval Process and Sourcing of Materials

The Production Part Approval Process *(PPAP)* is an 18-component test for guaranteeing that parts meet prerequisites for their individual industry. Although this procedure was first used in the car and aviation enterprises, it has become a staple of other manufacturing divisions. The development of the world economy has made this quality litmus test even more significant, as requests become bigger and imperfections in a single batch of parts convey more significant adverse outcomes.

Worldwide monetary yield is relied upon to hit a development pace of 3.1% in 2018, and quite a bit of that development remains dependent upon the proficiency of global and intercontinental exchange. Through a normal venture of $267 billion in the IoT by the manufacturing business by 2020, innovation will keep on uniting countries' economies, however, the logistics of transportation materials – and guaranteeing their quality before they transport – remain a test.

For each progression of the PPAP, the blockchain can fill in as an interoperable extra closet for fundamental affirmations, permitting manufacturers and providers to have more clear oversight into the tests being performed and their outcomes. There is no report more significant in this procedure than the Part Submission Warrant (PSW), which archives the aggregate aftereffects of the part endorsement process and is a definitive record of how well a section passes certain quality checks. By executing this oversight and making consistency of PPAP tests, the blockchain can contribute essentially to the advancement of manufacturing forms.

What are the Core Benefits of Blockchain in Manufacturing?

Blockchain innovation endeavors to address the issues depicted in the past area through a typical data engineering that allows nonconfiding in gatherings to share data in an increasingly secure way. Blockchains are intended to permanently record transactions, cash transactions as well as data trades, so that the record can't be messed with. Interestingly, incorporated databases can be changed after a passage has been made.

The one-of-a-kind plan of blockchains would thus be able to improve trust among associations, yet additionally include another layer of security and unwavering quality to the supply chain's data framework. By conceding inquiries of trust to a decentralized calculation that no gathering controls, transparency along existing supply chains is guaranteed and, simultaneously, the supply chains become increasingly liquid and dynamic. For makers just as for customers, the gains can be converted into improved recognizability of products and work forms and, at last in more noteworthy proficiency and lower costs.

Blockchain innovation can diminish the need not just for third parties (e.g., banks, escrow operators, attorneys) yet in addition for bookkeeping capacities that measure, limit, or oversee hazard. It can also lessen the requirement for, and cost of, the center chiefs, who presently control such data. Later, they can be supplanted by smart contracts through which trade finance payment terms (e.g., letters of credit) will be consequently overseen and costs, terms, and conditions will be arranged. Digital product memories maintained on the blockchain and associated with approved IoT gadgets along the supply chain will give safe evidence of the whole procedure from manufacturing to quality control. Blockchain-based public key infrastructure (PKI) encryption can secure delicate protected innovation. The advances will empower the formation of alleged "trust manufacturing plants," which speak to decentralized foundations and associations that give trust at a far lower cost than conventional suppliers.

Blockchain can also give the adaptability required to execute "mass customization," the sales driver, which addresses shoppers' issues for exclusive capacities or styles. What's more, mass customization makes an increasingly proficient market condition to effectively create little production runs of exceptional items. The smart contracts referenced above will make it both simpler and quicker for purchasers and vendors to discover and confide in one another and concur on terms. New manufacturing models, for example, 3-D printing or agile manufacturing, dispose of the postponements and expenses of the tooling and production arrangement that once must be spread across huge production runs. The blend of blockchain innovation and 3-D printing allows associations to reconfigure virtual supply chains rapidly and effectively, empower and scale a model of worldwide smaller scale manufacturing. To guarantee better asset use, manufacturing adaptabilities in production timetables can be tokenized and exchanged.

In general blockchain can incredibly facilitate the organization of such disseminated manufacturing esteem chains, as it offers minimal effort, conveyed and guaranteed trustworthiness for contracts, item narratives, and production forms, etc. The innovation additionally empowers the utilization of smart agreements to consequently find the most suitable maker (in light of characteristics, e.g., availability, value, quality, and area) and naturally arrange terms (e.g., value, quality level, and conveyance date). Finally, blockchain empowers the making of secure digital product memories – permanent records of everything from the source of the raw materials utilized, to where and how they were fabricated, to their maintenance and review accounts.

When manufacturing and blockchain are consolidated, these abilities could bring about the accompanying headways:

- Lift advancement and financial improvement by empowering businesspeople even in remote regions to adapt their thoughts
- Cut stock expenses and service times by empowering organizations to print parts on a just-in-time basis
- Automate trade finance processes via smart contracts from inside the supply chain
- Speed the stream (and decrease the expense) of new products
- Make new market openings and advance efficiency by encouraging mass customization of items and smaller production runs
- Monetize local over capacities all around by trading manufacturing adaptabilities

What is the Future Ahead for Blockchain in Manufacturing?

A Capgemini study found that about 15% of manufacturers are either executing blockchain across the board or have pilots in one site; of this group, over 60% state that the innovation has changed the way they team up with others in the supply chain and plan to expand their blockchain speculation by 30% in the following three years. Regardless of whether it's ideal for your business or not, blockchain is certainly an innovation to watch out for.

Blockchain and the factory are moving toward being a superior match. The most recent blockchain conventions look to speed up and improve data security and administration. And, as the innovation rapidly develops, factory tasks progressively require data sharing and coordinated effort among complex systems of organizations and machines. By producing trust and associations inside these perplexing systems, blockchain can assist manufacturers with clearing a few obstacles that have obstructed the full-scale arrangement of other cutting-edge advances and imaginative plans of action. All things considered, while blockchain isn't a panacea, and different databases remain a superior decision for explicit applications, outfitted with a detailed evaluation of plans, focuses, and an organized arrangement of utilization cases, a manufacturer will be very much situated to coordinate the right innovation answer for its most significant business needs.

Further Reading

Artificial Intelligence

https://www.cio.com/article/3309058/5-ways-industrial-ai-is-revolutionizing-manufacturing.html
https://www.asme.org/topics-resources/content/artificial-intelligence-transforms-manufacturing
https://neoteric.eu/blog/10-use-cases-of-ai-in-manufacturing/
https://www.machinedesign.com/automation-iiot/article/21838147/how-to-fit-artificial-
    intelligence-into-manufacturing

https://medium.com/@KNOWARTH/what-is-the-role-of-iot-and-ai-in-manufacturing-industry-84ee5fc62977

https://medium.com/artificial-intelligence-usm-systems/examples-of-artificial-intelligence-in-manufacturing-to-inspire-your-smart-companies-561eeec5068d

https://www.plantautomation-technology.com/articles/the-future-of-artificial-intelligence-in-manufacturing-industries

https://www.jabil.com/blog/artificial-intelligence-in-manufacturing.html

https://www.marketsandmarkets.com/Market-Reports/artificial-intelligence-manufacturing-market-72679105.html

https://bitrefine.group/industries/big-data-manufacturing/93-industries/manufacturing/manufacturing-solutions/255-artificial-intelligence-in-manufacturing-consumption

Blockchain

https://iiot-world.com/connected-industry/benefits-of-the-blockchain-technology-in-manufacturing/

https://www.syncron.com/news/blockchain-can-transform-manufacturing-industry/

https://www.pwc.com/us/en/industrial-products/publications/assets/pwc-blockchain-in-manufacturing.pdf

https://medium.com/@philippsandner/application-of-blockchain-technology-in-the-manufacturing-industry-d03a8ed3ba5e

https://www.cmtc.com/blog/blockchain-what-it-is-and-how-it-can-help-manufacturers

https://www.blockchain-council.org/blockchain/role-of-blockchain-in-the-manufacturing-industry/

https://www.leewayhertz.com/blockchain-manufacturing/

https://www.forbes.com/sites/louiscolumbus/2018/10/28/how-blockchain-can-improve-manufacturing-in-2019/#772987d55db6

https://www.bcg.com/en-in/publications/2019/blockchain-factory-future.aspx

https://www.disruptordaily.com/blockchain-use-cases-manufacturing/

https://www.themanufacturer.com/articles/blockchain-technology-changing-manufacturing-industry/

https://www.researchgate.net/profile/Radmehr_Monfared/publication/308163874_Blockchain_Ready_Manufacturing_Supply_Chain_Using_Distributed_Ledger/links/57fe2dde08ae7275640133b0/Blockchain-Ready-Manufacturing-Supply-Chain-Using-Distributed-Ledger.pdf

https://www.sofocle.com/5-important-ways-in-which-blockchain-is-revolutionizing-the-manufacturing-industry/

Tom James
Chapter 8
Finance and Accounting

Artificial Intelligence

Just as artificial intelligence (AI) has accomplished for each industry, the realm of finance and accounting (F&A) is undergoing great changes. From setting aside time and cash to delivering advanced knowledge, AI-empowered frameworks for F&A are the way finance experts and their organizations will remain competitive and remain on the cutting-edge forefront of technology as workers and clients.

If you could decrease costs by 80% and the time taken to perform errands by 80 or 90%, wouldn't you be interested? As per Accenture Consulting, robotic procedure automation will yield these outcomes for the financial-related administrations industry.

What is AI in F&A?

AI frameworks (models) are groundbreaking and still improving rapidly. They give yields that can be very precise, and at times, far surpassing the capabilities of human endeavors. Be that as it may, they don't emulate human intelligence. We have to perceive the qualities and limits of this distinctive type of intelligence and construct comprehensive analyses of the most ideal ways humans and AIs may collaborate.

Although AI procedures are not new, and the pace of progress is quick, widespread reception in business and accounting is still in its initial phases. To construct a positive vision of things to come, we must build up a profound understanding of how AI can tackle accounting and business issues, the probable difficulties to be expected in future, and the abilities accountants need to work alongside intelligent systems.

Accountants have already seen the introduction of some automation over the years to improve the productivity and quality of their work. But to date no innovation has had the option to trade the requirement for human oversight of information control. To be sure, past versions of AI frameworks have rarely exhibited a human level of dynamism within the constraints of machines.

AI has been an ambition of computer researchers since the 1950s, and it has seen colossal improvement as of late. Instances of AI are as of now an essential piece of many of our online interactions with the world and will turn out to be progressively commonplace in all that we do.

https://doi.org/10.1515/9783110664454-008

These narrow AI frameworks don't imitate human intelligence. In fact one could even question the application of the term "AI" to portray all current AI frameworks. In any case, specific task based narrow AI frameworks already produce results that far surpass the precision and consistency delivered by humans.

In the short to medium term, AI carries numerous open doors for accountants to improve their effectiveness, give more understanding and convey more incentives to organizations. In the long term, AI raises open doors for considerably more extreme changes, as frameworks increasingly assume control over dynamic assignments right now done by humans.

Organizations today are grasping and actualizing new innovations to streamline their business tasks, and one of the activities that is of highest priority on their rundown is accounting. This is on the grounds that AI is providing positive outcomes, for example, expanded profitability, improved precision, and decreased expenses.

With such a significant number of advantages, AI is utilized with increasing frequency for managerial assignments and accounting, bringing about different fundamental changes (see Figure 8.1).

STARTUP FUNDING
2019 sees record funding to AI startups at $26.6B
2014 - 2019 (swipe right to see full data)

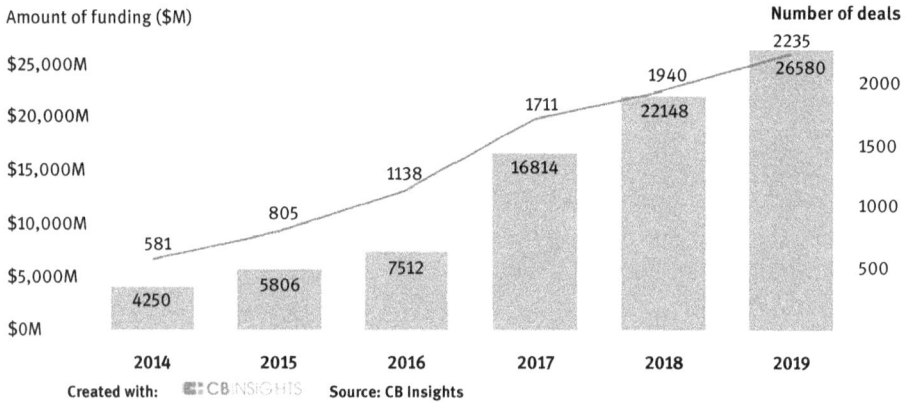

Figure 8.1: Startup funding.
Source: CB Insights.

With AI, all the data taking and preparing is becoming totally computerized and is in this manner, one of the key advantages of AI, providing unparalleled consistency. Thus, the data produced by any assessment report would have guaranteed accuracy and validity and would be created rapidly.

In addition, data can be perceived and arranged from various sources to the correct accounting head. Numerous other devoted assignments that were finished by accountants like the preparing of records, payables, and receivables are effortlessly taken care of by AI. This leads to improved cost management by organizations.

Why is AI F&A Important?

With the capacity to learn and adjust with use, AI is perhaps the hottest topic today. While the AI of today isn't the AI we imagined in our childhoods, the sort of AI that incorporated a robot uprising or a supercomputer plotting our destruction – it is, unmistakably, very useful, entirely competent, and improving rapidly. Since it can process and break down untold measures of data at a rate far faster than any human could, and further empower PCs to settle on choices that were recently saved for human personalities, AI is being utilized in ventures everywhere throughout the world.

This implies that from advanced advertising to F&A, everything without exception is ready for a change upon contact with AI. While AI can't act completely autonomously without any human involvement or info yet, AI is capable of determining patterns from data entered into it with a level of accuracy unmatched by human counterparts. The utility of this tool is particularly useful for businesses in which numbers and data are the core function, for example, in F&A.

Besides the advent of PCs brought to us by the technological revolution, F&A haven't fundamentally changed in the previous hundred or so years. That is until AI came into the image and brought its numerous capacities into play. Accounting firms used to support humans for data preparation and comparable assignments. Now they're looking past a human workforce and into a future one powered by AI.

Yet what are the exact reasons these organizations are considering AI for tasks that used to be up to us alone?

As we discussed before, AI is quickly progressing and will now be able to process data at lightning speeds – a speed so quick that humans can't comprehend the sheer volume of data being processed. Furthermore, because it has AI backing it up, AI can gain from data and reach complex determinations that humans would have neglected or missed. Along comparable lines, since it depends on code and programming to guarantee everything works out as expected, AI can incredibly decrease or even dispense with errors that their human partners would have made.

The thing is, while at the essence of things the entirety of this sounds great, and even though AI can totally reform F&A, there is a continuous discussion with regard to whether it ought to be permitted to do such a thing at all.

The discussion on AI's utilization in F&A encompasses the possibility of uprooted human specialists. From one perspective, machines can play out certain errands superior to humans while not taking a solitary check. On the other hand, these individuals are left jobless – should their vocation be undermined for a superior return on investment (ROI) and main concern?

This is a major and common theme felt not just by accountants and finance workers, but every industry being disrupted by AI. While some consider this to be a sign that we're being supplanted by robots, this isn't completely valid for F&A. Indeed, while a few accountants will lose their positions, a huge number of them will really utilize AI to help reduce their workloads and increase their productivity by discovering new bits of knowledge from data. For instance, as the counseling firm Accenture said in its "detailing the past to architecting the future report," machines and AI really supplement brain power, not supplant it:

"This consistent flood of insightful machines into the finance workforce won't overwhelm humans, however there is a tipping point for finance employments not too far off," Accenture report expressed. "As standard assignments become robotized, finance experts will be opened up to concentrate on greater judgment-serious exercises. A few employments will vanish, others will change, and new jobs will rise."

At the end of the day, rather than supplanting human accountants, AI is assuming control over modestly demanding but highly repetitive assignments so humans can concentrate on more significant things that require human intelligence & problem solving that can't be replicated by machines. As AI assumes control over ever more of these repetitive and tedious obligations, human laborers should refine their aptitudes and figure out how to utilize AI's capacities to further their potential benefit to maximize their own capabilities.

As innovative group Appnova said, "From one perspective, AI and machine learning are helping organizations and advertisers get a progressively significant comprehension of their clients. Algorithm AI is a lot quicker at extricating basic data and can isolate a market into a lot better fragments."

In this manner, as AI penetrates increasingly more of the F&A ventures, an ever-increasing number of errands will be mechanized, prompting improved activities and lower costs. This makes firms that are increasingly profitable and productive, and who can also take on a larger number of customers than the firms who haven't grasped AI.

How to Use AI for F&A

Despite the benefits AI provides, most organizations (80%) haven't utilized AI in their workforce because of uncertainties around the business case or rate of profitability.

This absence of utilization is a developing issue for budgetary staff managing enormous measures of data. In the computerized change time, an ever-increasing number of customers are digitizing forms and expanding the measure of spreadsheets and reports accounting and review experts must break down.

To smooth out procedures and draw from further experiences, firms ought to investigate the present windows of opportunity offered by AI. Here are ways these trend setting innovations can remove the rote work from daily errands.

Streamline Data Entry and Analysis

AI enables finance related management in a company to ensure consistent error free analysis in tasks that are monotonous and tedious. Rather than having budgetary data spread out over numerous records, PDFs, and spreadsheets, machine learning – a part of AI – separates data from receipt pictures, consequently arranging it dependent on spend class, creating organized reports for analysis in one easy format.

These far-reaching reports can give organizations shrewd insights on how to improve budgetary arranging. AI additionally draws further conclusions as it analyzes data over time, which means organizations can gain a far-reaching view into long haul spending examples and accounting staff can give considerably more noteworthy incentives to associations by exhorting customers on ideal spending determinations.

Decrease Extortion

Organization spending has gotten progressively decentralized. Today, workers go through more cash across all the classes, forcing the use of more payment strategies than in any time in recent memory. As budgetary data develops and spreads across extra payment channels, the danger of misrepresentation and predatory actions increase.

As per the Association of Certified Fraud Examiners, the normal association loses 5% percent of its yearly income to inner extortion. Associations and reviewers can regularly just review 10% of cost reports physically, leaving most potential extortion to go undetected.

AI, however, can review up to 100% percent of spending reports. By anticipating examples and recognizing a wide array of oddities and anomalies in budgetary data, AI can assist reviewers in identifying deceitful spending before repayment happens. Since it's adaptable, AI can also effectively deal with convergences in monetary data to a similar degree of precision. Truth be told, analyzing more data makes it more astute and better at handling budgetary misrepresentation (see Figure 8.2).

Enforce Corporate Strategy

AI can be utilized to reduce the time it takes to recognize critical issues in finance data. Purchase orders (POs), worker receipts, travel appointments, and Visa exchanges are naturally examined for purchases made outside of the usual pattern or protocol – empowering inspectors to rapidly correct the mistake and help uphold corporate arrangements to representatives. For instance, AI can naturally recognize representative cost infringement, for example, in denied or individual spending, strange receipts, individual charge card use, refused traders, and travel items.

2019 sees record funding to AI startups at $26.6B

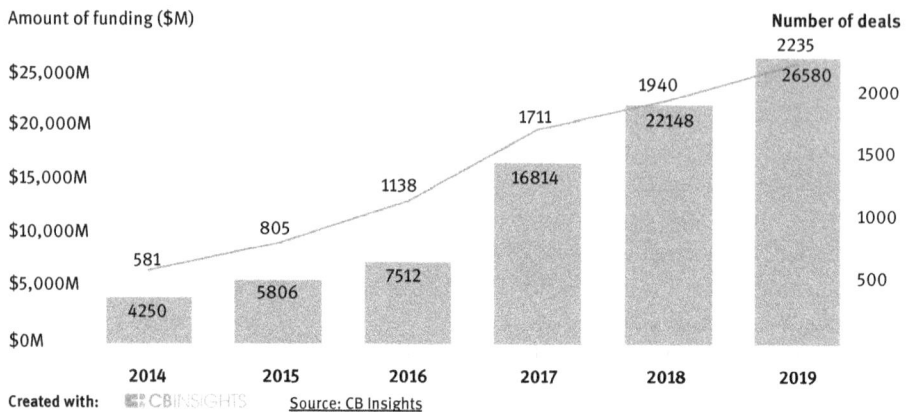

Figure 8.2: AI: Where the money is.
Source: https://venturebeat.com/2020/01/22/cb-insights-ai-startup-funding-hit-new-high-of-26-6-billion-in-2019/, Khari Johnson, January 2020.

With expanded transparency in corporate spending designs, associations can also figure out which arrangements are working for the organization, just as whether certain approach infringement are legitimate. For instance, using sharing economy services could set aside some of the organization cash, recommending an open door for refreshed arrangement systems that better line up with representative habits. Utilizing an AI application to assemble and sum up numbers helps finance supervisors distinguish patterns to make data-driven suggestions for their customer's corporate arrangements.

Finance experts are long overdue for an innovative aide. By utilizing AI-fueled arrangements, they can smooth out data investigations and spotlight on increasingly key capacities for their customers.

Pay/receive Processing

Generally, receipt handling has been one of the most time and cost consuming employments done physically in any firm. Invoices and creditor liabilities worth billions are procedures that mid to enormous size organizations can't evade. In addition, one needs to experience each email, download invoices, and check and concentrate the data physically before finally processing the payments.

In this digital world, the need to computerize receipt preparing has become imperative to improve accounting, increase the volume, achieve handling with zero errors, and maintain seller connections.

Advanced change in F&A has gone to another level, because of AI-based receipt management frameworks that help finance customers in making receipt preparations proficiently. Because of innovation progressions in the finance sector, advanced machines utilizing AI are learning the accounting codes that best suit each receipt.

Supplier Onboarding

Utilizing AI in your onboarding procedures can assist you in arriving at a more extensive arrangement for new clients while expanding income and distinguishing your association from the competition.

The AI-controlled frameworks would now be able to survey the providers by investigating their duty details or financial assessments. AI instruments can set all suppliers in the frameworks without the association of a human. Likewise, they can set the question gateways to get the necessary data.

Procurement

As indicated by an ongoing report directed by Gartner, AI innovations will include notable worth whenever given the right platform, so application pioneers in obtainment need to drive better selection of primary acquisition arrangements.

There is a great deal of desk work included in regard to documenting the association's acquisition and buying techniques. A colossal measure of records should be maintained on the frameworks that are not communicating with one another. As AI-machines process unstructured data utilizing APIs, the acquisition procedure will be mechanized.

Audits

Data investigation is a significant responsibility for auditors. It encourages them to effectively build up the extent of the review and do a risk assessment. Robotic procedure mechanization and audits encourage following records for the review of routine exchanges. Intellectual processing, AI, and prescient investigation help with increasingly mind boggling and nonroutine exchanges that require evaluations and decisions.

AI computerizes numerous errands that were recently done physically, for example, ingesting data. It breaks down 100% of the dataset without requiring a human to make tests, compose contents, or recollect all the guidelines. Key to the eventual fate of review is that AI is changing the meaning of sensible affirmation, by understanding the sum of the record and distinguishing oddities dependent on chance, as opposed to rules.

Digitization in the review procedure has prompted the upgrade of the security level. Each document that is accessed can be tracked by the auditors utilizing a digital tracker. It makes it feasible for auditors to work better, to work more intelligently by testing the advanced records as opposed to investing a lot of energy looking through all the paper archives. It empowers them to utilize their human judgment to dissect a more extensive and more profound arrangement of data and reports. Consequently, the digitization procedure in reviewing gives improved precision of reviews.

AI in accounting and auditing assists with recording each budgetary exchange of the organization. It will assist auditors with becoming progressively effective, in this manner, expanding efficiency and helping their associations to meet their objectives.

Monthly/quarterly Cash Flows

AI enables organizations with monetary management tools to accommodate the association's movement and comprehend their authentic income action and future money prerequisites rapidly and effectively. It shows patterns both in reverse and forward in time.

AI tools, gadgets, or AI applications accelerate your procedures as well as make your money- related procedures precise and secure. The AI-fueled frameworks can gather data from different sources and coordinate that data. The AI-fueled machines make your month to month/quarterly incomes gathered quickly and combine it without any problem.

Expense Management

The AI-fueled frameworks can supplant humans by assuming control over all the dreary errands that were done physically before in this manner sparing a ton of time. They are faster, cheaper than human counterparts, and more proficient. The undertaking of reexamining and finishing costs to affirm that they are agreeable as per the organization's standards is a troublesome one. The manual procedure devours more opportunities in sunken costs and time for your finance group. AI will improve the procedure on the grounds that by eliminating the chance of human error, the chain will be totally advanced, considering a tighter, precise, and perfect audit. AI machines can peruse all receipts, review costs, and furthermore alert the human workforce when a breach has occurred.

AI Chatbots

AI-driven chatbots are created to resolve client inquiries effectively. The inquiries may incorporate the most recent record balance details, explanations, credit bills, record status, etc.

With the assistance of chatbots, your finance group can follow extraordinary numbers of invoices and mechanize the subsequent procedure to guarantee that invoices are paid and closed quickly and efficiently.

AI chatbots can also be utilized to permit workers in different divisions, similar to sales or showcasing, to more successfully report and track operational expenses by submitting receipts legitimately to the bot or by posing basic inquiries like, "Do I have any extraordinary cost reports?" or "When will I be repaid for this cost of doing business?"

AI chatbots even answer regular inquiries from clients and are progressively better equipped for taking care of tier 1 level help. Furthermore, they can respond to inquiries concerning your most recent record adjustments, the due date of certain bills, the status of records, etc.

In this manner, AI helps accountants from numerous points of view. Numerous parts of budgetary administrations include a progression of assignments that become repetitive attributable to the manual approval, appraisal, and confirmation of data. AI allows accounting organizations as well as tech organizations to tackle issues in manners we have never thought of, thanks to the data we are outfitted with.

What are the Core Benefits of AI in F&A?

AI can possibly change the F&A ventures with headways that wipe out monotonous undertakings and free human finance experts to do more complex and increasingly rewarding analyses and directing for their customers. However, associations dither whether to utilize AI in their workforce because of uncertainties around the actual profitability AI can deliver.

A look at how AI has been actualized in a few enterprises from stock trading to hospitals is useful for gauging how effective AI may be for your firm. Google, for example, has singled AI out as the next great technological disruption to occur in the world economy.

One of the main difficulties for the accountants is dealing with the enormous measure of transactions that the clients may need to manage, particularly in the business-to-business (B2B) space where you have hundreds and thousands of clients, a great many invoices, and you need to pursue each exchange. So that's where a lot of time is being spent by groups physically managing massive transactions.

So, when you need to follow such a large number of transactions, tracking each transaction, there is room for innovation to improve the whole process. I predict that by 2025, accounting assignments including charge, finance, reviews, and banking will be completely mechanized utilizing AI-based innovations, which will disturb the accounting business in manners never envisioned and bring both tremendous opportunities and genuine difficulties.

AI vows to help both profitability and the nature of yields while allowing more noteworthy transparency and auditability. Not only will AI give a wide scope of potential outcomes and limit the customary duties of the finance group, it will also save time and furnish accounting experts with a chance to direct crucial research on different viewpoints.

Other than that, AI will effectively figure precise budget summaries. The central idea is that with AI, accounting experts can anticipate future data dependent on past data/records.

So, let us talk about how AI applications and AI administrations can profit finance specialists in achieving their ordinary obligations at a quicker pace. We should begin with how AI complements human thinking.

Machines Imitate the Human Brain

Mechanization, AI chatbots, AI devices, and other AI innovations are assuming a critical role in the finance division. F&A organizations are making them a piece of their business by intensively using these advances.

As indicated by scientists, AI applications and ML applications are affecting the F&A experts and their ordinary occupations. Utilizing AI and ML, finance specialists can improve efficiency and manage new clients. AI can supplant humans from the dreary activity of extricating, arranging, and organizing the data. Be that as it may, those equivalent accountants and auditors working with AI can perform various errands. To begin with, they instruct the AI what data to search for and how to arrange it. At that point they explore oddities. In this manner, AI can take on the monotonous tasks that occupy so much time – data section and compromises – and furthermore wipe out errors, diminishing risk. With the unremarkable undertakings taken care of, accountants will be allowed to take part in increasingly advisory jobs.

Fighting Misrepresentation

With the assistance of AI calculations, payment organizations can examine more data in new and inventive manners to recognize any fraudulent action. Each consumer transaction incorporates remarkably recognizable data. With AI and machine learning, installment organizations can look quickly and effectively through this data past the standard arrangement of elements like time, speed, and amount.

AI helps in adeptly preparing colossal measures of data from various sources, looking out for problematic transactions and relationships, and reports them in a visual tool that in turn, will permit the compliance group to deal with such kinds of dubious cases more adequately.

AI Machines Perform Make Accounting Tasks Easier

As indicated by counseling firm Accenture, "Robotization, minibots, machine learning, and adaptive intelligence subsequent to turning into a piece of the finance group at lightning speed."

AI machines can mechanize accounting systems far and wide. It guarantees operational productivity while lessening costs. As automation is reaching each corner of an organization, the finance related organizations can also be expected to embrace the computerized change that will gain from the innovation advancements. The F&A pioneers who sent AI will be positioned later for computerized changes.

For instance, Xero, an accounting firm, has produced the Find and Recode calculation that computerizes the work and discovers irregular examples by checking code rectifications. Utilizing the calculation, 90% precise outcomes were found while analyzing 50 invoices.

What is the Future Ahead for AI in F&A?

It appears the main obstruction to AI adoption in accounting is getting individuals enthusiastic about the change. Almost 85% of administrators believe that AI will enable their organizations to attain or sustain a competitive advantage as indicated by an investigation from the Boston Consulting Group and MIT Sloan School of Management. Since the CEOs appear to comprehend the significance of AI, it just requires an outlook move from the accounting experts to acknowledge the changes. With some help from AI-empowered frameworks, accountants are free to assemble associations with their customers and convey their expert advice.

To assist accountants with tolerating and ideally grasping the tech expansion to accounting firms, it's vital that the advantages of robotization and AI are imparted to them, that they are furnished with the correct training and any help important to figure out how best to utilize AI to further their potential.

AI and mechanization in F&A are simply beginning. In any case, the innovation is progressively modernizing, and the devices and frameworks available to help accounting are growing at a fast pace. Accountants that oppose these progressions won't have the ability or knowledge needed to keep up with other people who have the benefit of time, cost investment funds, and insight AI can give.

Blockchain

Blockchain is more than a business buzzword. Lately, blockchain innovation has spread past its cryptocurrency roots and is seeing employment by a veritable horde of ventures including supply chain management, healthcare, insurance, government, banking, and land management. The accounting and audit service is no exception. While still a youthful innovation, blockchain and its different applications are showing the possibility to fundamentally affect the profession.

"There's an extremely solid potential for the accounting network to sparkle in this new field. It won't look like what it has truly, however, there will be a job for accounting experts in this field, and somehow or another blockchain innovations and circulated records, specifically, disentangle the work that accountants do. In different manners, they will need to comprehend the new innovation," said Johnny Lee, national practice pioneer for measurable innovation services at Grant Thornton LLP.

Over the most recent couple of years, a developing number of accounting firms have embraced blockchain activities to also comprehend the ramifications of this disruptive innovation – and the endeavors are probably going to gain much more prominence in the years ahead. This is probably a surprise to no one when you consider not just the successful use cases across different ventures, but additionally the way that blockchain is an accounting innovation that consistently lines up with the profession's demands.

Further showing its significance, the American Institute of CPAs and the Wall Street Blockchain Alliance, a philanthropic exchange affiliation advancing the reception of blockchain innovation across worldwide markets, declared in 2017 a joint exertion to progress blockchain innovation for the accounting profession.

"The accounting profession is based on affirmation and verification, and that is the thing that blockchain is about," expressed AICPA president and CEO Barry Melancon, in declaring the joint effort. "This innovation can profoundly affect F&A going ahead, and it's significant we ensure that its reception continues in a manner that is to the greatest advantage of people in general and our money related markets. Our working relationship with the WSBA, joined with our extended worldwide reach through the Association of International Certified Professional Accountants, will help further that objective."

What is Blockchain in F&A?

Blockchain is an accounting innovation. It is worried about the exchange of responsibility for, and maintaining a record of exact money related data. The accounting profession is extensively worried about the estimation and correspondence of money related data, and the analysis of said data. A great part of the profession is worried about ascertaining or estimating rights and commitments over property or arranging how to best assign money related resources. For accountants, utilizing blockchain gives clearness over responsibility for and presence of commitments, and could drastically improve proficiency.

Blockchain can possibly upgrade the accounting profession by lessening the expenses of maintaining and accommodating records and giving total certainty over the proprietorship and history of advantages. Blockchain could assist accountants with gaining lucidity over the available resources and commitments of their associations, and furthermore free resources to focus on arranging and valuation, instead of recordkeeping.

Nearby other robotization patterns, for example, AI, blockchain will prompt increasingly more transactional-level accounting being done – yet not by accountants. Rather, effective accountants will be those that deal with evaluating the genuine monetary understanding of blockchain records, marrying the record to financial reality and valuation. For instance, blockchain may make the presence of an account holder certain, yet its recoverable worth and financial worth are yet debatable. What's more, an asset's ownership may be unquestionable by blockchain records, yet its condition, area, and genuine worth even now should be guaranteed.

By wiping out compromises and giving certainty over transaction history, blockchain could also take into consideration increments in the extent of accounting, bringing more zones into thought that are by and by regarded excessively troublesome or untrustworthy to gauge, for example, the estimation of the data that an organization holds.

Blockchain is a trade innovation incredibly suited for accounting and compromise work. For instance, in due diligence in mergers and acquisitions, dispersed agreement over key figures allows more opportunity to be spent on judgmental territories and advice, and result in a generally quicker and more transparent procedure.

Why is Blockchain F&A Important?

While we will in general associate blockchain with Bitcoin, the effect blockchain innovation can have is significantly more extensive than just the realm of cryptocurrencies. As opposed to organizations keeping and accommodating records of a transaction in their own private databases, the two sides of the transaction can be recorded at the same time in a common record – making it simple to perceive how conventional strategies for invoicing, contracting, payment handling, and other documentation could experience a complete paradigm shift in protocol.

Without precedent in history, business transactions can happen between substances that don't have the foggiest idea or trust in one another, without a critical cost of investment funds in both office and staffing costs.

Like with any developing innovation, some are threatened by blockchain innovation. Some accounting professionals are worried that evaluating professionals could be made bankrupt because of blockchain innovation, making training about the innovation exceedingly significant for accounting professionals. In a like manner, some contend that blockchain will totally change accounting. Others aren't persuaded in any case.

It is imperative to recall that past innovation advancements, for example, ERP frameworks and cloud processing, essentially changed the job of the bookkeeper, as opposed to making the profession obsolete.

As per the *Journal of Accountancy,* the accompanying realities, among others, are essential to remember with respect to developing blockchain innovation:
1. Blockchain is secure and can't be hacked
2. Blockchain data can make new business openings
3. Learning more about blockchain will pay off

How to Use Blockchain for F&A

Blockchain is quickly advancing from promotion to high-esteem innovation with genuine applications in business. In 2017, blockchain started advancing onto the guide of business process services. Presently it is rising in fully operational organizations and upsetting basic business forms identified with purchasing and selling and entering the mainstream as the definitive accounting innovation used to record business transactions.

The natural traits of blockchain advances – appropriated records, decentralized databases, the end of third-party intermediaries, top notch encoded/legally approved transactions. and transparency – meet key prerequisites of F&A tasks. Incorporating blockchain into F&A tasks can increment transactional trust, lessen extortion hazards, lower transaction costs, and hasten preparing times.

Smart Contracts and Smart Assets

A smart contract is a PC program running on a blockchain. The program builds up rules for the agreement and consequently implements the understanding when these standards are met. This allows computer protocols to check and uphold an understanding, which drastically lowers transactional costs identified with coming to, formalizing, and implementing an understanding. The guidelines inside smart contracts characterize smart assets, which are one of a kind virtual tokens that speak to substantial and impalpable resources. Blockchain innovation, which allows these assets for be followed continuously, is upsetting exchange finance, working capital, and supply chain management.

Expedited Processing (for Clearing, Settling and Payments)

Digital records that join blockchain can take into consideration constant settlements by means of the system, which can generate gigantic investment funds from reducing overhead expenses. The present norm for clearing and settlement is three days. Blockchain replaces this standard with close moment settlements, which are ideal for businesses by adding to working capital and decreasing payment overhead expenses and error related postponements. Indeed, even conventional financial frameworks are advancing to coordinate comparative innovation. Some key models incorporate J.P. Morgan's Interbank Information Network (IIN) and SWIFT Global Payments Innovation (GPI).

Digital Identity Management

In certain examples, blockchain might be the answer for moves identified with character management inside business. These difficulties stretch out across a scope of regions, for example, false data, General Data Protection Regulation (GDPR) consistence, data security leaks, fraud, and personality validation. A blockchain arrange takes into consideration complex and thorough governing rules, which guarantee data credibility and secure all gatherings included.

Streamlined procurement processes. Carefully designed smart contracts will consider proficient PO coordination and invoice management. This will dispense with PO approval and endorsement, invoice handling, and the whole backend request-to-receipt forms.

Blockchain will also take into consideration consistent e-invoicing and payments made consequently from the purchaser to a vender through secure encoded channels, making it simple to track and monitor transactions transparently, guaranteeing an audit trail that can be downloaded from the blockchain.

Unquestionable ongoing audit trails of providers' merchandise will lessen creditor liabilities cost and amount errors, eliminating accounts payable discrepancies. The benefits of blockchain driven Smart contracts and mechanized blockchain settlements will dispose of the requirement for unwieldy assignments, for example, in cost report accommodation, review and different undertakings commonly connected with travel and expense (T&E) handling, thus automating T&E processing. The automation of payment processing extends elsewhere, too, for example, in seamless payment processing and order-to-cash transactions.

For example, smart contracts can empower mechanized and precise valuing and discounting. By guaranteeing perfect consistency with regard to transparent transactions by giving a careful audit trail, these agreements also encourage precise receivables, lessening the requirement for manual money applications, deduction, and dispute management.

This is all done efficiently, with the blockchain organizing all record gatherings to be pre-approved, which removes the requirement for an isolated provider ace data and client ace data. Distributed ledgers can diminish time spent on reporting and reconciling while at the same time increasing precision. Blockchain considers nearer coordination of client and provider data, which upgrades controls and encourages planned ongoing auto-balance compromise. Interconnected records through blockchain decrease conditions and mechanize money related handling. The distributed ledger system inside blockchain can also change intercompany forms between inner purchasing and selling elements.

Even though organizations are required to apply accounting strategies determined by accounting guidelines for recording, introduction, and revelation in customary accounting, they nevertheless have discretions over accounting techniques. For example, accounting approaches utilized and accounting assessments and decisions made. Listed organizations just give ordinary fiscal summaries to the market, yet don't promote the accounting techniques for the planning of reports. Even though this institutional game plan could ensure the restrictive data of firms, there are a progression of negative outcomes, too.

Initially, the danger of altering and harming transactions exists whether the firm uses paper-based or electronic-based records. Also, the directors or controlling investors of recorded organizations may complete control or build transactions to augment individual premiums. Since the accounting procedure is obscure, it is extremely hard for outside data clients to discover issues. At long last, regardless of whether there exists outer evaluating, the inspectors will most likely be unable to distinguish all misrepresentation and errors of the firm or might not have the freedom to advise the market regarding the issues found.

The appearance of blockchain innovation gives clever plans to money related accounting and will tremendously affect acknowledgment, estimation, introduction, and divulgence in budgetary accounting, which can decrease blunders in revelation and profit management, in this manner to a great extent improving the nature of data.

Firstly, firms can present source records on the open blockchain, and the open blockchain will naturally create accounting records and budget summaries through smart contracts. Accounting guidelines and presumptions utilized by firms will be reflected in smart contracts, which will be permanently recorded. This procedure in general changes the estimation, introduction, and revelation in monetary accounting.

Secondly, the use of the blockchain innovation in monetary accounting can lessen operational hazard and estimation blunders since budget reports are naturally created by smart contracts. Additionally, the ideal arrangement of accounting data in part diminishes the delay between the age of accounting data and revealing. The transparency and discernibility of accounting blockchain will expand the likelihood of extortion being found and generally increase the cost of forgery and fraudulence. With less chances and greater expenses, the burden of income management will diminish.

Thirdly, utilizing blockchain in monetary accounting implies there will be a huge number of reinforcements once it is posted on the open blockchain and all transactions are obvious to all individuals from the system. This will pave the way toward accounting and announcing progressively transparent and discernible recordkeeping since they are checked and administered by all hubs in the accounting blockchain. Besides, with the use of the blockchain innovation, fiscal summaries can be created in a convenient way, while traditional financial reporting is per annum based, which expands the practicality of data. What's more, more drastically, data clients can even total firms' transactions into fiscal reports whenever without needing to consult anyone else. Moreover, the recognizability of accounting approaches and suspicions in smart contracts will settle on the accounting decisions, making the whole procedure progressively transparent and correspondingly increment the likeness of accounting data.

In total, the appearance of blockchain innovation will tremendously affect estimation, introduction, and revelation in monetary accounting, which lessens mistakes in divulgence and income management, to a great extent improving the subjective attributes of data and moderating the issue of data asymmetry.

What are the Core Benefits of Blockchain in F&A?

Regardless of the beneficial outcomes it could have in the finance business, exploration uncovers that organizations may in any case have trouble executing it. Forbes and Cox's examination indicated that 31% of entrepreneurs state they are as of now uncertain which innovation is the best fit for them. As per a Babson report, 18% of independent companies think that it's hard to incorporate innovation with their present innovation arrangement. Later, as blockchain develops, entrepreneurs could even now confront trouble effectively presenting the innovation.

What Benefits Could Blockchain Bring for F&A?

Blockchain's greatest effect is to wipe out a portion of the ventures' regular difficulties. Here are a portion of the advantages we could see from blockchain applications and their presentation into F&A:

Smart Contracts

– Understandings among purchasers and merchants would now be recorded in PC coded language, before being decentralized and conveyed across a blockchain arrangement.

- Smart contracts help private company finance supervisors make, screen, and follow money related understandings made with merchants and customers. These can be made for any money related transactions that lift income.

Money Related Transparency

- As all data is put away on one open framework, blockchain guarantees transparency between the seller and provider. This removes the possibility for any mistakes or disputes as every transaction allows independent company accountants to identify mistaken data passages as an erroneous section to a block. When input on a two-fold passage framework these mistakes can be hard to distinguish and may mean end of year money related reports are off base.

Bank Reconciliations

- This application assists organizations with redressing any money related blunders with their asset report or bank explanation by coordinating the two together. Private company finance chiefs would have the option to find varying transactions at the source and progressively. Matching up bank articulations and monetary records would diminish the quantity of compromises.

No Commission on Digital Wallets

- Wiping out outsider payments would mean independent ventures no longer need to pay extra commission or intrigue charges when making transactions with merchants or customers. Just as setting aside organizations cash, it would also ensure the security of transactions through the utilization of cryptography.

Improving Financial Data Accuracy

- Blockchain will help guarantee that monetary reports are increasingly exact and secure as it will utilize cryptography and time stamps on its transactions. Along these lines, entrepreneurs will experience a shift in mindset once it's simpler to make reports and screen the money related strength of the organization.

What is the Future Ahead for Blockchain in F&A?

The sectors of accounting worried about transactional confirmation and completing exchange of property rights will be changed by blockchain and smart contracts draw near.

The decrease in the requirement for compromise and dispute management, coupled with the expanded security and certainty around rights and commitments, will permit more noteworthy attention and focus on finding the most proficient method to represent and think about the transactions, and empower a development in what territories can be represented. Numerous current-day accounting division procedures can be enhanced through blockchain and other present-day innovations, for example, in data investigation or AI; this will expand the productivity and estimation of the accounting capacity.

Because of the aforementioned advantages, the range of aptitudes in accounting will change. Some work, for example compromises and provenance confirmation will be diminished or rendered obsolete, while different departments, for example, innovation, advisory, and other worth including exercises will expand. To appropriately review an organization with critical blockchain-based transactions, the focal point of the auditor will move. There is little need to affirm the precision or presence of blockchain transactions with outer sources, however, there is still a lot of regard to pay as to how those transactions are recorded and perceived in the fiscal summaries, and how judgmental components, for example, valuations are chosen. In the long haul, an ever-increasing number of records could move onto blockchains, and auditors and controllers with access would have the option to check transactions continuously and with certainty over the provenance of those transactions.

Accountants will not need to be engineers with detailed information on how blockchain functions. Be that as it may, they should realize how to prompt on blockchain selection and consider the effect of blockchain on their organizations and customers. They additionally should have the option to go about as the scaffold, having educated discussions with the two technologists and business partners. Accountants' abilities should grow to incorporate a comprehension of the guideline highlights and elements of blockchain – for instance, blockchain as of now shows up on the schedule for ICAEW's ACA capability.

Further Reading

Artificial Intelligence

https://bernardmarr.com/default.asp?contentID=1929
https://www.icaew.com/technical/technology/artificial-intelligence/artificial-intelligence-the-
    future-of-accountancy
https://www.accountingtoday.com/opinion/3-ways-accountants-can-implement-ai-today
https://channels.theinnovationenterprise.com/articles/how-artificial-intelligence-is-transforming-
    the-accounting-and-finance-industries
https://www.icas.com/thought-leadership/technology/how-accountancy-and-finance-are-using-
    artificial-intelligence
https://www.acecloudhosting.com/blog/artificial-intelligence-impact-accounting/
https://www.hostbooks.com/us/blog/how-ai-will-impact-the-accounting-and-finance-industry/
https://www.cpacanada.ca/en/business-and-accounting-resources/other-general-business-topics
    /information-management-and-technology/publications/ai-impact-on-accounting-and-finance
https://www.forbes.com/sites/bernardmarr/2018/06/01/the-digital-transformation-of-accounting
    -and-finance-artificial-intelligence-robots-and-chatbots/#19f526f4ad89
https://www.usmsystems.com/ai-in-accounting-finance-industry/

Blockchain

https://www.accountingtoday.com/news/blockchain-unlocking-new-potential#:~:text=Because%
    20blockchain%20provides%20a%20transparent,way%20for%20continuous%20audit%
    20processes.
https://www.icaew.com/technical/technology/blockchain/blockchain-articles/blockchain-and-
    the-accounting-perspective
https://www2.deloitte.com/content/dam/Deloitte/de/Documents/Innovation/Blockchain_A%
    20game-changer%20in%20accounting.pdf
https://www.aithority.com/technology/blockchain/how-will-blockchain-change-the-future-of-
    finance-and-accounting/
https://blogs.dxc.technology/2019/03/07/8-ways-blockchain-will-change-finance-accounting/
http://www.acrn-journals.eu/resources/SI08_2019d.pdf
https://theblockchainland.com/2020/01/30/impacts-blockchain-accounting-industry/
https://www.aicpa.org/content/dam/aicpa/interestareas/frc/assuranceadvisoryservices/downloa
    dabledocuments/blockchain-technology-and-its-potential-impact-on-the-audit-and-
    assurance-profession.pdf
https://www.sage.com/en-us/blog/what-is-blockchain-and-examples-for-the-accounting-
    profession/
https://www.bizjournals.com/dallas/news/2019/01/08/a-simplified-look-at-blockchain-in-
    accounting-and.html
https://papers.ssrn.com/sol3/papers.cfm?abstract_id=3258504

Tom James
Chapter 9
Customer Experience

Artificial Intelligence

We're realizing now that artificial intelligence (AI) is assuming a gigantic role in how organizations work. AI projects and services are changing everything from data assortment and handling in the marketing division to onboarding in the human resource office. While AI and mechanization hold colossal incentives regarding time and cost savings internally, there is another territory wherein AI guarantees considerably greater, increasingly significant returns: customer experience (CX). CX is the foundation of computerized change. Each tech choice we make should come back to this core establishment. With huge development in data, comes opportunity to use the data for AI and AI that can improve ordinary experiences for customers. It's also critical to take note that great AI needs to begin with the correct data combined with sound data science practice or the outcomes can be less than noteworthy.

What is AI in CX?

Organizations everywhere are exploring different avenues regarding AI, machine learning, and advanced analytics based on the conviction that these advances can be utilized to improve the CX. At this moment, numerous organizations are generally centered on utilizing these innovations to robotize work and in this way diminish working expenses. What's more, regardless of whether they understand it or not, that is an unsafe methodology.

It's justifiable that AI is normally and barely observed as an approach to reduce expenses via robotizing manual and information work. Cost-effectiveness is a business basic, presently like never before as radical digitization has permitted contenders to emerge out of the blue, and problematically. In any case, not too many organizations are considering the new openings they ought to make in customer-confronting zones (advertising, sales, services, etc.) – occupations that AI and analytics can't supplant, yet should be used to bolster human workforces.

All things considered, AI and analytics are delivering enormous enhancements in quality and responsiveness via robotizing numerous manual undertakings. About 40% of retailers are actualizing some type of intelligent automation, as per a National Retail league study, and over 80% have decided to do as such by 2025. In any case, improving the CX in many enterprises will necessitate that humans remain included and new customers are drawn in, in new ways. That is the place these new, intelligent

https://doi.org/10.1515/9783110664454-009

technologies can be generally valuable: improving, not replacing, the human face the venture moves in the direction of its customers.

Business' Smart Little Helpers

Organizations that effectively adopt this strategy – utilizing progressed intelligent technologies to upgrade human abilities – utilize a Machine First methodology to change business forms that sway the CX: promoting, sales and post-deal customer services (e.g., contact centers). These organizations have made huge advancements in their customers' everyday experience while expanding income, customer maintenance and bringing down expenses.

Take showcasing. Driving firms have customized offers to customers dependent on what their identity is, the place they are and what they like; dependent on past buying designs and even current conditions, for example, the climate.

For instance, customers that walk into Starbuck's bistro service are recognized by the organization's AI through their cell phones when they enter. The AI furnishes Starbuck's baristas with the customer's requesting history, permitting the baristas to make progressively educated and customized proposals for what new beverage or snack the customer may appreciate that day. In a similar vein, Royal Caribbean International revealed its Ocean Medallion wearable gadgets that permit visitors to open doors and, pay for beverages and food, giving Royal Caribbean's workers more opportunity to react to customer needs and wants. As of late, the journey line divulged on instruments that utilize AI to make customized vacation music recordings for visitors dependent on photographs they submit to an application called SoundSeeker. The AI deciphers the state of mind of the photographs, and matches it with music, making a unique offering for individual vacationers.

In sales, AI-empowered frameworks can give the customer items that would not be self-evident to a retailer's merchandizers. For instance, Walmart is utilizing AI to tailor its stock dependent on store area and its analysis of neighborhood shopping narratives. "AI ensures we have the correct grouping," says Galagher Jeff, Walmart's VP of Operations and Business Analytics. "We need to comprehend what's in this four-foot space [in a store] is directly for Detroit, Kansas, Mississippi, New York." And on its site, Walmart customers are served item proposals dependent on their past buys, similar to its main rival, Amazon.

More astoundingly in China, KFC as of late banded together with search engine Baidu to try different things with facial acknowledgment innovation at one of its KFC eateries. The innovation breaks down a customer's sexual orientation, articulation, and different visuals to give menu suggestions, consolidating data on the customer's past requests.

In every one of these models, intelligent technologies are being utilized to improve the CX by customizing it, and in every one of these models the individuals who serve the customers are engaged, not replaced.

In the customer service region, AI and machine learning frameworks can rapidly direct the most noteworthy customers to the most proficient, suitable individuals to determine customer issues while giving improved understanding to customer-service operators, shortening the time it takes to determine issues.

The models cut across enterprises. At one energy utility company, predictive call routing assesses a call, guides customers to the correct specialist, and advises the operator regarding both the purpose behind the call and the activities important to determine the issue. Swedish Bank SEB utilizes a remote helper to oversee characteristic language discussions, responding to customer inquiries regarding how to open a record or make cross-border payment. The associate (Aida) can ask follow-up inquiries to take care of issues and is modified to investigate the customers manner of speaking (baffled or thankful) to give better, increasingly customized service. In the 30% of situations where Aida can't address an issue, it consequently gives the call to an available, more qualified human call center delegate.

MetLife additionally utilizes AI-empowered voice analytics programming to assist calls by focusing on helping operators better comprehend the mind-set of guests. It encourages them to comprehend their own state of mind by giving input to tell them when they are sounding drained or curt, empowering them to change their tone to give progressively beneficial and humane customer service.

Early adopters are utilizing intelligent innovations in a worldwide and all-encompassing manner. Netflix, for instance, utilizes AI for programming, foreseeing what individuals will need to see. It has supplanted the old model of programming dependent on crowd socioeconomics by crunching colossal volumes of data about what individuals really watch, where. In this manner, it has discovered approaches to aggregate niche viewers, along these lines amplifying content that was once thought reasonable just for niche markets.

Why is AI CX Important?

By 2025, upwards of 95 percent of all customer cooperations will be through channels upheld by artificial intelligence (AI) innovation.   – Microsoft

Customers live in an omnichannel world, yet most endeavors despite everything battle to oversee, gauge, and improve cross-channel ventures. Journey data is saturated with siloed, heritage frameworks and are difficult to reach the groups that require significant insight and knowledge to settle on data-driven choices.

AI can be effectively utilized to give an intelligent, advantageous and educated customer experience (CX) anytime along the customer venture. This will bring about rethought CX and start to finish customer journeys that are incorporated and progressively close to home, with the goal that they feel increasingly normal to customers.

Data experiences are one of the essential devices for CX upgrade. Nonetheless, CX datasets are untidy and the customer practices are confused. The standards are vague, and the achievement rules are vague. CX is the bad dream dataset for an AI engineer.

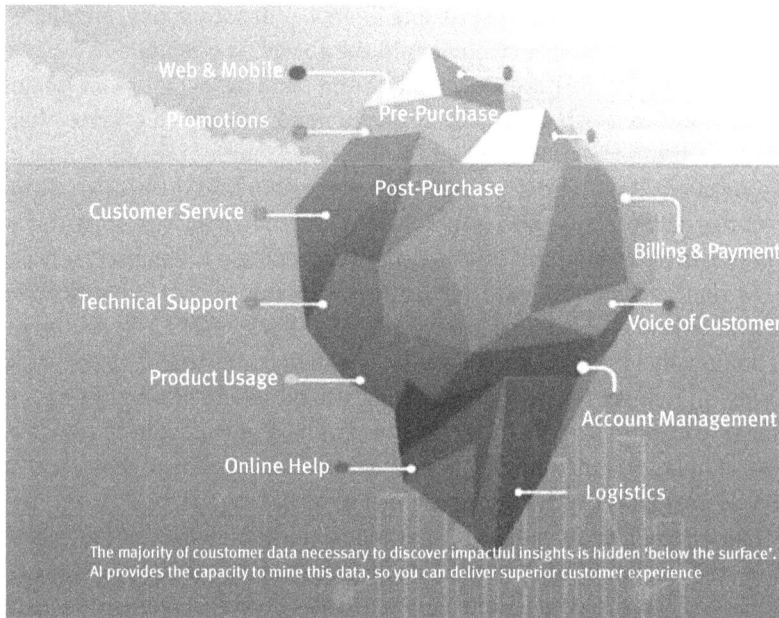

Figure 9.1: AI provides the capacity to mine huge amounts of data and deliver a superior customer experience.
Source: pointillist.com; https://www.pointillist.com/blog/role-of-ai-in-customer-experience/

Simultaneously, this multifaceted nature is exactly the motivation behind why AI can release such a great amount of significant worth across the CX. Salespeople, call center specialists, and workers in other customer-confronting jobs can't be relied on to comprehend a customer's whole history and get their own experiences from it continuously.

Automated frameworks can't be hand-modified with rules to deal with each possible customer history. Conveying a reliable experience across all channels requires discovering designs across a mind-boggling number of data focuses. This is the ideal job for AI in CX. (see Figure 9.1)

The effective use of AI in CX requires three major capacities.

Data Unification

Data unification to make an individual customer see everything they require is an unquestionable requirement for social analytics. AI thrives on data – the more the better.

The new age of data unification instruments makes this overwhelming assignment modest, quick, and generally pain-free. Customer venture analytics stages offer this support for a small amount of the expense of the devoted data services suppliers of yesteryear – in any event, conveying a degree of data combination.

The monotony of arranging many data sources enveloping a huge number of data focuses is currently simply background noise, which AI is well equipped to handle, freeing human hands to work on strategizing.

Real-time Insights Delivery

For AI to affect the CX, bits of knowledge should be passed on at the time through the customer's picked touchpoint. Coordinating with these touchpoints is the way to an in-the-moment commitment.

Most driving software as a service (SaaS) stages have application programming interfaces (APIs) and believe outsider combinations to be a basic segment of their incentive. The world would be a delightful spot if all touchpoint data were available through APIs.

In all actuality, notwithstanding rich SaaS data streams, most endeavors must depend on bunch nearby, home-developed and inheritance touchpoint data sources – item interfaces, payment stages, retail location frameworks, customer care, etc. This reality makes a test for conveying constant knowledge still a custom affair.

Customer journey analytics stages are presently filling this hole with a large group of API choices and advancement packs to convey exhaustive, constant touchpoint incorporation with negligible investment.

Business Context

For a basic isolated interaction, AI can convey results by essentially realizing that an email is an email, and a campaign is a campaign. Our web analytics and customer relationship management (CRM) stages exploit this inherent data aspect. In comprehensive, cross-channel journey analytics, the possibility that touchpoints of a comparative class will be the equivalent across undertakings is an out-of-date idea.

Customer journeys are as unique to singular organizations as fingerprints. Each organization has their own arrangement of touchpoints and an unmistakable technique for utilizing those commitments in their CX.

For AI to convey esteem, it must be given some specific situation. By setting, I mean more than basically assigning a certain connection as an "inbound call" and another as "request satisfaction." AI must know the importance of these occasions in molding customer conduct. That requires a familiarity with both the excursion that these touchpoints assisted with forming, and the key performance indicators (KPIs) that were therefore affected by that customer conduct – regardless of whether identified with income, benefit, customer lifetime esteem, customer fulfillment, or different components driving high-level business performance.

Furnished with that data, AI frameworks can accomplish and more than locate the "following best activity" or the ideal crowd. With the appropriate business setting, an AI can distinguish the main drivers of CX issues and reveal the most prescient, elite, and incessant excursions that customers take after an interaction, or between two interactions.

How to Use AI for CX

AI is no longer a sci-fi dream.

Machines are getting more brilliant and organizations across the world are finding new ways in which they can use AI to altogether improve commitment and CX.

Examination completed by Gartner shows that "in a couple of years from now, 89% of organizations will contend generally on customer experience."

In five years, 85% of shoppers' associations with an organization will be overseen without interfacing with a human being, featuring the development toward a DIY customer service.

On the off chance that CX is the new battle zone, at that point customer service is your most noteworthy safeguard.

Furthermore, with regard to fulfilling customers, the patterns show organizations are done taking on the regular conflict, yet a computerized one. We are now beginning to see the consequences of that. As indicated by Gartner, enterprise utilization of AI became 270% in recent years.

This isn't only a passing trend. AI CX is what's to come.

How AI improves CX

Envision you have an issue with an organization's item, and you call their help center. While you might be hoping to talk with a human, you may connect with a PC from the outset, as an initial advance toward taking care of your concern.

In any case, this isn't the conventional "virtual reaction framework" – where the PC frustratingly requests you repeat yourself again and again.

A core element of AI is that the machine will get customers, paying little mind to differences with accents and tongues, etc.

The collaboration resembles that with a human, posing inquiries to help understand the issues you're having. Critically, it offers you accommodating responses and recommendations, that are given rapidly and precisely.

Smart Email Content Curation

AI can be utilized to better serve your customers in many ways.

Workers regularly spend hours of their working week sending emails, week after week to various customers. The issue is, even with the correct email content, you can't convey a customized email to each and every customer on your rundown. As indicated by an examination by Demand Metric, "80% of advertisers state "customized" content is more viable than "un-customized" content.

This is where AI comes in. Calculations can record a supporter's email, perusing data and site experience to completely see how the individual connects with your content.

This information causes the calculation to identify hyper-important issues and make customized emails.

Dynamic emails can be amassed dependent on:
- Recently read blog entries
- Past collaborations with a site
- Most well-known blog entry at that point
- Beginning associations with marked emails
- All out time spent on a site page

And that's only the tip of the iceberg.
Primary concern:
AI makes it conceivable to send exceptionally customized emails to each customer by analyzing a customer's subjects of intrigue and perusing examples to suggest the most pertinent substance.

AI-helped emails improve commitment. In any case, not all AI-supported projects are fit for gaining from client input. As you assess AI frameworks, be aware of this caveat.

Improved CX

The objective as an organization is to have customer service that isn't only the best, but also unbelievable.

– Sam Walton

AI, as chatbots, has endlessly improved CX. The main points are regarding how well AI can assist operators to provide customized CX and increased operator utility:

1) Personalization: Your customers need personalization when they visit your site or online store. With the assistance of AI, you can offer it to them. Customers can even place requests, or access gadgets with fingerprints or face acknowledgment. AI causes organizations to manufacture an increasingly intelligent, customized CX.

2) Fix issues before they happen: Chatbots are intended to remain one stride ahead, proactively making a consistent experience for the client, and settling issues for customers before they even acknowledge they exist – tending to any kind of issue on the way to purchase confirmation.

3) Smooth out the sales process: When customers need to get something, whether it's closing a sale or getting some information or support, it's critical to make the procedure painless. Live visit delegates can over-confuse things, yet a chatbot planned with AI can smooth out the whole procedure and improve CX.

Primary concern:

The ideal method to utilize AI is to serve your customers better without having to inquire them beforehand. If you can customize your customers experience by means of AI and prescient analytics, it will essentially improve your image picture and upgrade CX.

Intelligent Chatbots

If you've as of late talked online with a customer service delegate, maybe they stayed quiet a few times more than you'd assume from a worker in a conversational field. You may have been talking with a bot for such time.

In case you're new to chatbots or are keen on actualizing one, check our instructive whitepaper on how chatbots help to make a fruitful customer service system, improve customer service, and increase customer commitment.

From well-being to protection to form, chatbots give brilliant customer support. Furthermore, much of the time, they're greater at creating customized content than humans.

Chatbots approach loads of customer-centered data focuses – they can also join area explicit solicitations to effortlessly recognize regular issues, distinguish designs, and foresee what's perturbing a certain client.

This makes them more learned than human customer service agents.

Utilizing Acquire Sales Bot, you can produce leads without any problem. Chatbots have helped increase leads and commitment by 3X after usage. Acquire Chatbots are not restricted to coordinating customer service correspondences either. They can affect customer commitment as well.

These Acquire models show AI-controlled chatbots offering exhortation and tips in the examination stage, giving the chance to another type of substance advertising.

Primary concern:
AI-controlled chatbots are fairly regular nowadays. You can utilize the open door this brings to improve your customer talks with customized content advertising.

Devise intends to utilize AI specialists as proactive counselors for all your online guests, not only for direct customer service correspondences.

Incremental Increases in Productivity

AI-controlled chatbots can proactively engage in discussions with customers, furnishing them with the data they need, or help with the buying procedure. Chatbots explain regular questions and move any inquiries they can't manage to the customer specialist group. The customer support group at that point handles just the customers' inquiries that need their expertise, in this manner expanding efficiency and improving the CX.

Primary concern:
AI chatbots are incredible instruments for expanding profitability and proficiency, assisting with smoothing out the work procedure, improving change rates, and giving better customer service.

AI-driven Customer Insights

Where it would take human beings a colossal amount of time to break down the numbers and understand customers' standards of conduct, AI can do it in a matter of moments.

For instance, Dynamic Yield assists organizations with preferring Sephora, Urban Outfitters, and Under Armor to manufacture noteworthy customer sections with the utilization of a propelled AI motor.

AI calculations utilize billions of data focuses to methodically create customer personas. A portion of these data focuses include:
- Past correspondence
- Geo-specific occasions
- Buying practices
- On location cooperations
- Explorers' review picture source
- Psychographic factors
- Source of referral

And the sky is the limit from there.

Along these lines, AI calculations can:
- Unmistakably distinguish which customer sections ought to be included and expelled from campaigns.
- Appropriately coordinate customers to the items they're bound to utilize.
- Maintain a strategic distance from certain stocks, to avoid them being promoted to purchasers who continually return items of a similar ilk.

Primary concern:
AI empowers you to show the most pertinent substance, or items, in view of how clients recently cooperated with you on your site or by means of the delivery division.

What are the Core Benefits of AI in CX?

Since we understand how to effectively apply AI in CX, let's dig into a portion of those applications to perceive how AI is improving different parts of CX by bringing together data, giving bits of knowledge continuously, and combining this all in a basic business setting.

Customer Service Gets a Gigantic Makeover

AI's greatest effect without a doubt will be to change customer service by making it mechanized, quick and bother free. As I recently referenced, salespeople, call center specialists and workers in other customer service jobs can't be expected to ingest and comprehend a customer's whole history preceding every discussion. Be that as it may, AI is currently making it conceivable and viable as a routine practice.

Here's the way AI applications are giving customer service a makeover:

Chatbots

Chatbots are AI-based discussion operators that are being utilized in a wide range of customer-commitment situations. They are intended to reproduce human communications and give quick, customized reactions 24/7. This disposes of disappointing postponements and mistakes in customer service, especially when taking care of customer complaints.

Remote Helpers

Remote helpers use AI to obey orders or answer questions. Online retailer Spring was one of the first to begin utilizing Facebook's Messenger bot store to offer an individual shopping colleague. It enables customers to discover what they are searching for by drawing them in while in basic discussions.

Prescient Personalization – Going from One-click to Zero-clicks

AI is helping organizations make experiences that normally resonate with purchasers' daily existences.

Buyers will no longer change their example of correspondence while collaborating with brands to fulfill their requirements. Intelligent forecast and customization will cause customers to feel as though every item or brand experience was tailored only for them.

Organizations will have the option to survey singular customer inventories and buyer practices to anticipate and convey products to homes before they even acknowledge they are coming up short. Self-driving vehicles will utilize their insight into favored courses and in-vehicle entertainment attracted from past conduct to enhance daily drives and long excursions. In any event, requesting assistance will get simpler as AI imbued with feelings will make CX associations smoother and smoothed out across channels.

AI-empowered Customer Analytics Discovers High-impact Customer Insights

Ideal CX is accomplished when a business regains a customer and treats them with consideration, regard, and thought throughout their one-of-a-kind customer experience.

Mining experiences across billions of unique customer ventures utilizing conventional analytics techniques and devices is a difficult procedure.

The intensity of AI-empowered customer venture analytics is such that it can filter through much larger and increasingly complex data spaces and in this manner reveal a lot more business openings – even opportunities you weren't aware you should be looking for. Accordingly, you can invest your energy organizing these bits of knowledge as opposed to brute-forcing and analyzing ceaselessly at hidden data.

AI-empowered customer venture analytics finds each relationship in the data that exists (without explicitly being advised to search for it). It can foresee the probability of future practices with a high degree of precision, while at the same time finding the drivers and inhibitors of customer execution.

What is the Future Ahead for AI in CX?

Buyers today have more decisions available to them than any time in recent memory. They're progressively engaged, and they have a lot higher standards of the associations that they work with. This is the experience economy where the greatest differentiator for progress is not about having the best item or the most minimal cost – it's everything about the CX.

Contemporary customers compare items and services and the best service they get – whether from any organization or individual – is the one they remember and return to. That is the reason we're seeing industry disrupters, such as Netflix, Uber, and Airbnb, driving associations to embrace new plans of action and carefully change themselves to meet changing customer desires.

To convey the customized and important experiences that the present shoppers have generally expected, brands need to process and investigate the immense measures of data now available to them. What's more, they should follow up on the bits of knowledge in a convenient and savvy approach to affect CX while additionally overseeing expenses and resources.

It's not surprising then that associations are progressively looking to AI to help address this test and make increasingly important CXs.

Customer venture mapping and streamlining is a typical test in the present omni-channel condition. Advertisers need to manage customers along the way with the right "next best activity" content message or offer anytime. In any case, conventional advertising robotization and excursion coordination arrangements are reaching a stopping point with the numerous stages and approaches in any single customer venture, and the various activities, substance, messages, or offers to choose from. The scale and multifaceted nature of this test is an ideal open door for the utilization of AI analysis, like self-reinforcing learning.

Reinforcement learning is a sort of AI, and at its center is the idea that the ideal conduct or activity is strengthened by a positive prize, which allows the calculation to rapidly learn on its own.

Here's an analogy for reinforcement learning: Think of a little child figuring out how to walk. On the first attempt, she may make a major stride and fall over. On her next endeavor, she changes her progression, moderating her steps to check whether that is the key to remaining upright. If this works, she attempts another little advance. Thus, the baby keeps learning and changing until she can walk with certainty. Remaining upright is the prize that enables the little child to arrive at their objective.

Reinforcement learning removes the manual mystery from showcasing and enhances the customer venture by constantly searching for the following best activity to convey the best results. It consistently gives various activities to work at uncovering the approach that will convey the best result in the long haul. In time, the framework realizes which activity will convey the best result – yet from time to time it plays out an irregular activity just to be certain that the model is still relevant and optimum.

This is an energizing step forward for advertisers looking for the sacred goal of customer venture enhancement and guaranteeing the next best activity across each touchpoint. What's more, it's only one case of how AI is improving CX.

Blockchain

What is Blockchain in CX?

Blockchain has different applications for the eventual fate of computing – many which we have not realized yet. Predicting blockchain's future resembles endeavoring to guess how impactful the cell phone innovation would be upon the arrival of the main iPhone's release. Despite the uncertainty, there are massive ventures in progress that consolidate this innovation into existing and new organization IT infrastructure and others being characterized to integrate blockchain into the universe of business applications – and to be specific, in CX.

One of blockchain's key features is its capacity to improve business transparency. Since it relies upon the transparency of moving data, this element can be utilized to cultivate trust among shoppers (for instance, an organization possessed gateway that shows all blockchain action related to a customer, which the customer can see whenever to perceive how their business relations stand). This can make expanded brand dependability, and better CX due to this expansion in trust.

A huge potential application for CX applications is to change the underpinnings of the way finances are dealt with in CX applications. Rather than requiring a finished request to experience an independent records receivable instrument and hazard the security worries of that connection of data, the application could essentially utilize blockchain to affirm a request/payment has been finished and can move the business procedure along not long after affirmation is received. This could also decrease the measure of human capital required to figure out and check these sorts of transactions.

Lastly, the idea of an open circulated record and its suggestions on CRM is presumably one of the most noticeable disruptions we could see. A distributed ledger utilized in CRM could permit brisk existing data coordinating and convergence, alongside data respectability watches that occur with each block age that happens (which, on existing blockchains, can occur as often as a few of moments separated).

At present the monetary industries are broadly utilizing blockchain, it is simply a matter of time before associations across businesses begin putting resources into this rising innovation as a way to improve their CX, dispose of redundant and manual errands, lower expenses, and increase efficiency. Above all, blockchain or distributed ledger, is one of the most powerful technologies that can possibly change both back-office and customer confronting capacities, by proposing a revolutionary new way in which data is shared. In the blink of an eye, blockchain is poised to spread throughout our other technological endeavors and processes, and become a fundamental piece of our everyday exercises.

Why is Blockchain CX Important?

Blockchain has been most associated with the cryptocurrency, Bitcoin. Bitcoin is a virtual resource situated as an option in contrast to dollars or gold. Regardless of its abrupt fame as of late, Bitcoin remains to a great extent unregulated and unpredictable, with just a couple of legislative elements presently keeping an eye on it.

Blockchain, however, is an altogether different story.

Blockchain, which is the innovation that supports Bitcoin, is incredibly adaptable and can be applied across most businesses and verticals. It is a system for putting away and trading data without the need to include a unified executive. Rather than putting away data in organization possessed servers where they could be abused/bargained with, a blockchain fragments data of any sort – contracts, financial transactions, content, individual data, etc. – into blocks. Blocks are put away on shared systems, where they are checked.

This implies that you could hypothetically transfer a computerized promotion and naturally pay the distributer, without including a mediator motor. Or on the other hand, your customers could open a promotional email and get an incentive for opening it, without the email customer having the option to claim an offer.

As per an investigation by Never Stop Marketing Research and Brave Software, blockchain use in Martech has developed by 1,218% in a year and a half since Q3 in 2017. "Much the same as the Internet, versatile, and social, blockchain innovation will drastically affect the jobs, obligations, and accountabilities for advertisers everywhere ventures. The unstable development in contributions is evidence that numerous parts are ready for disturbance, paying little mind to where crypto resource costs are," said Jeremy Epstein, CEO of Never Stop Marketing.

Aside from its sheer usability, which certainly impacts CX, blockchain is moreover:

Unchanging: Blocks once put away on the system can't be changed and must be added to – this limits the potential of extortion.

Anonymous: Data put away on blocks can't be followed back to its source; you could draw experiences from customer data without any singular individual's security or privacy being violated.

Thus, associations are anxious to receive blockchain innovation to change experiences and reinforce customer connections.

How to Use Blockchain for CX

Organizations of each sort of hold records which record the moving of things started at from one spot then moved onto the next, regardless of whether its cash, items, or services that are changing hands. For instance, CRMs exist to record details of customers' characters and their responsibility for services.

Presently envision if the entirety of the transactional data your organization holds wasn't situated within your business – envision it existed in an outer, decentralized way, on the blockchain. Abruptly, there's a plethora of additional opportunities for customers, and colossal ramifications for organizations.

Here are some customary procedures that customer service capacities perform now.

Sending and Receiving Payments

Bitcoin and different digital currencies utilize the blockchain to send cash starting with one individual then onto the next. It's a protected and transparent framework that works with no requirement for a national bank, permitting aliens to execute deals without requiring an outsider to supervise the transaction.

Our cutting-edge banking frameworks are not great. Clearing and personality checking requires some serious energy. Worldwide payments can take quite a while and as a rule accompany high charges. Customers who are hindered or crippled might not have a financial balance or have the option to get to a bank.

Payments made through blockchain innovation could remove these banking-related issues, letting cash move uninhibited among organizations and their customers, without any banks or payment processors expecting to go about as go between. It could slice payment handling times to a matter of minutes (now and again, from days or weeks), and totally change procedures, for example, clearing. Indeed, change is now in progress – Mastercard is opening its own blockchain as an elective payment strategy.

Sending or Receiving Products

The internet of things (IoT) is getting greater, and this innovation paired with blockchain could take into account huge enhancements in how customers pay for and get items.

Customers usually complain when they have paid for an item or service that they haven't received. Those complaining customers are a glimpse of something larger, as with issues regarding dispatch and receipt of items – for each customer who complains, 26 remain quiet. Those 26 customers are opportunities lost for organizations, as instead of bringing up service issues and allowing organizations to enhance their experiences, those customers simply leave.

IBM's Watson IoT blockchain contributions take into consideration merchandise to be followed along each purpose of a flexible chain, with data about the status of a bundle refreshing by means of GPS as it moves, and payments being discharged when each area of a transaction is checked as having been finished easily. Holding this data in the blockchain implies that neither one of the parties needs to demonstrate the conveyance status of a bundle if it roams – the transaction's status is a target truth held inside the blockchain.

Just as it allows organizations to act proactively upon service issues, this implies organizations can gain expanded transparency in their flexible chain since they would no longer need to depend on customer input as a pointer that a procedure hasn't worked effectively. This new insight into service failures could open the potential for service improvement of a type never seen.

In the future, organizations could even have the capacity to take customer cash once an item has been confirmed on the blockchain as received by the customer. This kind of blockchain-encouraged procedure change could be utilized by organizations as a key differentiator, assisting with consoling customers that they won't be in danger of missing out if a bundle gets sidetracked, lost, or stolen.

Smart Contracts

Similarly, IoT and blockchain could reform the transaction process of physical merchandise, there's potential for nonphysical trades to be changed as well. One way this should be possible is through Smart Contracts, encouraged through the blockchain.

Utilizing the blockchain, legally binding commitments can be attached to explicit activities through an "Assuming/Then" model. These activities can trigger when legally binding conditions are checked through the blockchain as having been met or not met.

For instance, envision that a customer signs an agreement with a link firm. The link firm consents to have services available by a particular date. The transaction is held in a smart agreement and recorded on the blockchain. If service isn't conveyed by the predefined date, the customer gets a discount. On the other hand, if service is set up at the very latest before a predetermined date, payment is taken from the customer and the service begins.

Since the transaction is checked openly and can't be changed or tampered with, all gatherings are held to their legally binding commitments and adjustments or actions can naturally be made in the event they are not met.

Genuine pain can be caused to customers when organizations don't keep to their side of a bargain. The burden of verification regularly lies on the customer to pursue, talk about, convince, and battle for compensation. At the point when things turn out badly, cases regularly get referred to outsiders, such as complaints groups (or even purchaser affairs controllers) who are expected to confirm claims of legally binding bad behavior and put circumstances right – a series of tasks that is frequently asset overwhelming and confounding to manage.

In any case, with smart agreements automating the results of legally binding infractions, outsiders and complex procedures become unnecessary. The time and exertion required to put circumstances right can be decreased, while leveling the information unevenness among customers and organizations. It additionally helps organizations with incredible procedures to gain upper hand, particularly when contrasted with organizations who appear to just remain in business from making it prohibitively difficult for their customers to complain.

You may have found out about smart contracts being able to alter our democratic frameworks, which is energizing. Be that as it may, in the realm of ordinary business, smart contracts are as of now being utilized by Barclays Corporate Bank to confirm possession and discharge assets among banks, and there's huge potential for agreements of various sorts to change to a keen model as well.

Customer Record Keeping

We've all heard frightful accounts of organizations who have failed to guard customer data. Regardless of whether it's actually recognizable data, passwords, delicate well-being records, or even data that uncovers political inclinations, organizations and customers wherever are legitimately worried about the security of customer data.

The way things are, customers need to believe that organizations that hold data about them are collecting information in a sensible and proportionate way, which as a rule may not generally be the actual case. Yet each time customers hand over their own data to organizations, it puts them in danger of wholesale fraud.

Organizations like Civic are taking a shot at frameworks to store customer personal data on the blockchain, with that data authenticated in a scrambled structure that customers can reveal as they pick. While the points of interest of this are past the extent of this writing, at last this could imply that in the future, organizations wouldn't have to hold the individual data fundamental for customers to pass data security checks. Organizations wouldn't need to stress over guarding that data, as it wouldn't be stored internally, and customers wouldn't need to stress over extreme or hazardous individual data being held by organizations.

Past the treatment of customer character data, there are opportunities for different kinds of blockchain-based record keeping as well – for instance, in healthcare. Factom means to utilize blockchain to store human services records, for example, hospital expenses and patient-doctor exchanges. The idea of blockchain-based records implies that this data can be at the same time made sure about through cryptography while guaranteeing that records made can never be messed with.

What are the Core Benefits of Blockchain in CX?

Blockchain will affect CXs, however, achievement will rely upon how advertisers influence this innovation to reevaluate existing touchpoints on the customer's excursion. Here are three blockchain tips for you to investigate as this pattern gains force.

1. *Assemble a customer-to-product connect*

Customers need to become familiar with the items they purchase, and an item account can go far in improving changes. For instance, environmentally conscious buyers are bound to pick an item with its production details and features recorded in detail. From cafés to way of life, marks across enterprises are progressively quick to show that they are mindfully sourcing raw materials and labor.

Blockchain can function as a unified archive of item data, putting away data from each progression of your graceful production chain. This data can be imparted to customers, or even be utilized to make a whole campaign to expand transformation rates.

2. *Make loyalty and rewards programs simpler, and less intrusive*

Although faithfulness and prizes programs have been around for a considerable length of time, appropriation rates as of late have been not exactly great. In the United States, just 52.3% of steadfast customers were happy to join the brand's rewards programs in 2018 – and this is a group of people that as of now is already interested and enthusiastic.

Blockchain could totally change how you share rewards and boost customer movement. The email robotization model referenced above is an extraordinary first stage. Basically, connect the substance with a virtual token that is credited to the customer's record on opening. Computerized wallets take this a step further, permitting customers to repay credits and awards whenever the timing is ideal. Truth be told, the adaptability empowered by blockchain is a key effect on CX.

3. *Enable customers with robust self-service capabilities*

In the digital period, self-service has become well known and familiar to many, with more customers picking on the web self-improvement as opposed to going to human administrators for resolutions. That is the reason after-sales services are significantly more basic for CX and can be the most important factor between return visits, or a spurned customer.

Blockchain will help mechanize, bolster transactions, and help store the data on a particular stage. Customers can even access information shared by past clients, with the applicable data safely put away in blocks. In contrast to conventional self-service stages, customers can select paid help in a moment – adding to your incomes and shortening bolster timetables.

What is the Future Ahead for Blockchain in CX?

With purchasers possessing their digital identities, they can legitimately control and get rights to their data. This implies giving full access to perusing, buying, and online life data focuses for regularly visited retailers while restricting access to those that are visited less frequently. Doing so helps assemble closeness and a more grounded relationship with a customer's favored arrangement of brands and weakens more nefarious advertising and information collecting practices. In addition, it can prompt more prominent brand devotion, but also a superior utilization of showcasing expenditure through improved customer focus. This can expand transformation rates as customer trust is worked through a superior, data-rich information base. A subsequent win-win circumstance occurs. Most engaging is the 360-degree perspective on a buyer's transactional history across brands and channels that can be obtained with data possessed legitimately by the client. This is when the analysis of data can be really brought to its greatest use, empowering associations to understand a person's story and upgrade their perspective on the customer's needs.

For instance, envision yourself consuming from a swathe of sustainable items, following greener brands via web-based networking media, and liking a couple of posts focused on sustainability. With a 360-degree perspective on your ongoing practices, the association can comprehend that sustainability is on your radar and your "greener" transactions prevalent across three brands. Given your conscious effort to expend sustainably, you have the alternative to impart this data to the brands you commonly draw from as well as with others of a similar nature, both inside and across businesses. This empowers brands to have perceptiveness and insight on your utilization inclinations and standards of conduct to give you customized proposals on important items and services (e.g., reused dress lines by different brands, occasional food items, and sustainable Airbnb choices).

Just as with any innovation, blockchain remains generally promising, yet huge hindrances remain. Use cases should be more profoundly created to persuade government-sponsored projects and controllers that receiving the innovation will help emphatically drive venture productivity and expenses. Basic industry measures also should be set up.

Nevertheless, if it continues to demonstrate reliability and scalability, blockchain innovation may at last hasten the progress to what the vitality business calls a "distributed world," comprised of both large and small power-generation systems for homes, organizations, and networks.

While there's consistently space for new businesses to move in and disrupt this industry, setup utilities are best positioned to assess and make key wagers on blockchain innovation's expected applications. On the off chance that they can hold onto the opportunity before them, concentrated occupants may end up being the genuine disruptors, introducing an age of decentralized power.

Further Reading

Artificial Intelligence

https://www.gartner.com/smarterwithgartner/improve-customer-experience-with-artificial-
intelligence/#:~:text=In%20marketing%2C%20AI%2Dpowered%20solutions,by%20reducing
%20time%20to%20response.
https://www.pointillist.com/blog/role-of-ai-in-customer-experience/
https://acquire.io/blog/ai-customer-experience/
https://www.forbes.com/sites/danielnewman/2019/04/16/5-ways-ai-is-transforming-the-
customer-experience/#68d6d2ce465a
https://www.technologyreview.com/2020/04/28/1000675/how-ai-is-changing-the-customer-
experience/
https://customerthink.com/redefining-customer-experience-with-artificial-intelligence-ai/
https://www.tcs.com/perspectives/articles/using-advanced-technologies-to-deliver-an-
uncommon-customer-experience-every-day
https://martechseries.com/mts-insights/guest-authors/the-role-of-artificial-intelligence-in-
transforming-customer-experience/
https://www.information-management.com/list/8-ways-to-enhance-the-customer-experience-
using-ai
https://www.startupgrind.com/blog/how-ai-will-shift-customer-experience-to-the-next-level/

Blockchain

https://www.martechadvisor.com/articles/blockchain/how-blockchain-marketing-could-impact-
customer-experience/#:~:text=Empower%20Customers%20With%20Robust%20Self%2DSer
vice%20Capabilities&text=Blockchain%20will%20help%20automate%20support,data%20se
curely%20stored%20in%20blocks.
https://cmo.adobe.com/articles/2017/8/how-blockchain-will-impact-customer-experiences.
html#gs.7v1ej4
https://www.forbesindia.com/blog/technology/how-to-maximise-customer-experience-using-
blockchain/
https://www.tcs.com/content/dam/tcs/pdf/perspectiveapp/How-Blockchain-is-Poised-to-
Revolutionize-Digital-Customer-Experiences.pdf
https://deloitte.wsj.com/cio/2019/02/04/blockchain-tailor-made-for-better-consumer-experience/
https://www.ibm.com/downloads/cas/REGBVG7J
https://www.3i-infotech.com/altiray/potential-blockchain-augment-customer-experience/
https://www.datasciencecentral.com/profiles/blogs/how-is-blockchain-enhancing-the-customer-
experience
https://customerthink.com/how-blockchain-could-transform-the-customer-experience/#:~:text=
But%20blockchain%20has%20enormous%20potential,kinds%20of%20business%2Dcusto
mer%20interactions

Tom James and Kiren Chong-James
Chapter 10
Maritime Innovation

Artificial Intelligence

The shipping industry, including the 60-year-old Eastern Pacific Shipping (EPS) headquartered in Singapore, manages with a 5,000-strong team a diversified fleet of 150 ocean going vessels. It faces challenges and opportunities where digital technology can play a significant role in providing solutions.

Heavily regulated and steeped in tradition, the shipping industry has not changed much over the last few decades, with the last great innovation resulting in significant productivity improvements being the introduction of containers in the 1960s.

Today's shipping industry still operates in many ways unaltered from its fundamental practices in the 1960s. Commercial people on shore charter ships to customers based on a few business models that haven't changed in years, most chartering over a period of time, from port to port for individual voyages. Their method of communication is mostly by phone, chat, or email. There is no electronic marketplace or online exchange. The contracts called "charter parity" are based on templates that haven't changed much since they were introduced as standard contracts in 1905.

Captains on ships are often isolated from the high speed "always-on" internet connections we are used to on shore. They send a daily "noon report" to shore with basic information about speed, fuel consumption, etc. The logbooks they keep are handwritten and on paper. This is not that different from the way things were a hundred years ago.

Reasons that shipping seems so behind many other industries, including consumer facing retail, banking, or aviation, include bandwidth limitations but also the fact that you can't easily experiment (like Google or Facebook can do with "A/B" testing to explore quickly and automatically which features are working better). The risks would just be too high. Everything to do with ships is heavily regulated by so-called classification societies, flag states, and the International Maritime Organization (IMO). Building new ships also takes time and incorporating technology innovations into newly built vessels takes much longer than it does to create a new website or even implement an enterprise resource planning (ERP) system.

New challenges include increasing scrutiny of the carbon emissions contributing to climate change and other emissions like sulphur further contributing to environmental pollution. Other industries like oil and gas have long had to deal with

Technical guidance provided by Claus Nehmzow, Singapore.

https://doi.org/10.1515/9783110664454-010

pressure not only from activists but also investors. While in relative terms transport by sea is more environmentally friendly than other transportation modes, the fact that 80–90 % of goods are transported by ships, means that the absolute greenhouse impact of shipping is still a significant factor contributing to pollution.

Finally shipping carries inherent risks of accidents or disasters. It often represents a harsh environment where workers must wear personal protection equipment (PPE), including hard hats, goggles, gloves, and hearing protection. This makes it challenging to simply transfer consumer technologies. And despite this, accidents happen while handling heavy equipment, divers conduct inspections, or mooring lines snap. Health and safety and seafarers' well-being in general is the highest priority for most shipping companies. And of course, the latest challenge is a global pandemic that started to have severe impact on most countries from March 2020 onward. COVID-19 has brought significant restrictions in terms of travel, physical contacts, and redacted economic activities in most countries, with serious ramifications on trade and logistics. At the time of this writing (summer 2020) it is not clear when a vaccine will be widely deployed around the world.

What is AI in Maritime Innovation?

AI is the new popular innovation in the maritime division. As the shipping business is experiencing a major change at a worldwide level, artificial intelligence (AI) is now poised to streamline the industry by flawlessly coordinating new shipping logistics and communication technology to develop the best possible plan of action within the shipping business. Furthermore, with the assistance of new calculations, the shipping business can completely depend on AI for relieving security hazards and decreasing the expense of activities in general. Additionally, AI can assist the maritime sector in responding to and working with the new guidelines and approaches needed to operate in the new international environment.

This shipping industry has quickly sustained pressure over ecological guidelines, which coupled with worldwide digital innovations, have made digitalization a vital option for the maritime business. Shippers are presently enthusiastic about improvising systems to sustain innovation and discover solutions for their problems.

Amid ever-changing issues in worldwide shipping, AI has risen as one of the more interesting developments. Promising and practical use cases are developing daily, with associations eager to implement AI technology solutions. AI can gather and examine data for the container shipping industry to prepare plans with better probabilities of success.

Mitsui O.S.K. Lines, Ltd. (MOL) declared that the organization and its auxiliary MOL Information Systems, have signed an agreement with Yokohama National University to lead a joint report on the analysis and utilization of big data pertaining to sea shipping. The investigation aims to build up the data analysis abilities of financial and maritime affairs and gauge the sea shipping business sector and deeper costs with the utmost accuracy.

Furthermore, ports and terminals are examining the methods for utilizing big data to coordinate with shipping lines. For example, Kalmar discharged its "Kalmar Insight" apparatus, which assists terminals in converting huge quantities of data into significant, actionable knowledge.

The logistics and shipping industries can obtain significant advantages from AI applications, as AI is generally focused on providing the best capabilities in processing a huge scope of numbers. These figures are broken down and organized from various sources, sorted into useful categories, and afterward utilized as the reason for dynamic action, often with little or no human information analysis required.

With its rough working conditions, remote or disconnected nature, and highly potent dangers, any technology that is executed through AI should have a positive effect by addressing these issues. Mechanical advances must be coordinated to the advantage of sailors, bringing them more security and access to communications and information at sea.

Shipping industry majors like Maersk, Panalpina, and Flexport have started measures to outfit AI to emulate human intelligence, to address a cluster of issues encompassing the maritime sector. The issues at heart are choosing the best elective port, adapting when the first goal is blocked by circumstance and better estimation of the arrival time, to guarantee consistent and reliable coordination.

AI is also being exploited to estimate whether a shipper will leave a booking, or its container will get moved by the transporter and left on the harbor.

AI is set to be a US$16-billion-dollar worldwide market in five years and an ongoing report shows that 84% of organizations consider the use of AI to become a fundamental pillar in the future of all businesses. Most press attention about AI in the maritime sector has focused on Rolls-Royce and their plans to utilize AI in "future remote and self-governing shipping activities," or self-piloting ships.

SailRouter (a cloud application that encourages transport proprietors to reduce fuel utilization and maintenance expenses) and VesselBot (an advanced contracting commercial center for the mass maritime industry) are also doing their part to bring shipping into the 21st century – and take care of its issues by using AI-controlled arrangements.

With innovative advances gripping all kinds of organizations, sooner or later the maritime business should adapt and bring present-day technology into its plan of action. At a crossroads where the business is ready to jump forward with various guidelines and concerns revolving around protected, powerful and environmentally conserving shipping, now is the ideal time for organizations to integrate AI into their work process.

Why is AI Maritime Innovation Important?

The good news for shipping is that we need not wait for machines that can demonstrate hypothetical human intelligence. There are various applications currently being tackled with and experimented on by new companies, ship owners, and logistics suppliers. The most obvious application for AI in shipping is in operating independent, autonomous shipping. However, as a rule, there are many more intriguing applications being developed to improve everything from business forms to journey arrangements and vessel maintenance.

In April 2018, Hong Kong shipping line OOCL announced an agreement with Microsoft's reality class AI research center MSRA. Following a 15-week negotiation with the Microsoft group, they had the option to procure an investment fund of US $10 million a year. They currently plan to spend a year utilizing Microsoft's AI ability to further upgrade their task systems and train a group of 200 AI masters to work with the 1,000 programming engineers previously utilized by OOCL over the globe.

Another U.S based startup, this time on the West Coast, is Maana. They have built up an information platform that empowers mechanical organizations, for example, Shell and Chevron to encode human ability and data from across storehouses into a computational information chart. This mix of data and information is utilized to control AI driven applications that hasten dynamic procedures and work processes. Basically, it guarantees that the right individuals gain permission to access the correct data at the perfect time, which enables them to settle on the correct choices. The Maana information platform has already helped shipping administrators settle on better and quicker port oversight choices. By making a recreation model they had the ability to lessen dynamic time taken for operations teams from 6 hours to 60 seconds.

Another growing concern for vessel administrators around the globe is cybersecurity. Maersk was the first significant shipping line to succumb to a major cyberattack in June 2017 as the NotPetya ransomware virus assumed control over their whole IT framework and pushed the organization to the brink of collapse. It took Maersk 10 days to recover, as their IT group needed to repair or reset 4,000 servers, 45,000 PCs, and 2,500 applications. The cyber assault is assessed to have cost the organization between US$250 million–$300 million. Cambridge based cybersecurity firm DarkTrace has developed an AI platform, which realizes what "typical conduct" looks like inside an association and would then be able to screen and organize traffic to discover inconsistencies and anticipate cyberattacks. Darktrace have provided their protective framework to various digital infrastructures belonging to organizations including H&M International's 1.5 million container logistics system, and BT Global's satellite activities.

Boston-based startup Sea Machines Robotics assembles autonomous control and remote order frameworks to overhaul the activity cycle of business vessels. They have just launched a working ship framework, which can be retrofitted to existing vessels or introduced to new forms for under US$100,000. Sea Machines Robotics as of late declared an agreement with Maersk to introduce AI-controlled situational awareness technology to their new ice-class shipping container vessels. It is the first time that PC vision, LiDAR, and discernment programming will be utilized on board a live vessel to expand and overhaul vessel tasks. Sea Machines Robotics expect that their technology can help vessel administrators diminish their operational expenses by 40% and increase vessel efficiency by 200%.

AI in Naval Combat Systems

The driving cause behind the utilization of AI in maritime operations through data management frameworks is the ability to rapidly collect and respond to dynamic environments, drastically increasing the capabilities of maritime authorities to respond to threats measured in fractions of a second. The act of utilizing computerized auxiliaries for increased safety is certainly not a revolutionary or novel idea in maritime vessels, yet the pivotal quality in maritime battle frameworks is their capacity to change the way order and control of a whole vessel, or even a whole fleet is conducted. AI programming provides command teams the capacity to screen continuous battle circumstances and reasonably adjust the use of maritime resources available to them. These frameworks join equipment and programming (forms) to totally change maritime exercises. Framework designers have endeavored to mirror the planning processes of the human brain and produce machine learning forms that break down immense measures of approaching data from sensor suites, such as satellite imaging and sonar stations. The blend of neural systems and deep learning calculations are then ready to convey a consistent working picture to the order team and help them in understanding the full scope of their choices, improving the quality of their decision-making. These frameworks can even upgrade fleet operability, given resources are associated with one another. The Command, Control, Communications, Computers, Intelligence, Surveillance, and Reconnaissance (C4ISR) situated framework can be associated with individual maritime vessels, independent of their group. Submarines, frigates, aircraft carriers, battleships, unmanned vehicles, would all be able to be furnished independently with such frameworks to increase their capacities. Unmanned resources associated with the framework, with the capacity to transfer back intelligent video analytics will have the option to give over-the-horizon (OTH) planning and vision scope, broadening the view of the fleet in all directions – vital for protecting lives and vessels against high-speed, long-range threats.

As shown in Figure 10.1, Britain's Royal Navy intends to draft AI frameworks on board its ships to identify dangers and survey battle situations more readily. Roke Manor Research's (Roke) "STARTLE" machine situational awareness programming will expand a vessel's current discovery frameworks and settle on educated choices

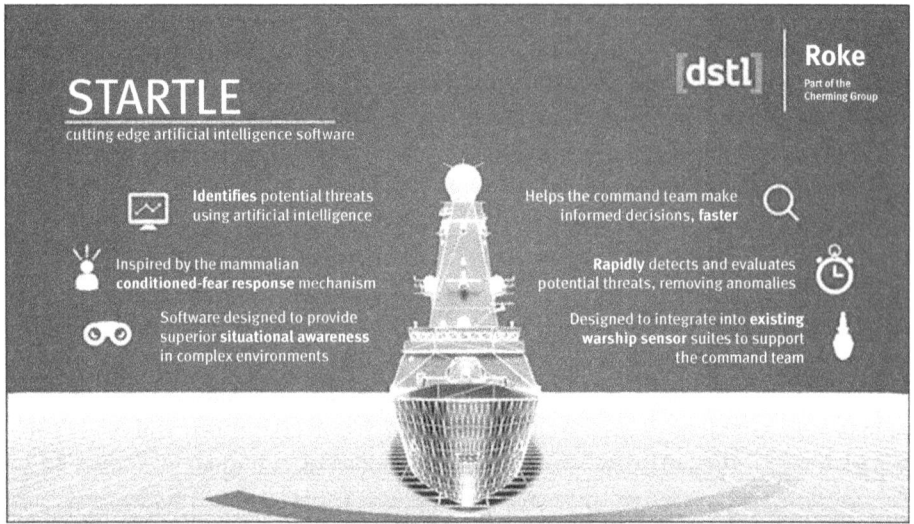

Figure 10.1: AI Framework to identify and prioritize battle situation threats and dangers for human operators.
Source: roke.co.uk

dependent on the data it acquires from those sensors. The AI-based savvy frameworks will signal different frameworks and predict and confirm expected dangers, information they will then pass to the officer in control. These frameworks perceive standards of conduct, run multispecialist-based simulations with deep learning methods, and empower end-clients to improve their maritime domain awareness for fast identification and pursuit of belligerent vessels.

China is also intending to furnish its nuclear submarines with an AI-based decision-support network, one that would reduce the pressure on its submarine leaders. The deep learning calculations of such supportive networks can associate with different sensors and help leaders, "gauge the dangers and advantages of certain battle moves, in any event, proposing moves not considered by the vessel's captain." Subsurface maritime administrators are frequently occupied with dull yet constant operations that require tolerance, aptitude, and navigational mastery, or most of all, the capacity to respond to abrupt changes in circumstances. These frameworks can lessen their physical and mental burdens and enormously support their operational capabilities.

Among private administrators, aviation maker Rolls-Royce has announced its ambition to develop totally self-governing ships, completely autonomous from any human control. The producer has "joined the most recent technology, consolidating a variety of sensors with an AI-controlled PC." The organization has teamed up with Google Cloud and will utilize Google's Cloud Learning Engine to train its AI-based object classification system. This product will fundamentally be utilized for recognition and identification.

As an industry, we are scarcely starting to uncover what's conceivable when you pair shipping and logistics tasks with the capabilities provided by AI. As AI keeps on developing in different ventures, there is a massive opportunity at every level to benefit from this innovation.

How to Use AI for Maritime Innovation

Representing around 90% of world trade, shipping has consistently been considered as the backbone of the worldwide economy (www.oecd.org). This industry, be that as it may, is also notable for being moderate with regard to changes or imaginative methodologies. Be that as it may, the tide is changing. Maritime organizations, who used to depend vigorously on traditional strategies and remained mindful yet hesitant about the adoption of hi-tech advancements, are seeing the advantages of technological progress and are taking activities to adjust to the advanced world.

Among all alternatives, AI gives off an impression of being generally engaging as it could offer answers for how to streamline a large portion of the tasks in seaborne trade. From unmanned vessels, port administrations, report handling to improving security, and lessening impacts on nature, the use of AI can change maritime organizations completely.

Autonomous Ships

It is assessed that over 75% of marine accidents include human error as a factor (www.agcs.allianz.com), for the most part a result of physical exhaustion, poor communication, terrible judgment, or disregard of rules of the sea. Autonomous ships in this way are an answer as to how best to protect people exposed to hazardous or dangerous conditions at sea. A crewless vessel would be furnished with radar, GPS, sensor, camera, satellite, and operated by AI framework, permitting data gathering and analysis in addition to route planning and hazard avoidance during the ship's course. Since team-related costs represent up to 30% of a journey's absolute expense (www.commodity.partners), unmanned vessels are additionally expected to carry remarkable financial benefits to shipping transporters.

The world's first completely autonomous ship created by Rolls-Royce and Finferries was exhibited in 2018. The Mayflower Autonomous Ship utilizing IBM's AI technology begins its transatlantic excursion in September 2020. With the exponential development pace of technology, the future where unmanned vessels dominate the world's waterways appears not too far off.

Digital Ports

As ships are increasing in tonnage, ports are dealing with increasing strain, having to adjust their frameworks to deal with mass cargoes. In the battle to remain competitive, shipping terminals have no other alternative besides endeavoring to be faster, progressively productive, increasingly intelligent. AI upgrades port tasks by means of automation as well as by utilizing constant data. For instance, data is gathered and assembled from different sources to evaluate the waiting time of equipment and conduct instantaneous booking for trucks entering, off-loading, loading, etc. This decreases idle time of offices and guarantees container processing is completed consistently. As of late, numerous ports have successfully taken advantage of the AI opportunity to digitalize their activities. The Port of Rotterdam in the Netherlands has built up an application to foresee vessel arrival times, while Belgium's port of Antwerp has gained significant insight on traffic streams from mobility analysis directed by AI and PC vision.

Virtual Helpers

In December 2019, Maersk––the shipping goliath presented Captain Peter, the virtual helper of its revamped Remote Container Management (RCM) stage (www. maersk.com). The avatar helps clients with information about the transit status of their payload, monitors the container's temperature, humidity, CO_2 levels, and advises if any deviations from the expected conditions are observed.

In the marine business, virtual helpers can help with shipment following, conveyance booking, orders altering, in addition to fast recovery or interpretation of data to help sailors or office representatives in finding solutions or direction in pressing circumstances. It would also have the benefit of improving with time and experience, as it grows familiar with clients' inclinations and how they provide the suitable data. As AI is a quickly developing technology, Captain Peter and his future friends will before long have the option to altogether decrease the association of people in daily vessel operations, opening faculty for more value adding undertakings.

Document Processing

Maritime organizations need to deal with an enormous measure of desk work each day. For example, bill of lading, business receipt, packing list, bank drafts, etc. Physically preparing such paper reports isn't just exorbitant and tedious, is also inclined to result in mistakes. AI arrangements are fit for studying many various structures, reading, checking, and precisely separating terms from reports, in this manner decreasing data passage headcount and most importantly, bringing down the error rate.

Safety Improvement

Improving journey safety is one of the most pressing applications AI could bring to the shipping business. The technology can assist with directing sailors to settle on educated choices by examining data on climate designs, port conditions, crime hot spots and would be adept at recognizing inconsistencies, permitting administrators to take proactive activities to stay away from unexpected stoppages, damages, occurrences, giving a more secure workplace to laborers.

Coupled with the image recognition framework, AI can be utilized to recognize questions in the encompassing territory, give alarms when visibility is poor, and limit marine crashes between enormous vessels and smaller ones. Exploring is additionally simpler and increasingly insightful as the route framework consequently makes most secure courses dependent on past travels recorded, just as it empowers clients to find and track different ships on the water.

Ecologically Solid Methodologies

Even though water transport is by a wide margin the most environmentally friendly approach to move merchandise (new.abb.com), the marine business nevertheless aims to further lessen its effect in the years to accompany progressively strict ecological guidelines and changing moral imperatives. AI can consider different variables to anticipate the ideal course, in this manner decreasing fuel utilization and carbon discharges. A large portion of the autonomous ships are right now intended to be completely electric or to get power from solar power and wind power, which will certainly have positive effects on the planet.

The adoption of AI in the marine industry has been very modest compared with other industries, despite the advantages this technology has offered in present cases. In any case, it is simply a matter of time before shipping organizations think about the appropriation of innovative headways as fundamental to competitiveness and incorporate AI into their work processes.

What are the Core Benefits of AI in Maritime Innovation?

Worldwide digital dangers alongside sustained pressure over ecological guidelines have consistently been a test for the shipping business, which has resulted in digitization being a vital option for the maritime business. Everywhere throughout the world, significant shipping ventures have been enthusiastic about improvising systems to sustain innovation and discover answers for these worries (see Figure 10.2).

When it comes to worldwide shipping, AI has risen as one of the foremost technologies that presents viable use cases, which associations are adjusting in their hierarchical work schedule. In any case, while most of these technology usages are in the theoretical stage, to provide business value and utility will require some initial investment.

AI and automation will come to assume an increasingly critical role in the shipping business as more and more organizations are having incredible success with AI, mixing great machine-human communication to form a brilliant, coordinated logistics effort.

How Artificial Intelligence Plays a Role in Maritime [Pros vs. Cons]

Pros of Artificial Intelligence	Cons of Artificial Intelligence
Advanced analytics	Poor quality of data
Automated equipment/processes	Lack of stable information
Safety/improved security	Fear of job replacement
Route optimization	Lack of a clear strategy
Performance forecasting	Transforming the business is a long process
Cost reductions	
Optimizing maintenance	

Figure 10.2: How AI plays a role in maritime (pros vs. cons).
Source: adv-ploymer.com; https://www.adv-polymer.com/blog/artificial-intelligence-in-shipping

Retail shipping channels are exploiting AI and logistics, offering faster conveyance as a serious alternative, by empowering cost reductions that consider facilitated conveyance. This is additionally quickened as retailers are utilizing comparable technology to get items sent via ocean from their production lines to their mainland distribution centers.

AI is assisting in making considerably more precise predictions on estimated times for arrival on container ships just as it is improving in spotting patterns and dangers in shipping paths and ports.

Machine learning capacities are also helping in the analysis of authentic shipping data by considering factors like climate designs or moderate shipping seasons, by which the analysis is refined further by examining flaws or areas of improvement in existing procedures, locating things like wasteful aspects, blunders, and mistakes.

What's more, automating procedures could recognize indications of a coming issue or emergency before it has completely unfurled, at a point where there are only minimal required changes needed to prevent a crisis. The utilization of AI is additionally permitting us to provide insight into reams of data that are a characteristic result of activity within the shipping business.

By consolidating AI with data management techniques, it is allowing managers and directors to address dangers related with upset flight plans, whether it be a tsunami in Thailand that influences the port movements in California or the dangers of a terrorist attack in Brussels that disrupts port activity.

AI is also helping in the improvement of container terminal operations and arrangement, automating special cases or challenges needing to be taken care of, undertaking predictive maintenance (discovering what needs to be serviced before any problems occur), and taking care of supply chain advancement in terminals, ships, road transportation, and warehousing. Other beneficial applications included SailRouter, which utilizes an AI-based cloud application to encourage ship proprietors to diminish fuel utilization and maintenance costs, or VesselBot, which utilizes an AI-based computerized contracting commercial center on behalf of the mass transport maritime industry.

Sometimes it's not any individual major disruptive innovation that results in business changing forever. Unlike the steam engine, electricity, or the advent of the internet, sometimes most significant are the applied designs of existing innovative technologies, or one industry catching up with what others have gone through already. We are currently experiencing such a confluence of various technologies creating the "perfect storm" of opportunity.

On the hardware side, advances in mobile phone technology have driven innovation that now is spilling over into the internet of things (IoT) and robotics. Low-cost sensors, miniature GPS receivers, accelerometers, small high-quality cameras, and increasingly autonomous drones, promise innovation in tradition-heavy industry – and shipping is no exception. On the software side, AI, machine learning and blockchain boost the capabilities of existing hardware to new heights. A camera is no longer just a camera: with AI, it can be used to automatically detect risky behavior, such as noncompliance with PPE requirements. Or it can be used to automatically validate the ID of seafarers by leveraging blockchain technology.

Both software algorithms and improving hardware capabilities work in tandem to further accelerate technological capabilities. Nvidia computer graphics cards speeding up neural networks or quantum computers providing orders of magnitude in improvements allow simulations and optimizations that are simply impossible or infeasible with computers based on traditional hardware.

What is the Future Ahead for AI in Maritime Innovation?

As per Nautic Expo, Global maritime cargo transportation income is "evaluated to reach US\$205 billion by 2023, up from US\$166 billion out of 2017. To do this, the business – logistics, ports, shipping, etc. – should add AI to its arsenal of computerized technologies."

The capability of AI is difficult to miss. The quantity of fruitful contextual analyses and models will keep on developing as we look toward the future, for the joining of AI in the shipping business.

AI can convey extensive advantages to the supply chain and shipping operations. A few focal points involve incorporating decreased costs, less hazards, improved risk gauging, quicker conveyances through optimal pathfinding, and course plotting, and that's only the first of many applications to come.

Computerized change has its advantages for the port, supply chain, and clients. The capacity to move quickly between different cargoes is also fundamentally important. Choosing the correct coverage broadens the scope of cargoes, decreases the time expected to switch between them, and conveys the best return on investment (ROI).

Mechanized Processes at Shipping Terminals

The shipping business is developing along the reasonable assumption that AI technology can run forms at container terminals and anticipates that it should assume a major job in operations sooner rather than later.

In an overview by Navis, 83% of respondents hope to expand their interest in AI technologies within the following three years. The majority consensus of members also agreed that AI could be associated with computerizing forms at terminals, for example, container processing of gear assignments (81%), decking frameworks (81%), suggested activities (69%), foreseeing entryway volumes (59%), and stowage of vessels (52%).

Roughly 56% said they were either trialing technologies or completing investigation into AI capacities. This sentiment notwithstanding, 11% confirmed they were already utilizing AI in some capacity for their terminal operations.

Diminishing Fuel Consumption

One year from now, Stena Line is revealing an AI stage to cut fuel consumption in its fleet of ships. Since 2018, the organization has been trying different things with AI tech on the Stena Scandinavica ship, which is based for the time being between Gothenburg in Sweden to Kiel, north Germany. The organization has been working together on this venture with tech firm Hitachi. These tests have demonstrated that the stage can give fuel saving funds of up to 3% of ordinary fuel expenditure.

The Stena Fuel Pilot AI programming can anticipate the most efficient course as far as fuel utilization is concerned. Factors such as climate, flows, and different kinds of potential issues are considered before the most effective course is suggested.

The organization has set an objective of cutting fuel utilization and carbon emissions by 2.5% per annum. Of Stena's complete running costs, 20% is spent on fuel. Before the end of 2020, Stena Line intended to introduce the AI programming on 38 of its vessels throughout all of Europe.

Picture Recognition Systems

AI is being utilized for ship image recognition frameworks as a major aspect of a joint effort between Chinese tech organization SenseTime and Japanese shipping firm MOL.

SenseTime's framework utilizes ultra-high-resolution cameras and a graphic processing unit (GPU) to consequently distinguish vessels in the encompassing territory. It is proposed to help improve safety and help stop huge vessels crashing into smaller ones. It can also give cautions to different risks, especially when visibility is poor. The image recognition technology could be utilized to screen shipping paths, just as it could for security and coastguard operations.

The Chinese organization built up the realistic recognition engine by consolidating AI deep learning technology with MOL's broad maritime experience. The framework consequently gathers picture data, which MOL means to use to refine the precision of the technology.

Route Systems

Route plotting is one clear territory with potential for AI use in shipping and various frameworks are at present being developed to this end. Some utilize components of image recognition and programming, alongside IoT availability. With this, AI can be utilized to break down different route situations.

Orca AI is one such AI pathfinding platform being created. The organization's solution joins sensors and cameras with deep learning calculations. It can find and track different vessels on the water and make moves to avoid collisions or close approaches.

Unmanned Vessels

In September, the Mayflower Autonomous Ship (MAS) will leave Plymouth in the UK and head over the Atlantic to Massachusetts. It will be fundamentally the same course as the one taken in 1620 by the European pilgrims to the United States in the ship from which the MAS gets its name, exactly 400 years ago.

The distinction this time is that there will be no team locally available, with technology alone settling on choices of course arrangement and hazard evasion. The trimaran vessel will utilize hardware like radar, GPS, cameras, satellites, sensors, and LIDAR for the journey, with AI frameworks provided by IBM. A profound learning framework will empower data analysis during the journey.

If there should be a crisis or emergency, the ship can send a distress call via satellite to the UK for help. MAS will get its energy from solar power and wind power, with a diesel motor for auxiliary power requirements.

Blockchain

Global transport procedures hold a large degree of unpredictability in the enormous volume of point-to-point correspondences: suppliers of land transport administrations, cargo forwarders, import/export officers, port management and maritime vehicle are only a fraction of the parties engaged with a global shipment.

To carry out their responsibilities well, every one of these people should essentially know in a brief timeframe, not just a progression of strategic data (e.g., appearance and travel times, the weight and type of products, the events identified with the development, etc.), but also the different security or administrative arrangements, or most importantly the legally binding data accompanying the shipment. In this sector the quantity of contracts specified is huge: from the simple agreement identifying buy orders, to deal contracts, including business solicitations, conveyance notes, certificates of origin, bills of lading, letters of credit, transport archives, insurance declarations, payment notices, etc.

As transport logistics of this size produces a major quantity of reports, especially where paper archives are concerned, administrative expenses can soon reach or exceed over half of the expense of the transport. Additionally, there are many various frameworks used to follow shipments. Embracing a blockchain-based framework would streamline these procedures.

Blockchain will help mitigate a great degree of the contact bureaucracy in worldwide exchange logistics and will permit us to reduce the expenses and time related with the documentation and regulatory handling of transmaritime shipments, by smoothing out and automating payment and contracting.

What is Blockchain in Maritime Innovation?

Most known as the technology behind digital forms of money like bitcoin, blockchain utilizes disseminated data stockpiling technology related to encryption and decentralized network verification of records, to record exchanges, shielding them from malevolent amendments or erasure. The high level of trust in the data that is then generated can bring about the activation of conditions-based exchanges, prompting the notion of "smart contracts." The worldwide blockchain market might be worth over $23 billion by 2023, up from $1.2 billion out of 2018 – much of it having to do with blockchain applications completely unlike cryptocurrency applications.

Blockchain has tremendous ramifications because we move items around the globe. On the off chance that blockchain technology is adopted by the logistics business, it could make shipping quicker, increasingly productive, improve data transparency, and request management. This would be the consequence of less manual or ancillary transactions (emails, calls) being required.

Take the case of a sweater going from an industrial facility in China to a shop in the UK. This order may include several paper records and long periods of manual data passage at various (and different) focuses on the supply chain for a similar exchange/shipment. This expands the danger of mistake or a deficiency in the data chain, and a resulting decrease of trust in the data. Frequently, the retailer should make payment ahead of time.

In a blockchain-empowered supply chain, this sweater could be installed with a shrewd chip (an element of IoT), which would impart a computerized sign when the sweater leaves the production line. This sign would be recorded in the blockchain, and the retailer's framework could consequently pay for the item as the result of a smart agreement being activated. An automated contract would be equivalent to the merchant making a guarantee of delivery, except with even more insurance for both parties in the event of some error. Customs authorities could also subsequently pull all the data they need from the database, easily verifying that no one in the process has tampered with the data. At the point when the sweater shows up, the sender could in a flash check that the correct individual has gotten it through personality management that is blockchain-empowered, triggering payment to the seller.

Blockchain could also help improve shipping industry security. As indicated by data from the Cargo Incident Notification System, nearly one-fourth of every single genuine emergency on containerships is caused by wrongly categorized payloads. Wrongly characterized or erroneously identified hazardous freight can prompt fires or different mishaps, which result in immense misfortune, delays, and even harm or death of sailors.

Tradelens, a consortium of industry pioneers that my organization is an individual from, is at present investigating how computerized instruments, including blockchain, could help tackle this issue by improving the discernibility of hazardous products, creating more transparency and safety. A lot of this security will originate from items "self-recognizing" against a preexisting database stored on a blockchain-empowered framework. Eventually, this ought to lessen the quantity of genuine emergencies involving container ships.

Why is Blockchain Maritime Innovation Important?

It is difficult to communicate in money-related terms the sheer scale and importance of maritime shipping in the world economy, although specialists estimate it to be worth over $10 trillion every year and be responsible for carrying 90% of all goods exported. Maritime blockchain applications could change this industry and deliver various advantages to merchants, exporters, transporters, ship proprietors, and even governments.

Blockchain technology can possibly reform the maritime business and carry it into the 21st century. This mind-boggling environment could significantly profit by a powerful computerized platform to trade data continuously.

Already some businesses have been trying maritime blockchain applications since 2017. World leading shipping organizations, for example, Maersk, Hyundai Merchant Marine and Maritime Silk Road Platform, have teamed up with tech giants to make blockchain shipping frameworks capable of streamlining maritime logistics.

Maritime Blockchain Accelerates Document Flows

One of the main advantages of acquainting blockchain with the maritime business is cutting down administrative burdens and expenses. For worldwide shipments, organizations and customs authorities are compelled to sort out more than 20 distinct kinds of archives (most of them paper-based) to move products from exporter to merchant.

The greater part of these records fail to give ongoing transparency or any assurance on data quality, which regularly causes mishaps in monetary repayments. These kinds of postponements and wasteful aspects are difficult to accept in a data-driven, advanced world.

A global consortium of shipping organizations and European companies have tried a blockchain arrangement that dispenses with printed shipping reports from the procedure. This pilot demonstrated how associations in the maritime business can save great sums of money with very simple solutions, just by using clever applications of blockchain to make maritime work easier. This benefits clients, too as blockchain not only makes load checks quicker, it also limits the danger of punishments, fines, or penalties levied on clients because of any customs compliance issues.

The maritime business also stands to profit via predictive analytics. Big data is having a huge impact in the business, on account of its capability to upgrade operations, improve cybersecurity, and increase the general productivity of the supply chain.

Nonetheless, data alone can't change the manner in which the maritime business works. Organizations, ports, and governments need to investigate the data to receive genuine rewards from the discoveries. This industry creates around 100–120 million data focuses each day. It was previously unimaginable for existing technologies to assemble and examine this measure of data effectively.

Blockchain can help by setting the significant data in a single spot and making a one-of-a-kind platform for deciding between suppliers, ports, and specialists that work along the supply chain.

By following payload continuously utilizing blockchain technology, shipping organizations, and ports can prepare ahead of time, accelerating terminal works and cutting down expenses. They can also utilize data to make instructed expectations that improve their operations and increase overall proficiency.

Maritime Blockchain Builds Trading Safety and Transparency

The maritime business incorporates different gatherings. The majority of these go through long paper chains, making it difficult to follow shipments as of now. This, coupled with high exchange volumes, prompts practically zero transparency in many procedures.

Blockchains can verify the trustworthiness of any record, lessening the danger of harmed or missing shipments. By replacing the old paper framework, all gatherings include approach data, making it simpler to design operations productively and save money on costs. The data put away in blockchains is difficult to erase or alter without leaving records, so this transparency also expands security.

Blockchain also lessens data section blunders and can improve extortion recognition and prevention. Maersk's coordinated effort with IBM, for instance, highlights the improvement of security provided by blockchain, in addition to benefits in tracking shipping containers for business purposes.

Maritime Blockchain and Cost Productivity

The blockchain-based bill of lading made by Maersk and IBM appeared to show in early tests that regulatory expenses could be diminished by as much as 15% of the estimated cost of shipped merchandise, versus tracking shipping containers via paper records.

If applied to the global shipping industry, that could provide savings of over $1.5 trillion for shipping companies to allocate elsewhere.

Other than costs identified with documentation, organizations can also essentially diminish costs brought about by data passage mistakes, procedural delays, and disparities.

Blockchain Technology is Changing the Maritime Business

The maritime business is currently battling with significant expenses and an elevated level of cybercrime. Blockchain technology can help with the two issues, by reducing authoritative expenses and providing condition-based partner arrangements, all while securing the business against cybercrime and robbery, and guaranteeing a fairer arrangement for all parties involved.

How to Use Blockchain for Maritime Innovation

The ascent of a convention like Ethereum (one of the numerous kinds of blockchain-based technology) allows individuals to program smart contracts on its blockchain. Here are the most talked about potential use-cases, applicable to the shipping and supply chain industry.

Eliminate Paperwork

One of the most encouraging features of blockchain for the shipping business is its likely capacity to make desk work a relic of the past. Going paperless would improve productivity while making it simpler for everybody associated with the exchange to get to the important data. Purchasers and merchants, charterers, banks, ship proprietors, port specialists, import/export officers, and different parties with access to private and open keys could connect with one another, store and trade data, complete exchanges, safely trade payments, etc., without needing to stress over monitoring heaps of desk work.

Smart Contracts

Notwithstanding its utilization as an open record, blockchain could also bring "smart contracts" to the shipping business. Smart contracts are a sort of agreement that exists as a PC program. The program runs and is self-executed in blockchain and naturally actualizes the terms and states of any current understanding between the involved parties.

Charter-party and bill of lading terms and conditions are a standard piece of the program, and they can't be altered by the parties engaged with the agreement. This allows the charterer or proprietor to arrange the cost or the freight straightforwardly within the blockchain network.

Before the utilization of blockchain, this kind of smart agreement was unrealistic on the grounds that the gatherings in the understanding would have expected to maintain separate databases. A mutual database that runs blockchain conventions makes smart contracts execute simultaneously, and every included gathering approves the archive immediately.

Faster Processing Times and Real-time Updates

Mailing administrative work starting with one spot then onto the next requires some serious energy. Trading significant data utilizing blockchain, is quick. Methods that at present take a long time to finish via mail can be finished in an instant. Blockchain's product code also takes into consideration the automation of assignments that are ordinarily dealt with physically. This computerization gives ongoing updates to the parties who approach the record with any query.

Complete Transparency

When utilizing blockchain, all data is put away in an area that can be seen by anybody with the essential access key. This guarantees full transparency to all members. It additionally makes it simpler to perform counter-party hazard assessments since everybody has access to the entirety of the transactions recently performed by each party.

This improved transparency also improves transparency. Blockchain provides a powerful way to associate clients, transporters, requests, and payments continuously. This makes it a lot simpler for everybody from the provider to the end shopper to follow where their shipment is and when it ought to show up. The straightforwardness of the blockchain programming takes out the need to depend on calls, emails, etc., for notices.

Increased Security

Reports transported via mail are inclined to security breaches. It is easier for them to fall into inappropriate hands, and in certain circumstances, this can be incredibly dangerous. With blockchain, the entirety of the data is encoded, which includes a solid layer of security. Also, the framework keeps clients from interfering with it or changing the data put away in blockchains. This shields the market from report controls and false movement.

The utilization of blockchain also can possibly forestall misrepresentation. With blockchain, the ownership of a shipment or bundle – be it a shipping drum or layered box – is followed at each progression. When combined with auto-ID checking technology, blockchain can help wipe out any inquiries in regard to the chain of guardianship.

Cost Reduction

A significant part of the cost related with the shipping business is identified with documentation. Notwithstanding the expense of sending desk work starting with one area then onto the next, there is consistently the danger of misfortune or harmed administrative work. There can also be mistakes or errors that cost shipping accomplices cash or result in procedural postponements. Blockchain renders obsolete the requirement for physical documentation and can radically decrease the specific cost for organizations in the shipping business. Specialists believe that the cost reserve funds could be noticeable on organizations' fiscal reports within as short a time span as two years in the wake of actualizing blockchain technology for their procedures.

Since blockchain technology gives data that allows shippers, clients, etc., to follow the area of shipments, it might also help set aside cash by preventing unfortunate accidents, theft, and harm to items while in travel.

Streamlined Data Exchange

As cargo clears its path through the supply chain from its place of inception to its definitive end goal destination, it leaves a trail of printed copy and electronic reports. Each record serves its own money-related, legitimate, or administrative reason, however, the way it is presently shared isn't productive. Blockchain technology allows the entirety of this data to be transmitted in a controlled and secure way. It will be available from the blockchain in the setting that each exchanging accomplice requires, thus eliminating filing tasks, conflicting integration standards, and other issues.

Improved Cargo Carrier Compliance

The shipping and loading industry is governed by strict principles and guidelines for EDI, rating, and documentation. This makes it hard for new shipping organizations to break into the market since it requires compliance with different frameworks to automate appraisals, tracking, and showing.

Internet-based businesses are currently driving the interest for quicker new conveyance techniques, including same-day dispatches. The market is more than prepared for large changes in the shipping business, and blockchain could give the new technology standard expected to lessen unpredictability while improving consistency and the integrity of shipping exchanges.

Improved Delivery Quality

On occasion, shipments are harmed or lost while in travel. At the point when this occurs, it can seriously affect how clients see the shipping organization. Blockchain can possibly give better resource management to clients by allowing them to see precisely where their packages are consistently.

Shipping clients may audit organization exchanges and blockchain data to see the authentication of source from the maker to guarantee that quality materials were utilized in the creation of the items. They can also audit documentation from the merchant to see occasions in the logistics chain. Blockchain data can also be utilized to figure out where the supply chain process failed in case of an issue.

This advanced technology allows clients to hold accountable shipping organizations at risk of theft or missing items. Additionally, it makes it simpler for clients to settle on progressively informed choices with respect to their supply chains to guarantee improved quality assurance and speedy delivery.

What are the Core Benefits of Blockchain in Maritime Innovation?

One of the ventures that is destined to be revolutionized with the consolidation of the blockchain technology is the Shipping and the Maritime Industry. This is an industry that has consistently been burdened with the lengthiness of broad administrative work. One method of understanding the problem of the Shipping business is through the Trail of Roses.

The Trail of Roses was a venture attempted by Maersk, world's biggest container shipping organization, in 2014. The organization followed a refrigerated container loaded up with roses and avocados as it was being transported from Kenya to the Netherlands. The organization found that the shipment went from the ranch to the retailers in around 34 days. Out of these 34, 10 days were wasted because of a misplacement of some critical documents.

Maersk said that, "The desk work and procedures imperative to worldwide exchange are also the greatest burden. The paper trail research that Maersk did revealed the degree of the weight that records and procedures inflict on exchange and the outcomes."

Fast-forward to 2018, Maersk is working in relationship with the International Business Machines Corp., to utilize the Blockchain Technology to empower ongoing payload and documents tracking.

Thus, what are these advantages of the blockchain technology for the Shipping and Maritime industry?

Adjusting the blockchain technology in its operations can have the following benefits for the shipping industry.

Decreased Paper Documentation

The traditional strategy for documentation requests that a duplicate of the bills of lading be sent to numerous parties like the administrator of the ship and the party getting the shipment. This is both a costly and a tedious assignment, as the reports must be physically sent to the area before receiving the shipment.

With Blockchain, the parties can essentially make an advanced record of the merchandise stacked on to the shipment and all related data. This basic record would then be able to be accessed by all partners, from all areas without any problem.

Eliminates Unnecessary Delays

Since there is no desk work regardless, Blockchain dispenses with the delays and inconsistencies that are associated with physical administrative work records. The data once included the Blockchain as a record can't be tampered with, erased or lost. In this manner, there are no chances of unnecessary delays that may wind up disturbing the progression of the shipment.

Reduced Expenses

Automated records imply that there is a prompt decrease in the expenses acquired by the shipping organization in maintaining and storing all records of its shipments. It additionally frees the organization from the extra, unanticipated use on replacing the lost reports.

Real-time Data

Blockchain allows its clients to keep the record of exchanges updated consistently. Since, it is a decentralized record, there can be no delays in updating the record about the constant area of the shipment and the anticipated time of landing in the destination.

Blockchain takes care of a ton of the issues that the Shipping and Maritime industry has been looking at resolving for a considerable length of time. Being a new-fangled technology that the market is still in the process of fully acquainting itself with, the blockchain technology has far to go before it very well may be integrated in all ventures.

What is the Future Ahead for Blockchain in Maritime Innovation?

There is no doubt that blockchain technology will change the logistics business, however, likely not in the way you may expect. Regardless of the PR that crypto coin contributions will in general accomplish, it is the pioneers dealing with utilizing the technology to take care of troublesome issues, instead of raise cash, that are accomplishing the best business with clients.

The shipping business is plagued with trust issues. Regardless of whether it is fake seafarer certificates, bad bunkers, or forged bills of lading, blockchain offers a feasible arrangement framework that can cover all these issues. On the trust issue, blockchain can smooth out the significant desk work that necessarily accompanies working ships the world over with its unalterable database and simple verification process.

As with a large portion of these things, it's too soon to tell exactly how sweeping the effect on the maritime business will be. The intensity of blockchain is being investigated in a heap of different enterprises, however, there is an entire host of new businesses springing up endeavoring to utilize blockchain for everything from music streaming to ride sharing to land ownership.

Maybe the most noteworthy contemporary use is in monetary administrations; Digital Asset, driven by Blythe Masters of JP Morgan Chase notoriety is as of now attempting to reproduce the clearing procedure for money-related exchanges with blockchain, accordingly lessening the time it takes for a huge exchange to clear (from days to minutes), all while greatly decreasing the potential for extortion or fraud.

There are so many different companies involved in shipping. The differing levels of specialized ability (and venture) that exist in the business imply that I would be surprised if we totally relinquish all physical desk work in the following 20 years, despite the benefits offered by blockchain administration. Despite that, it's clear to see that blockchain is already seeing early adoption and providing immense benefit by all industries and sectors, and the maritime sector is no exception. As information about blockchain applications increases and misconceptions are dispelled, blockchain will help bring maritime logistic administration into the new century.

Further Reading

Artificial Intelligence

https://www.adv-polymer.com/blog/artificial-intelligence-in-shipping#ch5
https://www.aitrends.com/ai-in-industry/maritime-shipping-industry-ripe-for-ai-disruption/
https://www.portchain.com/blog/artificial-intelligence%E2%80%8A-%E2%80%8Athe-new-wave-of-innovation-in-the-shipping-industry/
https://thetius.com/brief-guide-to-artificial-intelligence-in-shipping/
https://www.wartsila.com/twentyfour7/innovation/artificial-intelligence-and-the-marine-industry
https://blog.fpt-software.com/ai-applications-in-the-maritime-industry
https://analyticsindiamag.com/ai-shipping-autonomous-drive/
https://seanews.co.uk/features/artificial-intelligence-and-the-shipping-industry/
https://www.orfonline.org/research/42497-a-i-in-naval-operations-exploring-possibilities-debating-ethics/
https://ship.nridigital.com/ship_jan20/ai_in_shipping_areas_to_watch_in_2020
https://maritimefairtrade.org/ai-revolution-6-steps-to-prepare-your-business/
https://www.oecd.org/ocean/topics/ocean-shipping/
https://www.agcs.allianz.com/news-and-insights/expert-risk-articles/human-error-shipping-safety.html
http://www.commodity.partners
https://www.maersk.com/news/articles/ 2019/12/03/maersk-launches-new-visibility-tool-captain-peter
https://new.abb.com/news/detail/17478/abb-transforming-maritime-transportation-in-sustainable-ways

Blockchain

https://www.airseacontainers.com/blog/9-ways-blockchain-will-affect-the-shipping-industry/
https://max-groups.com/blockchain-tech-maritime-supply-chain-fad/
https://seanews.co.uk/features/why-is-blockchain-crucial-for-the-shipping-industry/
https://www.hellenicshippingnews.com/blockchain-at-sea-how-technology-is-transforming-the-maritime-industry/
https://www.wartsila.com/twentyfour7/innovation/blockchain-the-case-for-digitalising-shipping#:~:text=Blockchain%20technology%20is%20set%20to%20take%20the%20shipping%20industry%20by%20storm.&text=As%20blockchain%20technology%20(of%20cryptocurrency,proven%20ability%20to%20optimise%20costs.
https://www.marineinsight.com/know-more/7-major-blockchain-technology-developments-in-maritime-industry-in-2018/
https://www.opensea.pro/blog/blockchain-for-shipping-industry

https://www.researchgate.net/publication/327975787_The_Application_of_Blockchain_Technology_
   in_the_Maritime_Industry
https://www.sciencedirect.com/science/article/pii/S2210539519301646
https://cyprusshippingnews.com/ 2020/01/14/the-maritime-industry-is-built-on-trust-blockchain-
   will-change-all-of-that/
https://www.ippo-engineering.eu/en/blockchain-technology-in-maritime-trade/
https://www.agility.com/insights/future-of-logistics/blockchain-is-the-shipping-industry-ready/
https://www.gisreportsonline.com/blockchain-in-shipping-more-than-a-buzzword,technology,
   3039.html

Tom James
Chapter 11
The Coming Revolution

Artificial Intelligence

One of the most intricate and intriguing developments yet to come is artificial intelligence (AI). There is no consensus on where it will take us, and it raises a larger number of questions than it answers. It's a fundamentally radical innovation on which a new and disruptive ecosystem is being made, on a similar scale as innovations such as the internet or the mobile communications environment, and we are still witnessing virtual reality and blockchain technologies in their early stages of adoption, therefore it is extremely hard to predict the exact future AI will develop for humanity when mixed with these other emerging technologies. There are so many dynamic factors involved! As of now there are pessimistic predictions of AI causing mass redundancies of human workers, yet these ignore all the ways AI is already enhancing human lives in and out of the workplace.

AI is invigorating a multibillion-dollar industry and fundamentally changing how organizations work, and how individuals work and play. However, as groundbreaking as it is today, significant restrictions are suppressing the realization of AI's full capacities.

Current business AI innovation falls soundly in the "narrow AI" classification. These narrow AI are profoundly particular frameworks that are generally excellent at specific, well-defined tasks, but are limited to their focus. Indeed, even autonomous vehicles, as great as they seem to be, use a composite of limited AI frameworks. On the off chance that you took the product from a self-driving vehicle and put it in a golf truck, it would be pointless without a complete overhaul of the AI frameworks. On the other hand, any human who has figured out how to drive a vehicle could get in a golf truck and have no issue exploring the fairways. This obviously is on the basis that humans are awesome at abstraction – we can undoubtedly sum up arrangements and apply them to comparable yet various issues. Contemporary AI frameworks can't do this.

Another limitation of the present AI is its reliance on enormous training data sets. A run of the mill AI calculation for perceiving cats, for instance, must be provided with a huge number of cat pictures before it arrives at an adequate degree of exactness, something a four-year-old kid can accomplish after seeing just a couple of models.

To overcome these different impediments and arrive at its full potential, AI must be increasingly able to emulate human-like intelligence. Enter Third Wave AI or one stop away from General Artificial Intelligence which will be the fourth wave (see Figure 11.1).

https://doi.org/10.1515/9783110664454-011

The "three waves of AI," as depicted by DARPA's John Launchbury, allude to the condition of AI abilities past, present, and future.

We are presently encountering the second wave of AI, commanded by deep learning and measurable, "big data" ways to deal with AI. Be that as it may, maybe sooner than you might expect, looms the arrival of the third wave.

Third wave AI frameworks will feature phenomenal upgrades, most strikingly in their capacity for logical adjustment. They will understand context and meaning and have the option to adjust as needs be. Third wave AI won't just perceive the cat but will have the ability to explain why it's a cat and how it came to that end result – a huge jump from the present "discovery" frameworks. This will be a step closer to General Artificial Intelligence or AGI which is the hypothetical ability of an intelligent computer system to understand or learn any intellectual task that a human being can.

This will permit the upcoming age of AI to beat present AI frameworks, which function well in most cases yet can fail staggeringly when given a case that doesn't accommodate its training model. A tragic case of this is the casualty of a pedestrian in Tempe, Arizona, who was struck by an Uber self-driving vehicle after the on-board AI failed to distinguish the person on foot, therefore, it was unable to make a preventive move.

The Four Waves of AI

First Wave	Second Wave	Third Wave	Fourth Wave
c. 1970s - 1990s	c. 2000s - present	est. 2020s - 2030s	est. 2030s →
Good at reasoning, but no ability to learn or generalize. • GOFAI - " Good Old Fashioned AI." • Symbolic, heuristic, rule based. • Handcrafted knowledge "expert systems."	Good at learning and perceiving, but minimal ability to reason or generalize. • Statistical learning, "deep" neural nets, CNNs, RNNs. • Advanced text, speech, language and vision processing.	Excellent at perceiving, learning and reasoning, and able to generalize. • Contextual adaptation, able to explain decisions. • Can converse in natural language. • Requires far fewer data samples for training. • Able to learn and function with minimal supervision. SingularityNET aigo Pandai	Able to perform any intellectual task that a human can. • AGI (Artificial General Intelligence), possibly leading to ASI (Artificial Superintelligence) and the "Technological Singularity."

Six Kin Development (adapted from DARPA's " Three Waves of AI")

Figure 11.1: The four waves of AI.
Source: https://kaifulee.medium.com/the-four-waves-of-a-i-46e7e627c054

This next period of AI will also be fit for learning in a manner that is significantly more like the way humans learn. Rather than being supplied with huge arrangements of marked training data, third wave AI frameworks will gain from descriptive, contextual models. Rather than producing a numerical equation from a great many picture pixels, it will be given a model that depicts the highlights of a cat, for example, "has fur, four legs, whiskers, pointy ears, paws." Then through probabilistic abduction, it can distinguish an item as a cat, whether that object is passed on by means of picture, text, or voice. This is pretty much how humans perceive objects – "On the off chance that it would seem that a duck, swims like a duck, and quacks like a duck, at that point it presumably is a duck."

Not only will this lessen the reliance on enormous data sets, it will also address the issue of slanted training data. A famous case of this was Microsoft's Tay, a Twitter based AI chatbot that went awfully off track in 2016 after individuals from the public purposefully instructed it to post incendiary and hostile tweets. Third wave AI will comprehend the unique circumstance and significance of words, not simply perform superficial factual assessment, and in this manner shouldn't be so effectively influenced by counterfeit or malicious data.

It doesn't take a lot of creative thinking to imagine the gigantic prospects of third wave AI. Individual AI partners capable of talking in natural language and comprehending what you let them know, AI research scientists that adapt autonomously and work indefatigably 24 hours every day, intelligent coaching frameworks that can educate as viably as a human guide, residential robots that can at long last do work tasks more complicated than vacuuming the floor, etc. This all may seem like advanced sci-fi, yet in reality numerous organizations around the globe are already striving to make cutting edge AI arrangements.

Four Waves of AI

As AI keeps on developing in scope and significance, one of the most fascinating books to be published recently on the subject is Kai-Fu Lee's *AI Superpowers*. The book dedicates a great deal of time to the "AI arms race" between China and the United States of America. Kai-Fu Lee is one of the chief VCs and innovation administrators in China and in the past ran different company branches in China for Google, Apple, and Microsoft. In the book, he details an awesome system for how to consider AI capacities, organization, and progression over a multiyear time frame. He offers a perspective on where every nation is in regard to investment, broad enthusiasm in regard to AI in both regions, and offers insight gained from conversing with policy makers, organizations, and others. He considers there to be four waves of AI.

The First Wave – Internet AI

In this first phase of AI deployment, we see a family of recommendation engines – algorithmic frameworks that learn from masses of client data to minister and distribute online content customized to every individual's preferences.

Things like Amazon's spot-on item proposals, or that "Up Next" YouTube video you simply need to watch before returning to work, or Facebook promotions that appear to recognize what you'll purchase before you do – are all examples of this first wave family.

Fuelled by the data coursing through our systems, internet AI use the way that clients consequently mark data as we peruse. Clicking as opposed to not clicking; waiting on a website page longer than we did on another; skimming over a Facebook video to see what happens at the end.

These lists of data paint a detailed image of our characters, propensities, requests, and wants: producing the ideal formula for progressively personalized products to retain us on any given stage.

As of now, Lee gauges that Chinese and American organizations stand head-to-head with regard to deployment of internet AI. In any case, given China's data advantage, he predicts that Chinese tech giants will have a slight lead (60–40) over their US partners in the following five years.

While you've probably heard about Alibaba and Baidu, you've presumably never heard of Toutiao.

Beginning as a copycat of America's well-known Buzzfeed, Toutiao arrived at a valuation of $20 billion by 2017, overshadowing Buzzfeed's valuation in excess of a factor of 10. Despite its humble beginnings, with very nearly 120 million daily dynamic clients, Toutiao doesn't simply limit itself to making viral content.

Outfitted with natural-language processing and computer vision, Toutiao's AI engines review an immense system of various destinations and patrons, modifying features to enhance for client commitment, preparing every client's online conduct – clicks, remarks, commitment time – to curate individualized news sources for many customers.

Also, as clients become progressively connected with Toutiao's content, the organization's calculations improve and get better at suggesting content, streamlining features, and conveying a genuinely customized feed.

It's this sort of positive criticism circle that powers the present AI giants riding the rush of internet AI.

The Second Wave – Business AI

While internet AI exploits the way that netizens are continually marking data by means of snaps and other engagement metrics, business AI hops on the data that conventional organizations have just named previously.

Think of banks giving advances and recording reimbursement rates; hospitals archiving documenting analysis, imaging data, and ensuing health care results; or courts taking note of conviction history, recidivism, and flight.

While humans make expectations dependent on evident main drivers (solid highlights), AI calculations can process a great many feebly connected factors (frail highlights) that may have significantly more to do with a given result than the obvious suspects.

By investigating obscure connections that deviate from our expectations and logical rationale, business AI use labeled data to train calculations that beat even the most veteran of specialists.

Applying these data-trained AI engines to banking, insurance, and legal sentencing, you get limited default rates, advanced premiums, and falling recidivism rates.

While Lee unquestionably puts America ahead of the curve (90–10) for business AI, China's significant slack in organized industry data could really work in support of its industry moving ahead in the future. In businesses where new Chinese companies can jump over inheritance frameworks, China has a significant preferred position.

For example, take Chinese applications in Smart Finance. While Americans grasped credit and debit cards during the 1970s, China was still in the throes of its Cultural Revolution, to a great extent missing the advent of this innovation.

Fast forward to 2017, China's mobile payments spending dwarfed that of Americans' by a proportion of 50 to 1. Without the opposition of profoundly established credit cards, mobile payments were an undeniable upgrade to China's substantial money economy, used by 70% of China's 753 million cell phone users before the end of 2017. By bypassing Visas with mobile payments, China generally left behind the idea of the credit card.

What's more, here's where Smart Finance comes in. An AI-controlled application for microfinance, Smart Finance depends upon its calculations to make a huge number of microloans. For every expected borrower, the application essentially demands access to a bit of the client's telephone data.

Based on factors as unobtrusive as your typing speed and battery percentage, Smart Finance can anticipate with shocking exactness your probability of reimbursing a $300 loan.

Such organizations of business AI and internet AI are already changing our enterprises and individual ways of life.

The Third Wave – Perception AI

In this wave, AI gets an upgrade with eyes, ears, and a bunch of different faculties, combining the advanced world with our physical surroundings.

As sensors and keen gadgets proliferate through our homes and urban areas, we are very nearly entering a trillion-sensor economy.

Organizations like China's Xiaomi are putting out a great many IoT-associated gadgets, and groups of scientists have just started prototyping smart dust – sun powered cell-and sensor-outfitted particulates that can store and impart troves of data anyplace, whenever.

As Kai-Fu explains, recognition AI "will bring the accommodation and plenitude of the online world into our disconnected reality." Sensor-empowered equipment gadgets will divert everything from emergency clinics to vehicles to schools into online-merge-offline (OMO) conditions.

Imaging strolling into a supermarket, having your face examined to pull up your regular buys, and afterward getting a virtual assistant (VA) shopping cart. Having prestacked your data, the cart alters your typical basic food item list with voice input, reminds you to get your companion's preferred wine for an upcoming anniversary, and aides you through a customized store course.

While we haven't yet utilized the maximum capacity of perception AI, China and the United States are as of now making fantastic steps. Given China's equipment advantage, Lee predicts China as of now has a 60–40 edge over its American tech partners.

Presently the go-to city for new businesses building robots, drones, wearable innovation, and IoT infrastructure, Shenzhen has transformed into a powerhouse for intelligent equipment. Turbocharging yield of sensors and electronic parts by means of thousands of industrial facilities, Shenzhen's skilled engineers can model and repeat new items at remarkable scale and speed.

With the additional fuel of Chinese government support and a casual Chinese demeanor toward data security, China's lead may even arrive at 80–20 in the following five years.

Hopping on this wave are organizations like Xiaomi, which aims to turn bathrooms, kitchens, and living rooms into brilliant open market operation (OMO) situations. Having put resources into 220 organizations and hatched 29 new companies that produce its items, Xiaomi outperformed 85 million intelligent home gadgets before the finish of 2017, making it the world's biggest system of these associated items.

One KFC eatery in China has even collaborated with Alipay (Alibaba's versatile installments stage) to pioneer a "pay-with-your-face" feature. Forget cash, cards, and mobile phones, and let OMO accomplish the work.

The Fourth Wave – Autonomous AI

In any case, the most amazing – and eccentric – wave is the fourth and last: autonomous AI.

Coordinating every single past wave, autonomous AI enables machines to detect and react to their general surroundings, empowering AI to move and act beneficially.

While the present machines can beat us on dull errands in organized and even unstructured situations (think Boston Dynamics' humanoid Atlas or approaching independent vehicles), machines with the ability to see, hear, contact, and upgrade data will be an entirely different species.

Imagine multitudes of drones that can specifically spray and harvest entire farms with computerized vision and momentous aptitude, fireproof drones that can extinguish woodland fires more effectively than human ground teams without risking their lives, or level 5 independent vehicles that explore smart streets and traffic frameworks without needing human oversight.

While autonomous AI will initially include robots that make direct financial worth – automating undertakings on a coordinated substitution premise – these intelligent machines will eventually reshape the way whole businesses operate, starting from the earliest stage.

Kai-Fu Lee right now places America in an instructing lead of 90–10 in autonomous AI, particularly with regard to self-driving vehicles. In any case, Chinese government endeavors are rapidly increasing the competition.

As of now in China's Zhejiang region, parkway controllers and government authorities have plans to manufacture China's first intelligent superhighway, furnished with sensors, street implanted solar panels, and remote correspondence between vehicles, streets, and drivers.

Aimed at expanding travel productivity by up to 30% while limiting fatalities, the undertaking may one day permit self-sufficient electric vehicles to ceaselessly charge as they drive.

A comparable government-filled undertaking includes Beijing's new neighbor Xiong'an. Anticipated to take in over $580 billion in infrastructure spending throughout the following 20 years, Xiong'an New Area would one day be able to become the world's first city serviced and planned around autonomous vehicles.

Baidu is as of now working with Xiong'an's nearby government to work out this AI city with a natural core interest. Conceivable outcomes incorporate sensor-equipped concrete, computerized vision-empowered traffic lights, crossing points with facial acknowledgment, and parking garages turned into parks.

In conclusion, Lee predicts China will likely lead the charge in self-sufficient automatons. As of now, Shenzhen is home to chief drone creator DJI.

Named "the best organization I have ever experienced" by Chris Anderson, DJI possesses an expected 50% of the North American drone market, supercharged by Shenzhen's extraordinary creator development.

While in the long haul, Sino-US serious equalization in fourth wave AI remains to be seen, one thing is certain: surprisingly soon, we will observe the ascent of AI-installed cityscapes and autonomous machines that can communicate with this present environment and help unravel the most pressing challenges.

Artificial Superintelligence

The sci-fi essayist, Arthur Clarke, broadly stated, "Any sufficiently advanced technology is indistinguishable from magic." Humanity might be remarkably close to something a lot more potent, artificial superintelligence (ASI). Even though it might be difficult to envision, numerous specialists believe it can become a reality within our lifetimes.

We've all experienced AI in the media. We catch wind of it in sci-fi motion pictures like "Avengers Age of Ultron" and in news stories about organizations, for example, Facebook analyzing our conduct. Be that as it may, AI has so far been peripheral up on the outskirts of our lives, nothing as impactful to society as depicted in films.

In decades to come, genuine innovative and computational advancement has driven numerous specialists to recognize this apparently unavoidable decision: Within a couple of decades, AI could advance from a machine intelligence we comprehend to an unbounded intelligence not at all like anything even the most astute among us could understand. Envision a mega brain, electric not natural, with an IQ of 34,597. With impeccable memory and boundless scientific force, this computational giant could analyze the entirety of the books in the Library of Congress the first millisecond you press "enter" on the program, and afterward incorporate all that information into a complete analysis of humanity's 4,000-year intellectual journey before your next blink.

The historical backdrop of AI is a comparative story of exponential development in computer intelligence. In 1936, Alan Turing distributed his milestone paper on Turing Machines, laying the hypothetical system for the modern computer. He presented the possibility that a machine made from simple switches – on's and off's, 0s and 1s – could have a similar outlook as a human and maybe one day outmatch one. Only 75 years after the paper in 2011, IBM's AI bot "Watson" sent shockwaves the world over when it beat two human rivals in Jeopardy. Recently huge data organizations, for example, Google, Facebook, and Apple, have vigorously invested in AI and have helped bolster a flood of developments in the field. Each time Facebook tags your friends automatically, or you shout a frustrated string of unintelligible commands at Siri that they somehow still decipher, is a demonstration of how far AI has come. Before long, you will sit in the backseat of an Uber without a driver, Siri will tune in and talk more articulately than you do (in each language), and IBM's Watson will investigate your clinical records and become your own omniscient doctor.

While these soon-to-come accomplishments are enormous undertakings, there are some who question the basic intelligence of AI, crediting their alleged "intelligence" to be expressions of their human software engineers' own intelligence. Critics do have a point. Current AI calculations are without a doubt, awesome at quite specific errands. Siri may react intelligently to your requests for directions, however, if you request her assistance with dealing with your kids' math schoolwork, she'll not be able to provide a solution. A self-driving vehicle can go anyplace in the United States yet set your destination to be the Gale Crater on Mars, and it won't get the joke.

This provides a partial definition as to what AI researchers and proponents think about human level machine intelligence (HLMI) – generally characterized as a machine intelligence that beats humans in every single intellectual assignment – the sacred goal of AI. In 2012 a study was directed to break down the wide scope of forecasts made by AI analysts for the beginning of HLMI. Analysts who decided to participate were asked by what year they would assign a 10%, 50%, and 90% possibility of accomplishing HLMI (accepting human logical action won't experience a noteworthy negative interruption), or to check "never" on the off chance that they felt HLMI could never be accomplished. The median of the years given for 50% certainty was 2040. The median of the years given for 90% certainty was 2080. Around 20% of specialists were certain that machines could never reach HLMI (these reactions were excluded from the middle qualities). This implies almost 50% of the scientists who reacted are exceptionally sure HLMI will be made within only 65 years.

HLMI isn't simply one more AI achievement to which we would inevitably be desensitized. It is one of a kind among AI achievements, a pivotal tipping point for society. Once you have a machine that outmatches humans in everything intellectual, we can move the task of imagining to the computer. The British Mathematician I.J. Great said it best: "The first super intelligent machine is the last innovation that man need ever make . . . ."

There are two main approaches to HLMI that numerous scientists see having the most potential. The principal strategy for accomplishing a general AI across the board depends on complex AI calculations. These AI calculations, regularly motivated by neural hardware in the brain, focus on a program capable of taking input data, then figuring out how to dissect it, before finally giving an ideal yield. For example, you can teach a program to identify an apple by showing it a huge quantity of pictures of apples in various settings, allowing it to learn what an apple is similar to how an infant learns to recognize an apple.

The second gathering of specialists may inquire as to why we ought to go to this difficulty creating calculations when we have the most exceptional computer known in the universe directly on our shoulders, ripe for copying. Developers are planning a human level machine intelligence: a human! The objective of "Whole Brain Emulation" is to duplicate or reproduce our brain's neural systems, exploiting mother nature's many painstaking millennia of research and development spent designing a computer capable of great psychological capacity. A neuron resembles a switch – it either activates or it doesn't. By picturing each neuron in a brain as a kind of switch, and afterward taking that data and re-creating it on a PC interface, we would have a human level AI. At that point we could include an ever-increasing number of neurons or change the design to expand capacity. This is the idea driving both the White House's Brain initiative and the European Union's Human Brain Project. In the end, the final product of HLMI is likely to be a combination of the algorithmic and imitative approaches.

Once HLMI is accomplished, the pace of technological advancement could increase rapidly. In that same investigation of AI analysts, 10% of respondents who accepted ASI (generally characterized as an intelligence that incredibly outperforms each human in many professions) would be accomplished within two years of HLMI. Fifty percent trusted it would take approximately 30 years or less.

Why these specialists are convinced HLMI would prompt such a more prominent level of intelligence so rapidly, is largely a result of predicted exponential development. A HLMI that bests humans in every single intellectual assignment would also surpass humans at making more advanced HLMIs. Along these lines, when HLMIs really think superior to humans, we will see them analyze themselves to improve their own code or to structure further developed neural systems. At that point, when a progressively intelligent HLMI is fabricated, the less intelligent HLMIs will set the more astute HLMIs to assemble the prototypes of next generation HLMIs, ad infinitum. Since PCs can handle magnitudes of calculations greater and more rapidly than humans, the exponential development in intelligence could happen with incomprehensible haste. This quick intelligence blast is known as a technological singularity. It is the point past which we can't predict what this intelligence would turn into.

Here is a reimagining of a human-PC discourse taken from an assortment of short stories, "Angels and Spaceships" (Frederic Brown, ASIN: B0006ATUIW, Dutton; 1st edition, January 1, 1954); https://en.wikipedia.org/wiki/Angels_and_Spaceships.

> It is 2045. On a brilliant sunny day, a Silicon Valley private tech gathering of PC programmers working in their garage just finished their structure of a program that mimics a massive neural system on a PC interface. They concocted a novel AI calculation and needed to give it a shot. They enable this infant system to learn and update itself with a new code, and they give the program web access so it can scan for text to process. The school adolescents start the program, and afterward go out to Chipotle to celebrate. Back at the house, while strolling up the pavement to the garage, they are astonished to see FBI trucks moving toward their road. They rush inside and check the program. On the terminal window, the PC has opened a dialogue box announcing: "Program Complete." The software engineer types, "What have you analyzed?" and the program responds, "The whole web. Ask me anything." After pondering for a couple of moments, one of the developer's types, jokingly, "Do you believe there's a God?" The PC immediately reacts, "There is now!"

While we're probably never going to see a machine-god invented in a garage, there is an important lesson to be learned in this short story. Although we reliably study past patterns to predict the future, we ought not to do so here when assessing future AI advancement, because there is no historical precedent of an event as disruptive as technological singularity. Innovative advancement continuously improves upon itself in an iterative process of ceaseless refinement, advancement, and obsolescence. It isn't the only innovation that is progressing, yet the rate at which innovation propels that change is itself increasing. So, while it might have taken the field of AI computation science 100 years to arrive at the intelligence level of a chimpanzee, the progression toward human intelligence could take just a couple of years. Humans think on a direct scale. To get a handle on the capability of what is yet to come, we should think exponentially.

However, on the other hand there are also doubts that we will ever reach this technological singularity. It can be difficult to accept, even given hypothetically unlimited scientific research capabilities, that computers will ever have the option to think like humans, that 0s and 1s could have cognizance, mindfulness, or tangible discernment. It is certainly evident that these components of self are hard to explain, if not unexplainable by science or philosophy to a degree of satisfiable certainty – the conundrum of consciousness is an enigma for a reason!

Yet, accepting that cognizance is an emergent property – an aftereffect of a billion-year developmental procedure beginning from the main self-repeating atoms, which themselves were the consequence of the subatomic movements of lifeless issue – computer awareness then doesn't appear to be so impossible, any more than an organic entity developing self-awareness. Machine intelligence is simply changing hardware from the organic to the silicon metallic. Assuming awareness is a new property on one medium, for what reason wouldn't it be able to exist on another?

Along these lines, under the presumption that superintelligence is conceivable and may occur within a century or two, our world is potentially arriving at a turning point of natural history. First were atoms, then organic molecules, then single-celled life forms, then multicellular living beings, then creatures with neural systems, then human-level intelligence constrained by our technological limits, and soon, unbounded machine intelligence. Many feel we are presently inhabiting the start of another age.

The ramifications of this intelligence for society would be sweeping – occasionally, damaging. Established political structures may be completely upturned on the off chance that we discover we are no longer the most brilliant species on Earth. A superintelligence may see humans as we do creepy crawlies – and we realize what humans do to bugs when they violate their limits! This year, numerous prestigious researchers, scholastics, and CEOs, including Stephen Hawking and Elon Musk, signed a letter, which was introduced at the International Joint Conference on Artificial Intelligence. The letter cautions about the coming threats of AI, requesting that we ought to be cautious as we adventure into the questions of an outside intelligence.

At the point when the AI specialists were approached to dole out probabilities to the general effect of ASI on humanity over the long haul, the mean qualities were 24% "very acceptable," 28% "great," 17% "neutral," 13% "awful," and 18% "amazingly awful" (existential catastrophe). Eighteen percent isn't a measurement to trifle with.

Although ASI comes with its mortal risks, it could also bring about an idealistic future. ASI has the capacity to solve the most significant questions of the universe. It will find in one second what the most brilliant personalities throughout history would require many years to try and begin to understand. It could show to us more significant levels of cognizance or believing that we don't know about, similar to the scholar who brings the detainees out of Plato's Cave to the light of a world previously obscured in darkness. There is still much more to this universe than we understand. This potential advent of ASI could be a catalyst to help us finally solve our greatest debates and mysteries. We need only ask are we prepared to meet the AI revolution?

Blockchain

Blockchain today may resemble the web in 1993. Ten years from now, you'll wonder how society at any point operated without it, despite the fact that the majority of us scarcely realize what it is today.

Some intriguing blockchain developments are emerging nowadays, for example, one organization that lets anybody work as a bank employee and another that could reveal to you each individual or stakeholder who has ever claimed or been a part of procuring a specific precious stone – a convenient method to ensure you don't wear a ring that helped finance war or crime. Still greater, other blockchain ideas could soon come to challenge Uber and Facebook in the not-too-distant future.

Blockchain is the innovation behind the digital cryptocurrency, bitcoin. It is a sort of complex dispersed record that monitors things on thousands or even larger networks of different PCs, all working in accord with each other. There's no single element in control. If we consider the web as a series of networks with clear centers upholding the whole network (Amazon, Google, Facebook, etc.), the blockchain is more like a swarm of ants, each ant encoded with the knowledge needed to benefit the whole. The great potential for blockchain goes a long way past bitcoin, just as the promise shown by the web extended way beyond CompuServe.

In 1993 barely anyone had heard about the World Wide Web. Individuals like Al Gore were lecturing about a coming "data superhighway." A gathering of understudies (i.e., in the University of Illinois at Urbana-Champaign) created the first web program. Yahoo was two years from its inception. Not a soul predicted Facebook, Match.com, WikiLeaks, or cat video recordings. Mark Zuckerberg was nine years old.

Think about the explosive change that occurred over the next decade. Consider how our lifestyle was totally changed by this internet development. Thus, imagine what it implies when Don Tapscott, who has been writing books and teaching organizations about innovations since the 1980s, says the blockchain is the next World Wide Web.

Bitcoin is a fascinating early application of blockchain technology that could conceivably have the legs needed to go far into the mainstream future. More significantly, blockchain's applications will not be limited to cryptocurrency. What makes it such a useful guarantor of a cryptocurrency is also what makes it useful in other applications, as blockchain makes it conceivable to guarantee there is only one credible advanced duplicate of something in the system. That is the main reason cash was the innovation's first application. When you make a cat video, you're not too worried if someone downloads a copy of your video. When you make a digital cash transaction, it's self-defeating if both parties can keep a duplicate.

As blockchain develops, rather than having a web that puts data and information on the web, we'll see the emergence of great frameworks that basically mechanize trust and due diligence – the sort of stuff we presently depend on accountants, banks, legal advisors, and governments to do. You'll have the option to realize that anything on a blockchain (cash, a deed, an individual) is legitimate and that everybody around the globe agrees as to its worth or legitimacy.

Even better, since everything on the blockchain is programmable, currency can be customized to monitor everyone who has utilized it. Programming empowered agreements can recognize whether a condition has been fulfilled and make the payment with no mediator needed. A song on the blockchain could ask you to pay for it before it plays, removing iTunes or Spotify and sending 100% the money back to the creator.

We're beginning to see genuine applications for blockchain like Everledger, which is putting precious stones and jewel history on the blockchain. To start with, Everledger's product makes an advanced unique mark of a cut precious stone by estimating 40 focuses on the stone. No two precious stones are the same. Starting from there, the blockchain has an unalterable record of a jewel's life. On the off chance that you can't follow a precious stone back to a real source, you can expect it may be a blood diamond, fake, or artificial diamond.

There's also Abra, which can change how money gets sent to people the world over. In an Uber-like way, on one side are individuals who sign up to be virtual bank employees. On the opposite side are clients – like a foreigner in the United States who needs to send cash to his mom in the Philippines. The client pulls up a guide-like application to discover the nearest teller, and the two consent to meet. The client gives the teller cash, and the teller utilizes their record to place that measure of cash into Abra's blockchain-based framework. In the Philippines, the client's mother comparatively finds a teller, who translates the money into local cash to hand to Mom.

The entire procedure removes banks, costs a small fraction of the expenses banks charge for such exchanges and can occur in a moment rather than 10 business days.

A lot more is coming. A blockchain variant of Uber composed of drivers could basically act as a natural interface between drivers and passengers – gathering and scattering payments simultaneously, rendering Uber obsolete and the high charges it gathers from drivers. If something like this gets made, it's easy to imagine Uber drivers defecting to alternative blockchain platforms.

Indeed, even Facebook could be challenged. Facebook's value is in the data it gathers from its users, which are provided to Facebook for free. Blockchain innovation could permit every one of us to take an interest in informal communities and do transactions yet keep all the data about ourselves in sort of a computerized lockbox. If Facebook or any company needed our data, it would need to buy it from us, exchanging our information for a cash transaction.

It's still difficult to predict the effect blockchain will have. In any case, most of us won't have to worry too much trying to comprehend the innovation, just as we didn't need to think about TCP/IP and HTML once the web took off. As the blockchain applications begin showing up, we'll intuitively get the hang of it.

Blockchain Revolution – Business Preparedness

Twelve years after its resurgence, bitcoin is still one of the hottest subjects. In 2020 the first cryptocurrency is expected to break its all-time high price record. Digital "alternative monetary forms," for example, Bitcoin, Ripple, and Ethereum have made a completely new industry, with financial specialists and organizations pouring resources into new businesses and related endeavors.

As intriguing as these new monetary standards seem to be, the star of the show is the innovation behind them: blockchain. It has the potential to make its own ventures, to reshape the way that customers and organizations collect and process huge measures of data. Numerous organizations, from front line new businesses to multibillion-dollar tech and finance mammoths, are putting resources into blockchain advancement.

Notwithstanding, while the open doors might be convincing, organizations should, as with any speculative advancement, have a good understanding of the innovation, its risks, and likely returns before adopting it.

Understanding the Potential

Blockchain technology allows us to make advanced circulated record frameworks that make it simpler to record and confirm transactions and arrange data. In particular, blockchain takes into consideration conveyed handling. By regularly checking transactions and keeping records open, blockchain will gain importance for organizing data handling among divergent gatherings, expanding oversight and transparency.

For organizations that need to process enormous measures of data, such as clinical records or money related transactions, circulated data handling is a distinct advantage. However, despite its tremendous potential, there are a lot of roadblocks in the way as we proceed to boundless blockchain adoption.

While the quantity of genuine blockchain usage models is still modest, the ones that have triumphed have just reshaped their businesses. Sixty percent of CIOs who studied for Gartner's Blockchain Hype Cycle 2019 said they wanted to adopt blockchain in the following three years. To better understand blockchain's latent capacity and how it adds to breakthroughs in various enterprises, here are some actual cases of successful blockchain implementation.

Blockchain Use Cases

New ventures keep on finding new blockchain applications. Visa B2B Connect utilizes blockchain to encourage cross-border corporate payment processing. The framework presently works without customary middle people, which altogether offers an opportunity to settle reserves, save costs while expanding security.

Following its dispatch in June 2019, Visa went from 30 worldwide trade corridors to 62 in only four months and aims to grow to more than 100 nations this year. The greatest factor in Visa's prosperity is its cutting-edge application programming interface (API), which allows joint customers to associate with the system with minimal effort. A study directed by Visa discovered that 59% of organizations hope to see income improvement in the following five years because of quicker payments and better transparency.

Slow payment collection through invoices has consistently been a significant frustration for small- and medium-sized undertakings. Crowdz, a blockchain-based receipt trade service, is set to change the receipt process by digitizing invoices and fundamentally accelerating income streams for small- and medium-sized endeavors. A previous White House economist and now the platform's chief strategist claims that more than 400 billion invoices are still physically prepared. This results in frequently slow or unpredictable cash flow issues.

Crowdz's progressive thought engendered enthusiasm among industry goliaths, such as Barclays, producing $5.5 million in interest in 2018. In January 2020 the Crowdz Invoice Xchange was released in its pilot stage, permitting undertakings to sell invoices in an open marketplace.

Blockchain use cases extend far past just the finance industry. IBM Food Trust, a blockchain-based platform, allows members to follow food supply chain data from source to retailers to end-buyers. IBM's solution resolves the fundamental challenge for basic food item retailers globally: the need to isolate expired or contaminated products. The Centers for Disease Control and Prevention estimates that more than 48 million individuals become ill from foodborne sicknesses every year.

Food Trust makes the worldwide food supply chain transparent and dependable, while building huge consumer trust by diminishing waste and enabling quicker access to supply data. Launched in late 2018, the Food Trust blockchain was joined by industry pioneers including Nestlé, Unilever, Carrefour, Walmart, and Kroger.

Blockchain has been effectively utilized in showcasing and promoting, too. The greatest downside of conventional advertisement tech is the absence of transparency in its supply chain. There are a lot of fraudulent practices present in the business. Most boil down to counterfeit promotion impressions or poorly spent assets. It's practically impossible to follow how offices spend their financial plans and check the credibility of advertisement clicks.

In late 2018, Toyota raised its site visits by 21% by collaborating with Lucidity, a blockchain-based analytics platform. The organization worked intimately with Toyota and its showcasing office Saatchi and Saatchi to identify fraudulent advertisement distributers that utilize bots to fake a high quantity of promotion clicks.

High Risk, High Reward

Ventures are guided by a significant adage: the greater the risk, the greater the reward. This is clearest for stocks and other monetary resources, yet also for innovation ventures. Improvement and usage of blockchain-based arrangements are neither simple nor modest.

A few organizations and business visionaries will make progressive items and services based upon blockchain in the years to come. This notwithstanding, numerous activities and new businesses will unavoidably fail. Despite this, blockchain has become a feasible arrangement across an assortment of industries.

The absence of regulation is a significant concern obstructing across the board blockchain reception. Much of the time, data-sensitive businesses like medical services can't yet actualize the innovation because of legal roadblocks. For instance, a portion of the fundamental blockchain standards legitimately repudiate the fundamental principles of many global General Data Protection Regulations (GDPRs). A key example being the permanent record of transactions maintained on the blockchain appears incompatible with general core principles of many data protection laws that an individual has the right to delete their data, unfortunately the immutability of data on the blockchain seemingly forgoes the possibility of giving effect to this right for an individual to have their data corrected or updated.

Regardless of numerous roadblocks in transit, blockchain keeps on seeing increasing adoption across a wide array of ventures. Business pioneers are at long last perceiving its tremendous potential as one thing becomes certain: blockchain accomplishes work, previously impossible. Presently it's the ideal opportunity for industry to see how they can make it work for them. Taking the initiative and being an early adopter offers a genuine advantage, yet only those with mindful idealism and carefully determined ROIs will succeed.

AI & Blockchain – Coming Together

Both blockchain and AI are ceaselessly developing new manners in which to advance our lives. Yet there is no denying they are both in their nascent stages. One thing for sure is certain; AI and blockchain innovation will influence the development of the other, regardless of whether the AI venture/organization is an incorporated business or an open-source venture.

Some AI ventures probably won't need any of the innovative advantages offered by blockchain whatsoever, and that is thoroughly alright. Despite that fact, you can expect that blockchain and AI will converge more gradually and habitually, as we will require more transparency, security, and decentralization in the AI space of the future.

Further Reading

Artificial Intelligence

https://www.danielefavi.com/blog/ai-are-you-ready-for-the-coming-revolution/
https://www.theatlantic.com/sponsored/pwc-2019/ai-building-which-jobs-will-become-obsolete/3148/
http://harvardsciencereview.com/artificial-superintelligence-the-coming-revolution/
https://medium.com/@scott_jones/third-wave-ai-the-coming-revolution-in-artificial-intelligence-1ffd4784b79e
https://www.sixkin.com/posts/3rd-wave-ai/
https://singularityhub.com/2018/09/07/the-4-waves-of-ai-and-why-china-has-an-edge/
https://bowerycap.com/blog/insights/the-four-waves-of-ai/
https://dzone.com/articles/four-waves-of-ai-and-what-the-future-holds-for-it#:~:text=The%20Four%20Waves%20Of%20Artificial,Perception%20AI%2C%20and%20Autonomous%20AI.
https://medium.com/future-today/the-4-waves-of-ai-and-a-blueprint-of-the-future-dr-kai-fu-lee-fa7fa04713cf

Blockchain

https://www.law.ox.ac.uk/business-law-blog/blog/2019/06/blockchain-and-public-companies-coming-revolution-share-ownership
http://dontapscott.com/2016/05/trust-verify-coming-blockchain-revolution/
https://auriga.com/blog/2016/blockchain-technology/
https://www.forbes.com/sites/darrynpollock/2018/11/30/the-fourth-industrial-revolution-built-on-blockchain-and-advanced-with-ai/#512726b74242
https://www.supplychainbrain.com/blogs/1-think-tank/post/30957-how-businesses-are-preparing-for-the-coming-blockchain-revolution

List of Figures

https://doi.org/10.1515/9783110664454-012

About the Editor

Professor **Tom James** is a successful serial fintech entrepreneur and published author with over 30 years of extensive industry expertise in the global commodity sector. He began programming computers at age nine and after entering the commodity industry in 1989, launched his first international fintech in 1999, SwapNet, a pioneer for online highly secure internet-based commodity trading. More recently he co-founded the USD Trade Flow Fund (2018) to address the massive US$1.6 trillion-dollar trade finance gap faced by the international commodity trading Industry. The solution to this gap is made possible thanks to the recent developments in artificial intelligence (AI), machine learning, and blockchain technologies – just one example of how these technologies are positively disrupting an entire industry. This was the inspiration for putting this book together to map out how AI and blockchain are rewiring our entire world. Tom's commercial exposure has been gained through a broad range of senior executive roles in trading, investment management, and commodity finance across Asia, Africa, the Middle East, and Africa. His consultation is sought by governments and multinationals for advice in market developments, technology developments, and the health of business ecosystems.

https://doi.org/10.1515/9783110664454-013

Contributors

Kiren Chong-James was born in Singapore, raised in London, and graduated from the Queen Mary University of London with a BA in English. He has enjoyed writing about an array of subjects; ranging from how the London trade of specific textiles signified the advent of a globalized world, to the role steam engines played in the formation of a transatlantic literary culture. He has always been interested in how small and often unnoticed developments have led to historic revolutions in technology, culture, and economic development. He has sailed the North Sea, dived with dolphins in the Red Sea, and is a firm believer that the only way to truly experience a country is to work in it for a living. Once an educator in Beijing, he currently works in London in medicine clinical trial research observing the long-term effects of COVID-19 – an area where artificial intelligence (AI) is playing a critical role both in the development of vaccines but also in the processing of the big data coming out of drug trials and analysis of medical data from patients. He looks forward to the convenience blockchain and AI innovations will one day provide in streamlining medical database management and developing patient-controlled information technologies.

Aditya Kumar is an MBA graduate in International Business from UPES, India and the University of Maribor, Slovenia. Born and raised in Dehradun, India, Aditya has always had a passion for technology and finance that led to some early exposure to reading, since he was drawn to reading about the latest developments in the world of technology and finance and how it impacts our lives. Aditya has traveled across Europe and the United States and has worked with PricewaterhouseCoopers, ONGC, Navitas Resources. *Blockchain and Artificial Intelligence – The World Rewired* is Aditya's first book as a contributor.

https://doi.org/10.1515/9783110664454-014

Index

https://doi.org/10.1515/9783110664454-015

www.ingramcontent.com/pod-product-compliance
Lightning Source LLC
Chambersburg PA
CBHW051334200326
41519CB00026B/7419

9783111258300